When Frankie Went to Hollywood

When Frankie Went to Hollywood

Frank Sinatra and
American Male
Identity

Karen McNally

University of Illinois Press
Urbana and Chicago

Manufactured in the United States of America
1 2 3 4 5 C P 5 4 3 2 1

⊗ This book is printed on acid-free paper.

Library of Congress Cataloging-in-Publication Data
McNally, Karen, 1964–
When Frankie went to Hollywood : Frank Sinatra
and American male identity / Karen McNally.
p.   cm.
Frank Sinatra filmography: p.
Includes bibliographical references and index.
ISBN-13 978-0-252-03334-6 (cloth : alk. paper)
ISBN-10 0-252-03334-5 (cloth : alk. paper)
ISBN-13 978-0-252-07542-1 (pbk. : alk. paper)
ISBN-10 0-252-07542-0 (pbk. : alk. paper)
1. Sinatra, Frank, 1915–1998.
2. Masculinity in motion pictures.
I. Title.
PN2287.S39M36   2008
791.4302'8092—dc22   2007030915

Contents

Acknowledgments

A number of people have helped this book along its way through their support and advice, and I am pleased to have this opportunity to express my gratitude to them.

A first and special note of thanks goes to Mr. Frank Sinatra. As an area of research, I could not have asked for any more fascinating or enjoyable a subject, and I remain a true fan. This book would have been far longer in the writing were it not for the financial assistance of the Arts and Humanities Research Council, which is gratefully acknowledged. A number of people are owed thanks for their input at various stages of the book's development. Mark Jancovich provided comments and observations, during the initial research, which were always constructive. Steve Neale's support of the project has been an encouragement at all times and is hugely appreciated. I am fortunate in the patience and editorial guidance I have received from my editor, Joan Catapano, and the staff of the University of Illinois Press, and I am grateful in addition for the comments of the external readers of the manuscript. Warm thanks go in particular to Sharon Monteith for her enthusiasm and insight throughout the course of this research. She has helped to make this the book I wanted it to be, and her unstinting support will always be valued.

Sections of this book have appeared as articles in amended form. An early version of material included in Chapter 5 appeared as "Films for Swingin' Lovers: Frank Sinatra, Performance and Sexual Objectification in *The Tender Trap* and *Pal Joey*" in *Scope: An Online Journal of Film*

Studies in May 2002. Portions of Chapter 3 were included both in "'Your Blood's the Same as Mine': *The House I Live In* and the Post-War Push for Tolerance" on the *Film and History* CD-Rom Annual 2003, and "'Sinatra, Commie Playboy': Frank Sinatra, Post-War Liberalism and Press Paranoia," was published in *Film Studies* (Winter 2005): 43–53. "'Where's the Spinning Wheel?': Frank Sinatra and Working-Class Alienation in *Young at Heart,*" in the *Journal of American Studies* 41 (2007), 115–33, contains elements of Chapter 1. The publishers' permission to include this material is gratefully acknowledged.

Finally, family and friends have provided invaluable support and encouragement. I would especially like to thank Paul for both his practical assistance with the illustrations included in this book and his periodic motivating words, Janet for her unwavering belief, and Kate for her empathetic phone calls. Without the influence of my late parents, Lena and Eddie, and their love of movies, the following would never have come to fruition. This book is dedicated to them.

When Frankie
Went to Hollywood

Introduction:
Meet Frank Sinatra

Sinatra long ago established a public character that is both
interesting and diverse. And the most interesting part of this
character derives from the fact that Sinatra is—well, there's
no better way to say it—not nice. He is tough, sardonic and
often funny in a rather rude way. Now there are plenty of
people who are not nice, but few of them earn their livings
as popular entertainers, and, in a world all too well supplied
with nice guys, we should be grateful for them. By their presence they suggest that all life does not exist on the level of
country-club chumminess.

—Robert Fulford

Robert Fulford's remarks in the *New Republic* in November
1957 articulated the popular perception of Frank Sinatra at the height of
his career. Prompted by the opening programs of ABC's *The Frank Sinatra Show,* the comments pointed to the combative, caustic, and sexually
potent male identity Sinatra conveyed in the 1950s on stage, screen,
and record. The series of variety shows and one-off dramas, which ran
between October 1957 and May 1958, highlighted the extent to which
Sinatra strayed beyond the conventional image of a mainstream entertainer. The television variety-show host epitomized the stable or "nice"
identity constructed around America's postwar white male. Performers
such as Perry Como and Steve Allen projected an uncomplicated image
of American masculinity into suburban homes: amiable, subdued, and
unfailingly uncontroversial. Sinatra, on the other hand, communicated
what the *New York Journal-American* television critic Jack O'Brian described as a "nouveau attitude which came through the X-ray eye of the
TV lens somewhere between arrogance and insolence."[1]

Stretching the limits of the variety-show host's identity, Sinatra's television persona drew on the cinematic image that developed around the star across the postwar period. Evolving through the varying contexts of the postwar era, Sinatra's screen persona constantly disturbed accepted definitions of American masculinity. Playing a World War II veteran in his first postwar feature film, *It Happened in Brooklyn* (1947), Sinatra presented an image of the American GI that disrupted gender norms while addressing anxieties about the veteran's ability to assimilate in a dispirited postwar society. Returning to his beloved Brooklyn, Danny Miller represents the working-class urban American male pursuing professional success and romantic domesticity in the aftermath of the war. Carrying a photo of the Brooklyn Bridge rather than a movie star pinup in his wallet, and exuding the type of shy innocence on which Sinatra's early screen persona was built, Miller points to the emotional vulnerability and distinctive sexual imagery that develops around Sinatra's star identity. Thirteen years later, Sinatra was reunited with his *Brooklyn* costar Peter Lawford in a fiesta of star power and masculine excess. Gathering famous friends Dean Martin and Sammy Davis Jr. together for *Ocean's Eleven* (1960), a mischievous tale of displaced veterans plundering the safes of the Las Vegas casinos, Sinatra displayed all the male bravado, sexual arrogance, and ethnic loyalties that his star identity had come to represent.

With Sinatra's cinematic performances as its central focus, this book explores the ways in which Sinatra's star image consistently challenges postwar notions of American male identity through its engagement with contemporary debates in Hollywood and the wider culture and by exposing limitations on the ways in which American masculinity is defined. The postwar years represent the most dramatic and creative period of Sinatra's career. From the collapse of his career in the late 1940s to his central position in Hollywood and as a recording artist by the end of the 1950s, perceptions of Sinatra as a star altered significantly. The 1950s also represent Sinatra's most prolific and critically acclaimed time frame as a creative artist. His influential mood albums with Capitol Records are widely acknowledged as his greatest musical legacy; films such as *From Here to Eternity* (1953) and *The Man with the Golden Arm* (1955) challenged the restrictions of the Production Code, and Sinatra permeated Hollywood film culture, from cameo appearances in *Meet Me in Las Vegas* (1956) and *Around the World in 80 Days* (1956), to his uncredited rendition of "Farewell Amanda" in *Adam's Rib* (1949) and his performance of the theme to the 1954 film *Three Coins in the Fountain.*

Shifting imaging around Sinatra from World War II through the postwar period occurred in the context of a constant negotiation of meanings about what constituted American male identity. As the middle-class male anguished over the loss of his individualism, ethnic culture was reduced to stereotypes, liberal Hollywood attacked racial inequality, male film stars expressed their vulnerabilities, and the hip bachelor was constructed as an alternative to the suburban husband, debates around ways to define American masculinity were a key feature of postwar culture and were represented in Hollywood in a variety of ways. This book frames Sinatra's image around these debates, considering Sinatra's identity as a synthesized collection of interconnecting personae that intersect with issues of relevance in American culture. Examining the construction of Sinatra's image through extracinematic performance and biographical commentary, and locating his star image in relation to cultural debates, provides a context for readings of Sinatra's film performances as they shift definitions of American masculinity.

The book's title, *When Frankie Went to Hollywood,* refers in part to the screen career that is at the center of this discussion, while "Frankie" also draws attention to the essential identity that builds around Sinatra during World War II. The title additionally references the cultural resonance of Sinatra's image evidenced by *Frankie Goes to Hollywood*'s use of a 1940s *Variety* headline as their band name. The stage shows *Sinatra: His Voice, His World, His Way* at New York's Radio City Music Hall in 2003 and *Sinatra at the Palladium* in London in 2006, featuring footage culled from the star's ABC television series, form part of the current fascination with Sinatra that has been developing since the mid-1990s. The appeal of Sinatra's 1950s persona in particular is built largely around the notion of the star as a male fantasy figure, inspiring both American and British men to emulate Sinatra's coolly confident masculine style. Films such as *Swingers* (1996) and *Strictly Sinatra* (2000) depict Sinatra as a role model for, respectively, young men aiming for style and sexual appeal in the Los Angeles club scene, and a Scottish nightclub singer requiring assistance to overcome his naturally shy persona. The 2001 remake of *Ocean's Eleven* and its sequels, *Ocean's Twelve* (2004) and *Ocean's Thirteen* (2007), equally draw on the sharp male persona Sinatra represents. Sinatra's identification with a specific brand of hypermasculinity is evident across popular culture of the 1990s and beyond. In a 1995 episode of *Frasier* titled "Martin Does It His Way," the radio psychiatrist and his brother Niles added music to lyrics their father Martin had written for Sinatra. Running through the completed song, "She's Such a Groovy Lady," was a healthy sprinkling of words and phrases such as "chick" and "ring-a-ding," which pointed to Sinatra's image as a swingin' bachelor. In

The Sopranos, the series that dramatized the business and home lives of the New Jersey Mafia, Sinatra is unsurprisingly revered as a figure of Italian American machismo, represented by a police mug shot of the star hanging on the wall of Tony Soprano's office at the Bada-Bing strip joint. In the 1998 novel *Underworld,* Don DeLillo placed Sinatra in the stands watching the New York Giants alongside Jackie Gleason, restaurateur Toots Shor, and J. Edgar Hoover. DeLillo describes Sinatra as a model of male behavior for those around him, or "a reference for everything that happens. Somebody makes a nice play, they look at Frank to see how he reacts."[2]

The ease with which Sinatra is used as a cultural reference for a heightened version of American masculinity attests to the sustained potency of the star's image in the popular imagination, even in these simplistic forms. The 1998 conference *Frank Sinatra: The Man, The Music, The Legend,* held at Hofstra University in New York State, was an initial attempt to interrogate Sinatra's cultural relevance through panels that tackled the complexity of Sinatra imaging from such varied perspectives as "Frank Sinatra and the Politics of Cool," "Philosophy and Iconography," and "Gender and Masculinity." The conference's resulting collections, *Frank Sinatra: History, Identity, and Italian American Culture* and *Frank Sinatra: The Man, the Music, the Legend,* are among a number of recent publications that have moved writings on Sinatra beyond the strictly biographical to more considered explorations of his identity and cultural importance.[3] While Will Friedwald and Charles Granata's impressive studies of Sinatra's career as a singer have acknowledged his musical influence, the star's cinematic significance has remained largely ignored. However, as Robert Horton's insightful article published in *Film Comment* in 1998 indicated, Sinatra's screen persona is more intriguing than those of other male stars who have tended to dominate retrospectives of postwar Hollywood.[4] Preoccupations with the impact of the Method school of acting and the sexual ambiguities of star imaging around actors such as Rock Hudson have obscured Sinatra's import as a mainstream performer whose screen image represents a highly masculine, white, heterosexual masculinity that, nevertheless, disrupts simplistic notions of male identity and Americanness.[5]

In cultural terms, the 1960s remains in the popular imagination as the decade in which America awoke from the complacent comfort zone of the previous decade. The civil-rights struggle, the dawn of feminism, and a new counterculture suggest a cultural eruption occurring as a reaction against a stagnancy that settled in after the upheavals of World War II.

On the contrary, however, such counterpoints hugely misrepresent the postwar period. The 1953–61 presidency of Dwight D. Eisenhower, the World War II general famous for his love of golf rather than his political courage, often characterizes this untroubled image. However, the 1950s was marked by political anxiety. The Korean War (1950–53) sent American troops back overseas, the 1955 Montgomery Bus Boycott signaled the first direct action of the Civil Rights Movement, and American fears of Soviet attack were intensified in 1957 by Russia's launch of *Sputnik*, its first artificial satellite. The country's domestic culture also reflected a disparity between image and reality. The 1950s is an era noted for the prominence of the suburban family, defined by strict gender roles and contented prosperity. However, increasing numbers of wives returned to the workforce in order to help maintain their families' living standards, while professional males grew frustrated at their lack of professional autonomy. Reports of the country's sexual practices published by Dr. Alfred Kinsey of the Institute for Sexual Research at Indiana University also disputed the fairy-tale image of the American family. *Sexual Behavior in the Human Male* (1948) and *Sexual Behavior in the Human Female* (1953) revealed levels of adultery, homosexuality, and diverse sexual activity largely concealed by popular imagery.

The extent to which American identities existed in an uneasy state of renegotiation is revealed in a range of contemporary texts, whether from the perspective of female dissatisfaction in Betty Friedan's *The Feminine Mystique* or the middle-class male's readjustment crisis in *The Man in the Gray Flannel Suit*.[6] This state of flux was represented nowhere more than in Hollywood cinema. Debates around male identity, in particular, are represented in a variety of ways in the films of postwar Hollywood. Films such as *Executive Suite* (1954) and *Woman's World* (1954) draw on concerns about the conformist demands of corporate life highlighted by, for example, *The Organization Man,* a study of middle management by William H. Whyte, which noted an unhealthy discouragement of individualism in the office environment.[7] An increasingly pressing civil-rights agenda could be seen reflected in more progressive representations of African American characters in films such as *The Pride of the Marines* (1945) and in narratives that directly addressed racial prejudice, such as *The Defiant Ones* (1958). The difficulties experienced by veterans as they attempted to redefine themselves in an altered postwar America formed a frequent theme across genres, as in the dark 1955 musical *It's Always Fair Weather* and the film-noir classic *The Blue Dahlia* (1946). Similarly, the apparent stability of the suburban marriage came under scrutiny in films such as *Strangers When We Meet* (1960), which portrayed the sexual and creative frustrations of an architect, played by Kirk Douglas, who had defined himself as a husband and father.

Each of these depictions of male crisis speaks to postwar conflicts that occur around the ways in which American masculinity had been traditionally defined. Similarly, star imaging often drew attention to anxieties about male identity. The emotional expressiveness of newer stars Marlon Brando and James Dean suggested a youthful abandonment of previous ideas of male certainty. Gregory Peck's honorable self-assurance was tested in films such as *Twelve O'Clock High* (1949) and *The Gunfighter* (1950), and James Stewart's performances in *The Naked Spur* (1953) and *Vertigo* (1958), among a number of films, moved his star identity away from comfortable amiability toward aggressive tension and psychological disturbance. Sinatra's significance can be seen in the ways in which his screen persona intersects with these images of male instability and circulating debates.

When referring to the postwar period, there are various definitions that can be applied to the term. For the purposes of this book, I have chosen to define *postwar* as the years from 1945 to 1960. Although the period can clearly be extended into the following decade, in relation to Sinatra's star image 1960 is an apposite place at which to conclude discussion of his postwar relevance. As the book's conclusion demonstrates, Sinatra's image begins to display further shifts in relation to the ways in which it defines American male identity around the year 1960. The films discussed in detail, therefore, were released prior to the end of the 1950s. In order to demonstrate both the early formation of the core elements of Sinatra's image and the shifts that occur over time, I have also examined his star identity in World War II. Highlighting the shifts that occur in the postwar period accents Sinatra's location in relation to specific cultural trends and new debates.

The manner by which this shifting image builds is complex. John Ellis's definition of a star as "a performer in a particular medium whose figure enters into subsidiary forms of circulation, and then feeds back into future performances"[8] describes the circular nature of image making around Sinatra. Yet it seems an inadequate summary of the ways in which the formation of a star image works in relation to this star. The "subsidiary forms of circulation" are generally taken to mean those texts which revolve around the star's Hollywood identity—i.e., material such as film posters, press books, and reviews that relate specifically to films in which the star appears, and articles in fan magazines and journals such as *Look* and *Life* that discuss the star biographically through his or her identity as a film star. However, commentary around Sinatra stems from a much wider variety of sources than those that relate specifically to film. This occurs in part because as a performer Sinatra is obviously not limited to the medium of film, and also because his star identity interacts with numerous political and social issues, provoking comment in diverse texts. To illustrate the contribution of assorted commentary to the construction of Sinatra's star image, I have drawn on articles and reviews from magazines, journals, and newspapers that cover a wide range of subject areas and styles, from the music journal *Metronome* and *The New Yorker,* to *Ebony* and *Playboy.*

The "subsidiary forms of circulation" to which John Ellis refers also need to be extended beyond commentary, whether specific to film performances or otherwise, to include other forms of performance. As both a singer and actor, Sinatra's performances occur across the breadth of popular media, on record, radio, and television and in nightclubs. These performances should not necessarily be considered subordinate to Sinatra's screen persona in the construction of his star identity. Certainly, Sinatra is best known and most respected as a singer, and, just as biographical commentary has a strong effect on his image, Sinatra's recordings and the imaging around them are arguably the most potent texts. However, since Sinatra's neglected film performances are the central focus of this discussion, all extracinematic performance has been considered as part of the circulating stream of texts that work toward the star identity revealed by Sinatra on film.

The necessity of stressing the intertextuality of Sinatra's star image is clearly demonstrated by his introduction as a screen actor. Following musical cameos with the Tommy Dorsey Orchestra in *Las Vegas Nights* (1941) and *Ship Ahoy* (1942) and a solo spot in *Reveille with Beverly* (1943), Sinatra's first acting role came in the 1943 musical comedy *Higher and Higher.* "Good morning. My name is Frank Sinatra" is Sinatra's opening line to the Drake family's maid, Mickey (Marcy McGuire), who responds by fainting into Sinatra's arms. Sinatra's film identity began as this overt combination of character and star image—an image that predates cinematic connections, reinforcing the importance of extrafilmic image construction. Cast as a shy romantic who serenades the film's female characters, Sinatra appears as a loose interpretation of what "Frank Sinatra" meant in the mid-1940s. The star's unmarried troubadour, who lives across the street from the main characters, draws on Sinatra's benign romantic image, developed through ballad singing and largely positive press publicity that represented Sinatra as a home-loving family man who caused bobbysoxers to faint. This confused mix of role and image sets a precedent for the extent to which extracinematic imagery consistently intervenes in the creation of Sinatra's screen characters. Sinatra's star image remains a constant reference point, even on the most superficial level. Ozzie's (Jules Munshin) mention of Ava Gardner in *On the Town* (1949), Charlie Reader's reference to wearing bow ties in *The Tender Trap* (1955), and Frankie Machine's speculation as to his possible appeal for bobbysoxers in *The Man with the Golden Arm* (1955) are just a few examples of the numerous occasions when the audience is given a direct reminder of the actor playing the role. The narrative of *Meet Danny Wilson* (1951) plays like a thinly veiled biopic in which Sinatra appears as a combative yet emotionally vulnerable singer, assisted on his way to New York's Paramount Theater by gangster connections. Reviews of the film inevitably centered on these similarities. In the *Los Angeles Examiner,* for example, Kay Proctor wrote: "As for Sinatra, the actor, for the first time on the screen he seems completely at ease, and sure of himself and what he is doing. There may be other reasons for this, but chiefly, I suspect, it is because the role of Danny Wilson quite openly parallels Sinatra's own career in many instances, and in a sense, therefore, he is just being himself."[9] Proctor's conclusion becomes a familiar theme of reviews in the wider context of Sinatra's star identity. Hollis Alpert, reviewing *Guys and Dolls* (1955) in *The Saturday Review,* contended that "Sinatra is Sinatra and in this is perfect."[10] *Variety* reported on *Can Can* (1960) that "Sinatra is Sinatra, ring-a-ding-ding and all."[11]

While these reviewers suggest that Sinatra's star identity extinguishes any film character, what appears on screen is a complex negotiation between the two—a character undoubtedly impacted by and changed by Sinatra imaging, and a Sinatra image altering as it is developed by this and other film roles. The result is that Sinatra's image carries a meaning beyond any specific narrative intent. The image may reinforce the thematic drive played out through the character, or add elements that are at variance with it, but it clearly has an effect when drawn into the text. As Lawrence Alloway argues: "The star whose personality and status are created as a product is, when photographed, continually present in a more powerful form than the individual roles he or she may be playing. It is not Beau Geste as interpreted by Gary Cooper, but Gary Cooper himself that is the point."[12] Alloway suggests that a potent star image may articulate specific themes across a number of films in a similar way to directorial authorship. Using Sinatra as his example, he argues that *Meet Danny*

Wilson, Young at Heart (1954), and *Johnny Concho* (1956) each center on the notion of "estrangement from society and from family, so that the content of identification with Sinatra was the pleasure of individualism expressed by bitter and equivocal independence."[13] Alloway simplifies Sinatra's image but correctly identifies the sense of resentful alienation that underpins his screen persona, as well as the consistency of imaging through which that persona brings added meaning to a film.

In examining individual films, therefore, my aim has been to consider the ways in which Sinatra's image works within the film, affecting readings of a film's themes and forming a context as significant as the postwar cultural framework in which the film is located. Barbara Klinger's description of these various contextual elements as "interpretive frames"[14] usefully articulates the need to examine the ways in which a film's meaning can be generated by factors beyond its narrative intent. However, Klinger dismisses textual analysis as the act of "rolling back the historical meanings to produce the 'real' meaning of the film in question or delineate what its resistances could be to the uses such contexts want it to serve."[15] No attempt will be made here to come to any such stark conclusions. However, to focus solely on context and ignore the film text to which it applies seems incongruous. Analyses of particular films therefore have a central position in this book, as narrative, cultural debates, and imagery circulating around Sinatra provide a way of finding meaning in the text.

In order to manage this synthesis effectively, I have structured chapters around specific aspects of Sinatra's identity as an American male, all the while demonstrating that these personae are not distinct but form interconnecting elements of Sinatra's image. Each chapter considers the development of a persona and its location in the context of postwar cultural trends, centering on an examination of Sinatra's expression of a certain aspect of American maleness through the themes and characters of particular films. Chapter 1, "The Postwar Success Story and Working-Class Alienation," examines the image of working-class masculinity that builds around Sinatra. In the midst of popular projections of America as a classless society, I argue that Sinatra's resolutely working-class identity reveals the extent to which American masculinity has by the 1950s fused into a middle-class notion of manhood. The specter of failure that looms around Sinatra because of his sharp career decline is considered in the light of connections made between professional success and male identity. Commentary that stresses the reinvented Sinatra's unabashed ambition and nonconformist behavior is explored in relation to press disapproval of the star's retained class markers, and working-class males' sense of identification with Sinatra's attitudes and values. Sinatra's roles in *Young at Heart* and *The Man with the Golden Arm* are analyzed as a thematic departure from the expressions of anxiety over white middle-class masculinity evident in books such as *The Organization Man* and films such as *Executive Suite*. *Young at Heart* provides an arena in which to consider two contrasting male identities, as Sinatra's portrayal of embittered alienation in a middle-class suburban environment reveals the minimal opportunities and frustrations open to the working-class American male. Rather than focusing on the drugs theme around which the narrative of *The Man with the Golden Arm* revolves, Sinatra's performance as heroin addict Frankie Machine is read as a representation of the alternative experience of an American underclass through which addiction becomes a consistent coping mechanism.

In Chapter 2, "Ethnic Stereotyping and Italian American Cultural Identity," I consider Sinatra's Italian American identity, contending that the stereotyping of Sinatra's ethnicity reveals much about the cultural exclusivity of the postwar period. Sinatra's ethnic identity is located in relation to shifting attitudes toward immigrant culture, from World War II's celebration of difference to a postwar promotion of assimilation. Sinatra's aggressive assertion of his Italian American identity is contrasted with the more obvious yet less troublesome ethnicity expressed by Dean Martin. Commentary that stereotypes Sinatra's ethnicity in terms of violent criminality is explored. An alternative interpretation of Sinatra's dress style and codes of loyalty connects these tendencies directly to Sinatra's cultural background, making negative stereotyping an illustration of a narrow American identity defined by a dominant white Anglo-Saxon culture. Sinatra's role as Private Angelo Maggio in *From Here to Eternity* is one of the star's defining screen performances. Yet analyses of the film tend to focus on Montgomery Clift's portrayal of Private Robert E. Lee Prewitt's struggle to maintain individualism in a community that requires conformity. In this chapter, the film is examined as Sinatra's illustration of an Italian American identity that rejects negative stereotyping. Through Maggio's friendship with Prewitt and the character's anti-authority stance, Sinatra depicts an alternative value system specific to an ethnic culture.

Tied to Sinatra's image of proud ethnicity is his insertion into the civil-rights debate, which is considered in Chapter 3, "Anticommunist Witch Hunts and Civil Rights." Here I examine Sinatra's involvement in liberal politics, subjecting the short film *The House I Live In* (1945) to close analysis in the context of Hollywood's attempts to address the issue of racial tolerance in the immediate postwar period. Sinatra's assertion of racial, ethnic, and religious diversity as intrinsic to American identity makes him a target for press attacks as part of the communist witch hunts of the late 1940s. Shifts in the star's approach to civil rights through the 1950s are studied in the light of the simultaneous increased urgency of demands for equality and cautious political climate. The 1958 film *Kings Go Forth* is examined as an illustration of Hollywood's desire to address the racial debate directly and the industry's still compromised ability to do so.

The book proceeds to a consideration of Sinatra's image as an emotionally vulnerable male in Chapter 4, "Vulnerable Masculinity and Damaged Veterans." The chapter traces the development of vulnerable imagery from World War II, when Sinatra's ballads associated the singer with the female experience of war, to the "saloon songs" of the 1950s, through which Sinatra's expressiveness claims emotional vulnerability as part of mature male identity. Connections are made between the narrative musical style and cinematic covers of Sinatra's albums, and the noir imagery evident in his films, illustrating a consistency of imagery across Sinatra's performances. Analyses of *Suddenly* (1954) and *Some Came Running* contextualize male vulnerability as part of the identity of the war veteran. In *Suddenly,* machismo is exposed as an outdated expression of masculinity. The impact of Sinatra's image on the film is considered as a disruption to narrative intent, enabling his character to stress the emotional damage of war. In *Some Came Running,* Sinatra conveys the instability of the American veteran. As author Dave Hirsh, Sinatra displays the machismo sanctioned by war and expresses the vulnerabilities of the postwar male in the context of the problematic assimilation of the veteran. Resisting the repression and conformity exhibited by nonveterans, Sinatra's characterization reformulates adult male identity to include an emotional expressiveness indicative of affective experience.

In Chapter 5, "Male Performance and Swingin' Bachelors," I interrogate Sinatra's image of male heterosexuality, dissolving the stark distinctions drawn between a perception of early innocence and later heightened virility. Sinatra's vocal eroticism and his position as an object of desire for female audiences during World War II establish a highly sexual but unconventional image for a male star. Sinatra's early screen roles draw on the objectification of Sinatra and the issue of performance raised around the star's physical inadequacy. The chapter moves on to examine Sinatra's swinger persona, locating this image in the context of the bachelor identity constructed by *Playboy* magazine. While *Playboy* deifies Sinatra as its Hollywood representative, the magazine's struggle to reconcile Sinatra's working-class links and unremarkable appearance with its definition of bachelorhood demonstrates the extent to which Sinatra's swinger veers from the playboy identity. An analysis of *The Tender Trap* (1955) considers the film's revelation of gender roles as social constructions and Sinatra's exposure of the playboy's hypermasculinity as a performed identity. Nightclub master of ceremonies Joey Evans, in the 1957 film *Pal Joey,* is Sinatra's best-known screen swinger, famed for his hip language, stylish suits, and sexual exploits. A close examination of the ways in which the film draws on Sinatra's willing self-objectification and consistently working-class identity argues that the popular casting of Sinatra's Joey as a playboy misrepresents this powerless character. Sinatra's star image combines with the film's depiction of distorted sexual relations to move the 1950s playboy beyond stereotype to more complex territory.

Each of these chapters demonstrates the mix of screen characters, extracinematic performance, and commentary that works to construct Sinatra's star image. Played out in films that reference contemporary debates around the American male, and drawn into press discourse locating the star in the midst of a variety of social, political, and cultural issues, Sinatra's distinct persona becomes a way of understanding the dominant attitudes existing in postwar America. This book comprehensively examines Sinatra's star image and uncovers the surprising masculine identity that image represents.

1

The Postwar Success Story and Working-Class Alienation

"Frank Sinatra," says an agent who wishes he had Frank's account, "is just about the hottest item in show business today" . . . his new success spreads like a Hoboken cargo net across almost every area of show business.

—Ezra Goodman

Goodman's 1955 *Time* magazine profile of Sinatra is a stark illustration of the star's developing class image. Essentially a comprehensive examination of the extreme successes and failures of Sinatra's career, the article's treatment of Sinatra's Hoboken background makes plain the location of his attitudes and behavior in a highly specific class identity. As *Time* applauds Sinatra's ability to resurrect his defunct career against all odds, the magazine's constant references to the star's urban, industrial upbringing in New Jersey tie Sinatra's story indelibly to an American working class. Sinatra's desire for the extraordinary level of success he achieves in the 1950s, and his public displays of resentment and hostility, in this way become an expression of a conspicuous working-class identity. The cover illustration with which *Time* accompanies the article illustrates the magazine's unease about these distinct class associations. An inset drawing of Sinatra in a pink shirt and fedora presents a familiar picture of the star, and surrounding newspaper cuttings highlight the impact of biography and commentary on Sinatra's image. In the midst of this imagery, the addition of a ravaged face resembling Dorian Gray's painting indicates a clear discomfort with the working-class male identity Sinatra presents.

The changes that occur around Sinatra's working-class identity and their illustration of shifting cultural attitudes toward class are the subject of this chapter. As ideas of the average American male alter from World War II to the 1950s, Sinatra's working-class image exposes the extent to which issues of class alienation and disenfranchisement are concealed in a postwar culture stressing the elimination of class barriers. The abundance of sociological texts and films of the 1950s focusing on the white-collar, middle management suburban husband highlights the cultural dominance of this definition of the American male. Equally, the concerns expressed in these texts with regard to a lack of ambition and a desire for conformity reveal the anxieties surrounding middle-class masculinity.

In the context of the prominence of the middle-class male, Sinatra's image introduces an alternative male identity into discussions of postwar American masculinity. Sinatra's class persona is established during World War II, when commentators reveal the ways in which working-class audiences engage with the star for the possibility he promises of career achievement. Sinatra's screen persona maintains this link with the working-class and ethnic identity that typifies the American male in 1940s Hollywood. The highs and lows of Sinatra's career impact substantially on the class element of his image. As postwar culture draws close connections between professional success and the middle class, Sinatra's highly public career slide challenges the certainty of upward mobility. Similarly, the level of success achieved by Sinatra following this decline, and the sense of resentment and nonconformity that circulates around him, makes his star image problematic. In the light of press portrayals of Sinatra, Herbert Gans's identification of his appeal for the working class of Boston's West End, where he was regarded as a "quasi–West Ender,"[1] indicates the potency of Sinatra's working-class persona by the late 1950s.

Sinatra's screen image works further to consolidate this class identity. In the 1950s, Hollywood increasingly focused on the middle-class American male's anxiety-fueled attempts to combine contented suburban family living with a manageable level of professional success and with expressions of individuality in a conformist environment. Sinatra's screen characters, however, invariably derive from an urban, blue-collar background, his medical student in *Not as a Stranger* providing his single middle-class role. Through these characters, Sinatra presents an alternative version of the postwar American male to the dominant middle-class model. In *Young at Heart* and *The Man with the Golden Arm,* Sinatra challenges assertions of postwar prosperity and social advancement, highlighting a sense of working-class alienation. At the same time, Sinatra's characters forcefully demonstrate distinct values that contest the ascendance of the middle-class male.

"Just a Kid from Hoboken Who Got the Breaks": The Cinderella Myth and the 1940s Everyman

During an interview in 1977, Sinatra discussed his rise to fame during World War II and observed, "I always felt that I was, in their minds, one of the kids from the neighborhood who grew up and became a success."[2] Sinatra's identification of his symbolic value as a working-class success story is confirmed by the conclusions of several commentators who sought to explain his extraordinary early popularity. Following his employment as vocalist with the Harry James and Tommy Dorsey orchestras, Sinatra's solo performances at New York's Paramount Theater in December 1942/January 1943 and October 1944 were notable for bearing witness to the uniquely enthusiastic reaction of Sinatra's audience, which consisted largely of teenage girls, nicknamed "the bobbysoxers." By 1944, Sinatra's popularity was such that disturbances arose outside the theater when thousands of girls were unable to gain entry, provoking what came to be known as the Columbus Day Riots. One of those who attended this second round of performances was the editor of the *New Republic,* Bruce Bliven. The attention paid to Sinatra by this weighty journalist, normally concerned with the country's economic and political affairs, suggested that Sinatra's popularity held a cultural significance, which Bliven concluded was in part related to class: "Although I am told that devotion to The Voice is found in all classes of society, nearly all of the bobbysockers whom I saw at the Paramount gave every appearance of being children of the poor . . . he represents a dream of what they themselves might conceivably do or become. He earns a million a year, and yet he talks their language; he is just a kid from Hoboken who got the breaks."[3] Bliven noted Sinatra's self-presentation as an ordinary American male and identified his particular appeal among the working class as a representation of the possibility of upward mobility. A series of articles by E. J. Kahn Jr. in *The New Yorker* made similar attempts to understand what Kahn termed the "social phenomenon" of Sinatra. Like Bliven, Kahn detected a central class element to Sinatra's image: "In public statements, he likes to describe himself as 'just a kid from Hoboken' and to imply that if a poor boy from a place like Hoboken can do as well as he has done in so short a time, this is indeed a land of hope and promise. His triumph has been as splendid as Cinderella's, and the storybook quality of his life is probably the basis of much of the appeal he has for young citizens who have never known anything even approximating success or prosperity."[4] In what becomes a trend of feminizing imagery, Kahn recognizes the mythology already being created around Sinatra as the subject of a 1940s rags to riches fairy tale. Sinatra's references to his urban, industrial New Jersey background establish a precedent for the ways in which he would continuously be associated with a working-class identity constructed as part of his star biography and developed through commentary and his screen persona.

The positive presentation and reception of Sinatra as a working-class male occurs in the context of the prominence of the "ordinary" American in the 1940s. One of the legacies of the Great Depression was that poverty, unemployment, and blue-collar work were viewed as the average American experience. Franklin Delano Roosevelt's New Deal policies, designed to assist the plight of "the forgotten man," and the documentary and arts projects of the Works Progress Administration (WPA) highlighted working-class identity in the lean years of the 1930s. This promotion of the working-class white male continued into the 1940s, and in 1942 FDR's vice president, Henry Wallace, gave a speech declaring the twentieth century the "Century of the Common Man." This came as a response to publishing magnate Henry Luce's "American Century" editorial in 1941, which had promoted private enterprise and economic freedom in preference to social reform. When Sinatra actively campaigned in 1944 for FDR's reelection for a historic third term, he drew on this class imagery surrounding both the president and himself, telling audiences: "The thing I like about the President, he's pretty fond of the little man. Well, I'm one, even with all of my good fortune."[5]

Hollywood cinema reflected this pride in the working man, most notably in the films of Frank Capra, which idealized the "Everyman" character portrayed several times by Jimmy Stewart and Gary Cooper. In Stewart's challenge to political corruption in *Mr. Smith Goes to Washington* (1939) and his struggle against unfeeling capitalism in *It's a Wonderful Life* (1946), and in Cooper's cynical abuse by a politicized media in *Meet John Doe* (1941), Capra reveres the smalltown, high-school-educated laborer or clerk as the embodiment of America's independent spirit. World War II combat films also celebrated the working-class male in positive representations of servicemen. Documentaries by Hollywood directors such as John Huston (*The Battle of San Pietro,* 1944), William Wyler (*Memphis Belle,* 1944) and John Ford (*The Battle of Midway,* 1942) paid tribute to the contribution of ordinary soldiers.[6] Feature films such as *Destination Tokyo* (1943) and *Battleground* (1949) foregrounded the working class, often immigrant male (immigrant usually implying working class) as a symbol of the ordinary American's fight against fascism. Combat units were therefore filled with "GI Joes" who worked as mechanics or served in their fathers' stores in their civilian lives.

Sinatra commenced his Hollywood acting career in this atmosphere of the normalization of the working-class male identity. His initial roles at RKO were unrepresentative of the class persona Sinatra would develop through his screen career. Thomas Cripps describes *Higher and Higher* as "an egalitarian affair that was a jiving civilian twist on the war movie genre," pointing to the role reversal required for the butlers' ball as evidence of its liberal tone.[7] However, in this tale of servants and their titled masters, Sinatra is, in part, connected to the upstairs class, playing singing neighbor "Frank Sinatra," who employs household staff. In *Step Lively* (1944), a remake of the 1938 Marx Brothers comedy *Room Service,* Sinatra's role again combines the loose class definition of the artist with upper-class associations, as he plays an aspiring singer and playwright who is also the nephew of a judge. At MGM, however, the class persona identified by Bliven and Kahn as a contributing factor to Sinatra's appeal as a singer begins to develop on screen. Sinatra's serviceman and veteran roles, in particular, connect with the working-class male identity made average by 1940s American culture. In *Anchors Aweigh* (1945), Sinatra plays U.S. naval man Clarence Doolittle, nicknamed "Brooklyn" after the New York district of which he is a native. As another sailor on shore leave in *On the Town,* Sinatra hails from the small town of Peoria and in *It Happened in Brooklyn,* he returns as an army veteran to his urban home. In a multitude of 1940s films, Brooklyn becomes synonymous with the idea of an urban, working-class, and often immigrant environment. The Danny Kaye comedy *The Kid from Brooklyn* (1946) and the family melodrama *A Tree Grows in Brooklyn* (1945) are among numerous films that use the New York district as a byword for a standard urban American community. When Sinatra's characters display traits that problematically distinguish them from the regular male identity Brooklyn represents, the narratives become involved in resolving such deviancies. In *Anchors Aweigh,* Clarence's fear of women is disbelieved by Gene Kelly's navy "wolf" Joe Brady, who argues, "After all, you're no yokel. You're from Brooklyn!" Clarence's explanation is that "even in Brooklyn, things can go wrong," and the remainder of the film works toward reconstructing Clarence's male identity to fit the romantically confident urban image. In the same way, in *It Happened in Brooklyn,* various characters attest to the sociable confidence of the community's men, a trait that Sinatra's Danny Miller initially fails to display. His retiring nature is, once again, discarded through the course of the film, and Miller is restored to a working-class masculine norm. Sinatra's association with Hollywood's standardization of the Brooklyn male illustrates the positive class identity established as part of his star image in the 1940s. As Sinatra's image develops in the 1950s and cultural attitudes to male class identity alter, his working-class persona becomes more complex, illuminating the postwar cultural dominance of the professionally successful suburban husband and defining an alternative version of the American male.

"Sinatra Is All Washed Up": Upward Mobility and Career Failure

From the end of World War II, America began experiencing an economic boom that reached its peak in the 1950s and had a substantial effect on perceptions of American identity. Technological advances, new electronics industries, a postwar population growth, and a growing demand for new consumer goods all led to an expanding economy and increased prosperity. The growth in service industries that had occurred since the early part of the twentieth century continued apace, until by 1956 there were more white-collar professionals than manual workers.[8] The subsidy of veterans' education through the GI Bill combined with these factors to indicate a trend of upward mobility, and the increased prosperity and change in professional status enjoyed by many Americans during this period of economic growth created an expanding middle class. The middle-class male was now defined by a middle-management level of white-collar success and a married life in suburbia, where the evidence of his success could be displayed. When William J. Levitt created a housing development in Long Island, his appearance on the cover of *Time* on July 3, 1950, illustrated the importance of lifestyle to the middle-class image, as the headline read: "House Builder Levitt: For Sale: A New Way of Life."[9] The suburban home, complete with television set and car parked in the driveway, was an emblem of the professional male's success and upward mobility, and the growth of the suburban lifestyle shifted perceptions of the average American male from the urban working class to the middle class of suburbia.

This image of America as overwhelmingly middle class was promoted throughout U.S. culture. In 1959, Vance Packard quoted recent proclamations about the disappearance of class. A national periodical claimed America had become the "most truly classless society in history," and the director of a market-research company argued the country was becoming "one vast middle class."[10] In 1959, Vice President Richard Nixon drew on the suburban lifestyle as evidence of the opportunities for social mobility created by the capitalist system. In his "kitchen debate" with Soviet Premier Nikita Khrushchev at Moscow's American National Exhibition, Nixon argued that the kind of machine-packed kitchen on display represented the prosperity and chances for professional advancement available to all American men and visible in the suburban family home. Elaine Tyler May explains: "In appliance-laden houses across the country, working-class as well as business-class breadwinners could fulfill the new American work-to-consume ethic. Home ownership would lessen class consciousness among workers, who would set their sights toward the middle-class ideal. The family home would be the place where a man could display his success through the accumulation of consumer goods."[11] For Nixon, the suburban home symbolized America's ability in the 1950s to pull all its citizens into an idealized middle class. These assertions of a predominant class defined the average American male in clear terms as a successful, upwardly mobile figure.

The direction Sinatra's career was taking in the late 1940s and early 1950s markedly differentiates him from this male model and the atmosphere of optimistic postwar prosperity in which it developed. The slump that devastated his career gave the impression that the "kid from Hoboken" was being swiftly returned to his roots. As early as 1948, *Modern Television and Radio* headlined an article with the question "Is Sinatra Finished?" The article, by *Metronome* coeditor Barry Ulanov, discussed rumors alleging "Sinatra is all washed up!" and "'The Voice' is now just 'The Gargle.'" Detailing the political affiliations, gangster connections, extramarital affairs, and poor recording and film choices that had contributed to these rumors, Ulanov nevertheless concluded that Sinatra's career misfortune was temporary.[12] His optimism was misplaced, however, and Sinatra's dual career as a singer and actor would continue to collapse.

The decline in Sinatra's popularity as a singer in the late 1940s occurred for a variety of reasons. The teenage fan base he had accumulated had matured at the same time that a different style of male singer was appearing. "Belters" like Frankie Laine, whose "Mule Train" was an instant hit in 1949, were replacing the restrained ballad style exemplified by Sinatra. A trend was also developing away from the lyrical artistry of Broadway composers such as Rodgers and Hart and Cole Porter toward the kind of novelty song that was neither admired by Sinatra nor suited to his vocal style. Columbia Records producer and artists-and-repertoire man Mitch Miller, who favored the throwaway lyrics and sales potential of the novelty song, brought Laine to the label and was also responsible for securing Rosemary Clooney's first hit, "Come on-a My House," in 1951. Although Sinatra was still recording the standards of Porter and Rodgers and Hart for albums such as *Sing and Dance with Sinatra* (1950), Miller was also steering him toward unsuitable material, such as "The Hucklebuck," released in 1949, and the infamous 1951 collaboration with the blond siren Dagmar, "Mama Will Bark," which featured a barking dog. Sinatra frequently expressed his dissatisfaction with this type of material in interviews, such as two published in *Metronome* in 1948 and 1953.[13] His recordings of novelty songs therefore suggested a lack of control over his career caused by his declining popularity and, at the same time, contributed to his increasingly poor reception. The throat hemorrhage Sinatra suffered on the stage of New York's Copacabana nightclub on April 26, 1950, added to this sense of a downward spiral, and in 1952 Sinatra was dropped from the Columbia label.

Sinatra's film career suffered a similar fate. In 1945 his star status ensured he was given top billing against costar Gene Kelly in his first MGM film, *Anchors Aweigh.* By the time *On the Town* was released in 1949, however, the two stars' names had been transposed in the titles, and in 1950 MGM declined to renew Sinatra's contract. In a lecture Sinatra gave at Yale University in 1986, he blamed his dismissal on a joke he made in the MGM canteen about the alleged relationship between studio head Louis B. Mayer and the singer Ginny Simms.[14] However, the bad publicity resulting from Sinatra's adulterous relationship with Ava Gardner could not have assisted his position in the studio famed for its family-oriented films. More significantly, Sinatra's career at MGM had never achieved the heights of his status as a popular singer. While his final film for the studio, *On the Town,* was a critical and popular success, his tenure at MGM was largely defined by mediocre films and unchallenging roles. The 1948 film *The Kissing Bandit,* in which Sinatra played a shy nineteenth-century Spanish Californian mistaken for a romantic outlaw, was a particular low point. The *New York Herald Tribune* critic described the flop as "a grand Technicolored vacuum . . . [and a] limp Spanish omelette."[15] Sinatra's departure from MGM was followed by further unsuccessful productions. RKO's *Double Dynamite* in 1951 and Universal's *Meet Danny Wilson* the same year both failed to make a mark and reiterated the direction Sinatra's career was taking.

Sinatra's appearances on television most visibly associated the star with failure, as *The Frank Sinatra Show* acted as the screen through which the prolonged deterioration of the Sinatra career could be viewed on a weekly basis. Sinatra's perception of the role played by television during this period of his career was strangely positive. During a 1955 *Person to Person* interview with Edward R. Murrow, Sinatra credited Bob Hope's invitation to appear on the variety show *The Star Spangled Review* in 1950 as an opportunity to revitalize his career, or "get off the canvas," as he expressed it.[16] Certainly, by 1953, television was providing one stage for Sinatra's revival. The star's confident performance of his new Capitol recording "I've Got the World on a String," and his role as a charming schemer in "Anything Goes," on episodes of the *Colgate Comedy Hour,* pointed to the upward path of Sinatra's career in 1953.[17] However, prior to this upturn, Sinatra's television appearances largely reinforced his image as a star in professional freefall. Sinatra's decreasing popularity was often illustrated through the lack of self-assurance evident in his performances, as well as the extent to which appearances traded on the star's earlier appeal. When Sinatra appeared on *The Dinah Shore Show* in 1952, a few weeks before his own show was to close, the two stars performed a sketch reenacting the WNEW radio show on which they appeared together in 1942. The changes that had occurred in the intervening ten years are apparent in the show's closing moments as Sinatra nervously falters over lyrics in a duet with Shore and attempts to promote what would soon be the commercial failure *Meet Danny Wilson,* while Shore silences him with a mute button.[18]

Sinatra's own series illustrates even more forcefully this reliance on past glories and the contrasts that were evident with the current state of his career. *The Frank Sinatra Show* ran on the CBS network between October 1950 and April 1952 and consisted of a series of one-hour programs mixing music and comedy in a variety format. In November 1950, *Metronome* predicted "a very bright season coming up for Frankie," based on the excellent reviews Sinatra had garnered for his appearance on *The Star Spangled Review.*[19] However, scheduled against the popular satirical program *Your Show of Shows* for its first season, and subsequently against the ratings-winning *Milton Berle Show,* Sinatra's television venture was arguably doomed to failure. The series's initial sponsor, Bulova watches, withdrew its support after only thirteen weeks, and the series stumbled along through multiple sponsors and low viewing figures until its final demise with the early termination of Sinatra's contract. With each show opening with a caricature drawing of Sinatra as the skinny singer with arms outstretched, a mass of hair and an oversized bow tie, the series draws the audience back to Sinatra's early image while emphasizing his current difficulties. A show broadcast in May 1951 makes these associations plain. Sinatra was appearing simultaneously on television and at the Paramount and took his stage show to the small screen, enabling immediate comparisons to be made with the frenzied days of bobby-soxer riots. Chatting to singer June Hutton, he jokes that the last time he played the Paramount he only had to sing, whereas "now, in the intermissions, I have to go out in the aisles and sell popcorn." In a further conversation with pianist Joe Bushkin, Sinatra moves talk toward their years with the Tommy Dorsey Orchestra and Sinatra's opening performance at the Paramount in 1942. These remarks place Sinatra's popular success firmly in the past. Dagmar's appearance on the show, and a sketch wherein Sinatra explains that his torn clothes are due to some fans—Frankie Laine fans—further reference the deterioration of Sinatra's career and the rise of his competition.[20] As other shows drew attention to Sinatra's lack of hit records and financial problems, the series presented a pitiful image of Sinatra as a fading star.[21]

"Busy, Busy, Busy—Frank": Resentment and Working-Class Identification

When Sinatra's career entered its third installment and he achieved even greater success than during his early years of stardom, he remained associated with downward mobility and its class connotations. Articles frequently concentrated on Sinatra's apparent resentment about his years of falling popularity and his nonconformist behavior, connecting both to the star's working-class identity. Sinatra's public ascendance began in 1954 with the simultaneous renewal of his film and recording careers. The singer had his first hit record since 1947 with the "Young at Heart" movie theme, signaling his new and effective collaboration with arranger Nelson Riddle and Capitol Records.[22] Sinatra also received the Oscar for Best Supporting Actor at the 1954 Academy Awards ceremony for his performance as Private Angelo Maggio in *From Here to Eternity,* which proclaimed the revitalization of his film career. Through the 1950s, Sinatra's career continued to flourish. His albums with Capitol Records received both critical and popular acclaim and established him as the foremost male interpreter of popular music. The albums' widespread appeal is evident in Sinatra's consistent topping of music polls. He won the *Down Beat* critics' Male Singer of the Year poll in 1955 and 1957 and the magazine's readers' poll consecutively from 1954 to 1962. Sinatra's film career was similarly healthy. He was nominated for an Academy Award for his role in *The Man with the Golden Arm* and successfully combined dramatic performances with musical roles in a wide range of films.

The extremes of Sinatra's career were, by the mid-1950s, the frequent subject of press comment, forming part of the mythology surrounding his persona. *Time*'s 1955 cover story, *Photoplay*'s "The Sinatra Story" from the same year, and *The New York Times Magazine*'s "The Rise, Fall, and Rise of Sinatra," published in 1957, are among numerous articles that traced the spectacular ups and downs of Sinatra's career.[23] In the light of Sinatra's decline and recent success, his attitudes and behavior came under increasing scrutiny. The ambition that had yielded the star's second wave of success was often viewed as peculiarly working-class. Prefacing discussion of Sinatra's professional aspirations with a tale of a bottle fight in his youth, *Time* inferred a direct class connection, warning: "It is well to remember the jagged weapon. The one he carries nowadays is of the mind, and called ambition."[24] The depiction of Sinatra as a star harboring resentment about his career slide also tainted his newly successful image with lingering associations of failure. Sinatra contributed to this imagery with public pronouncements intended to emphasize his career successes but that instead suggested an unwillingness to relinquish a festering sense of bitterness. In December 1954, Sinatra took out a fullpage advertisement in *Billboard* magazine listing the awards he had received during the year and the films he had on release and in progress, signing off, "Busy, busy, busy—Frank."[25] Having been named Top Male Vocalist by *Metronome* in 1955, Sinatra published a further advertisement in the magazine. Including a copy of the telegram informing him of the award, and concluding with the caustic remark, "P.P.S. Mitch Miller???," Sinatra's swaggering resentment toward his Columbia producer unsettled his image as a successful star.[26] Thomas Wiseman detected a similar bitterness in several interviews he conducted with the star in 1957 and commented: "Sinatra has always had the appearance of a man who has been ill-treated by life. Wealth, fame, adulation and a life as privileged as a sultan's have not deprived him of the starved, hurt, bitter look of an under-privileged citizen who is going to get his own back one day."[27] Describing Sinatra's "neon personality" and tendency toward physical aggression, Wiseman paints an image of Sinatra as a working-class American whose success has failed to rid him of his sense of exclusion.

Sinatra's bitterness is often displayed through nonconformist behavior and an antagonistic relationship with the press, which articles frequently connect to both his career decline and working-class background. In

1959, *Photoplay* discussed Hollywood talk of "The Mysterious Sinatra Hate Campaign," suggesting: "He has always been awkward. Recently he has become difficult. No one can get near him. . . . Sinatra is becoming maddeningly unpredictable and as morose as a backwoodsman. . . . The fact is that Sinatra learned to hate a long time ago and he hasn't forgotten how. . . . The scars that Sinatra wears today are souvenirs of Hoboken gang-wars and clashes with the cops. . . . He can't forget the savagery of Hoboken, the jeers that were showered at him on the way up and the ruthless verbal beatings he took from critics when he was down."[28] Like many articles published through the 1950s, *Photoplay*'s discussion presents Sinatra's unwillingness to conduct himself in ways expected of a star of his stature as part of a working-class sensibility.[29] A *Redbook* article published in 1959 made similar connections, alluding to Sinatra's underworld friendships and lack of cooperation with the press. The article concluded, "The most striking reason for the strong reactions he inspires is his refusal to change or disguise his way of living for the sake of appearances."[30] Vance Packard argues that crossing class boundaries requires a willing social conformity. For those who resist transforming their identity, success becomes problematic: "Others of us, less expert in the nuances of status symbols or more indifferent to them, persist in modes of behavior and in displays of taste that themselves serve as barriers in separating us from the group to which we may secretly aspire. They can keep us in our place. If we aspire to rise in the world but fail to take on the coloration of the group we aspire to—by failing to discard our old status symbols, friends, club memberships, values, behavior patterns, and acquiring new ones esteemed by the higher group—our chances of success are diminished."[31] As the articles described here indicate, Sinatra's failure to comply with standard codes of behavior consolidates his working-class image. Sinatra's retention of this class persona at the peak of his success is identified by sociologist Herbert Gans as central to his appeal to a working-class, particularly Italian American, audience.

Between October 1957 and May 1958, Gans undertook a study of the innercity neighborhood of Boston's West End, an area that had been declared a slum in 1953 and was set for inclusion in a program of urban renewal. Gans focused on American-born children of Italian immigrants aged in their thirties and forties. His conclusions about this "independent working-class subculture," or "peer group society," were driven as much by his subjects' class origins as by their ethnicity, since his studies of other working-class communities bore similar results.[32] Gans discovered a society separated from "the outside world" by both opportunities and values, where Sinatra was "almost worshipped." The West Enders' admiration for Sinatra stemmed from his ability to achieve success and prosperity while resisting the pressure for class conformity. The male subjects, in particular, cited Sinatra's proud defense of his Italian background, including his retention of his surname, his loyalty to childhood friends, a willingness to physically and verbally contest exclusion, and a lifestyle that included gambling and numerous sexual relationships as evidence of Sinatra's indifference to middle-class notions of respectable behavior. Gans observes:

> As an actor, he often plays the kind of rebellious roles with which West End men can identify. As a singer, the inflection he gives to the tune and the lyrics is interpreted as arousing his audience to action. As a West Ender said, "He gives you a little dig in his songs." . . . To them, he seems to be putting something over on the outside world, while at the same time taking its money and attractive women. He has risen to the top, failed, and come back again to even greater fame, to prove that downward mobility is not inevitable, that the "bum" can return to even greater heights than he achieved before. And, despite his success, he has not given up the old values; he has remained what he was originally—a seeker of action with peer group values.[33]

The West Enders identify strongly with Sinatra's nonconformity and view his displays of a working-class sensibility in the rarefied world he inhabits as an inspiring call to infiltrate the successful middle-class arena. The myth of Sinatra's career rise, fall, and further rise is equally evidence of Sinatra's defiant claim to success, extending the symbolic value recognized in the 1940s by Bliven and Kahn. Responding to Sinatra's Italian American and fundamentally working-class image, the West Enders view Sinatra still as one of their own, so that "they react not as fans but as quasi-colleagues or peers."[34]

"Everybody Can't Be Gregory Peck": Conformity and Ambition in the Corporate Male

The sense of identification with Sinatra amid Boston's "peergroup society" highlights the clear class distinctions that exist in 1950s America and Sinatra's place within them. Gans's study sheds light on the attitudes and ways of behaving of the urban working-class male, just as Sinatra's film roles of the period frequently reveal his experiences and values. American culture of the 1950s, however, often focused on the middle-class male, expressing concerns about this particular male identity and, in doing so, reiterating its primacy as a representation of American masculinity. Sociological texts such as *The Lonely Crowd* and *The Organization Man* reflect on the changing characteristics of the middle-class American male, David Riesman and William H. Whyte perceiving a trend away from a traditional sense of American individualism, toward a new desire for conformity. In *The Lonely Crowd,* Riesman uses the terms *inner-directed* and *other-directed* to differentiate between these old and new character types, defining the *other-directed* male in terms of his reliance on others for the development of his attitudes and behavior.[35] Whyte sees the "Protestant Ethic" of achievement through hard work and enterprise being replaced by a "Social Ethic," which he explains as "a belief in the group as the source of creativity; a belief in 'belongingness' as the ultimate need of the individual."[36] *The Organization Man* examines the middle-class male's conformist tendencies in the office and at home in suburbia. According to Whyte, the postwar middle-class male is dominated by a need to conform in businesses, where personality tests define employee suitability, and in the suburbs, where identical homes and a prescribed social life restrict individuality. He additionally perceives a lack of ambition in white-collar workers, who aspire to reach only "a sort of plateau," a safe level of success that requires little personal enterprise or risk.[37] Whyte suggests this male type governs postwar American society in relation to both status and cultural impact: "They are the dominant members of our society. . . . They have not joined together into a recognizable elite . . . but it is from their ranks that are coming most of the first and second echelons of our leadership, and it is their values which will set the American temper."[38] The conformity and lack of ambition exemplified by Whyte's "organization man" sets the tone for 1950s America and emphasizes the cultural dominance of the middle-class male as a representation of the country's male identity.

This concern with the changing character of America's middle-class male was equally evident in the literature and films of the 1950s. Sloan Wilson's *The Man in the Gray Flannel Suit* (1955) is the most famous of the novels that deal with the postwar anxieties of the business executive, providing a label for the middle-class white-collar male. The 1956 film version of the novel starred Gregory Peck as World War II veteran Tom Rath. By the mid-1950s Peck was being referred to in films such as *All About Eve* (1950) and *The Seven Year Itch* (1955) as a male ideal, and his performance in *The Man in the Gray Flannel Suit* expresses American culture's concern about its favored class of men.[39] Through Tom's wife Betsy, the film raises the problematic issue of Tom's need for security. Betsy pushes her husband into a public relations position with a Madison Avenue broadcasting company, which epitomizes the superficiality of corporate life. As his friend Bill Hawthorne remarks when advising him of the opening: "You have a clean shirt. You bathe every day. That's all there is to it." Writing speeches for his employer's proposal of a mental health campaign, Tom attempts to negotiate his way around the immediate seniors, who undermine him, and company president Hopkins (Fredric March), who warms to him. Debating with Betsy whether to tailor his comments about a speech to what he anticipates Hopkins will want to hear, Tom reveals the conformity required in corporate life: "I never wanted to get into this rat race, but now that I'm in it I think I'd be an idiot not to play it the way everybody else plays it." Tom eventually relays his negative views about the speech to Hopkins, resisting this definition of the corporate male. At the same time, the film validates Tom's lack of ambition. Hopkins is an entrepreneur with a failed marriage and dilettante daughter. Tom's decision to decline a position working directly with Hopkins, which could advance his career, in favor of spending more time with his family, endorses the kind of mediocrity identified by Whyte.

In the 1954 film *Woman's World,* three local carplant managers and their wives spend a weekend in New York being assessed for the position of general manager.[40] Company president Ernest Gifford (Clifton Webb) scrutinizes the couples' personalities and the men's professional attitudes to determine the most suitable man for the job. At the elimination stage, one unsuccessful couple is relieved to be able to return to suburban anonymity. The other failed contender sees defeat as an opportunity to repair his health and failed marriage. The successful candidate is required to discard his overambitious wife before achieving his goal, thereby proving his ability to conform to the group ethic. In *Woman's World,* success, gained without the zeal of ambition, is a single man's game.

In the same year, *Executive Suite* presented an array of ideas about the corporate male. When Avery Bullard, the president of a furniture business, dies suddenly of a heart attack, the other members of the board scramble to appoint a new leader, each negotiating to secure his own position. Accountant Loren Shaw (Fredric March) is most eager to gain support for his nomination. His open ambition and nightschool qualifications mark him out as the film's negative representation of working-class male identity. Designer McDonald Walling (William Holden) is unsure whether he wants the post, aware that success and the drive for profit have altered the company as well as Bullard's character. Walling ultimately wins the position of company president by declaring his intention to raise the standard of the company's product and consider the welfare of its employees. The dilemma in the film is how to remain a creative individualist and empathetic employer while improving the company's profits. Walling's messianic speech amid the stained-glass windows of the boardroom demonstrates how the middle-class individualist with minimal ambition might save the corporation.

"Where's the Spinning Wheel?": Americana and Class Alienation in *Young at Heart*

The era's corporate films epitomize Hollywood's expression of a postwar focus on the middle-class male. Affirming his lack of ambition, yet critical of his conformity, the films reiterate America's confused attitudes toward its white-collar male and highlight the cultural dominance of his class. Sinatra's screen persona in the 1950s contests this normalization of middle-class masculinity. From the cynical reporter among Rhode Island's elite in *High Society* (1956), to the ambitious Miami hotel owner destined for failure in *A Hole in the Head* (1959), Sinatra's characters are urban working-class versions of the American male. Pitted against successful professional males or a disinterested middle class, they dramatize the class alienation denied by middle-class hegemony and validate alternative values. In *Young at Heart* and *The Man with the Golden Arm,* these class conflicts are enacted most effectively, as Sinatra's characters are located in environments that highlight their exclusion from the postwar American success story. Both films connect Sinatra in different ways to John Garfield, making Sinatra's working-class male almost an updated version of the identity created by Garfield in films such as *The Postman Always Rings Twice* (1946), *Humoresque* (1946), and *Body and Soul* (1947). While the two stars share a close association with working-class masculinity, the shifting context of the 1950s means that Sinatra's films use narrative and star image to confront the sense of alienation provoked by American attitudes toward class.

Young at Heart is a pivotal film in terms of the construction of Sinatra's 1950s screen image. Sinatra's performance commences a shift away from the feminizing vulnerability of his 1940s persona to an emotional expressiveness conveyed from a more masculine perspective. The role additionally defines the bitter and alienated working-class persona that underpins Sinatra's screen image through the 1950s, as both character and star are closely associated with career failure. Sinatra plays composer and musical arranger Barney Sloan in this remake of Warner Bros.' 1938 film *Four Daughters,* which starred John Garfield as, on that occasion, Mickey Borden. The *New York Times* congratulated Garfield on the "acidity" of his performance, although the script prepared by Julius J. Epstein and Lenore Coffee clearly articulated the fundamentals of the character: "His manner is indolent, his expression wry, almost surly. His humor is ironic. When he smiles (which is seldom), his demeanor is sardonic. Mickey Borden doesn't think well of himself or the world. Poverty had done the trick."[41] In his film debut, Garfield carries with him none of the filmic and extracinematic class associations that accompany Sinatra's portrayal of Barney Sloan. Equally, the variant contexts of the Depression era and postwar prosperity provide contrasting approaches to issues of American class. In his brief analysis of *Young at Heart,* Thomas Schatz is singularly concerned with the generic and star imagery conflicts in the film, which he views less as creating points of interest than as poorly conceived. The casting of Doris Day and Dorothy Malone, and Day and Sinatra, therefore becomes evidence of the film's "generic schizophrenia."[42] On the contrary, however, the tensions that build around Day's ebullient musical style and Sinatra's film noir–like presence form part of the struggle that occurs between the narrative's attempts to incorporate Sinatra's character into suburban domesticity, and the class alienation that ensures his exclusion.

The first section of the film builds a picture of middle-class American contentment. The audience is introduced to the Tuttle family, who live in a picket-fenced house on a quiet, tree-lined street in the heart of Connecticut. The nominal head of the household is widower Gregory Tuttle (Robert Keith), the dean of faculty at the local Music Foundation. The Tuttle home is a largely feminine arena, however, led by Gregory's unmarried sister Jessie (Ethel Barrymore) and completed by his three daughters, Laurie (Day), Fran (Malone), and Amy (Elizabeth Fraser). These early scenes quickly establish the middle-class family and its suburban lifestyle as American normality. Highbrow culture provided by Gregory's flute playing is softened by the boxing match on the television set viewed by Jessie, and the lace curtains and fireside rug mark this location as a typical American family home. These introductory scenes also highlight the significance of marriage and professional achievement to the male identity. When Fran arrives home from a date with local businessman Bob Neary (Alan Hale Jr.) and excitedly announces their engagement, she proudly boasts that Bob is "the biggest real estate operator in Connecticut." Fran is emotionally uninvolved in the relationship and demonstrates a lack of physical attraction to her overweight fiancé. While Fran is drawn to Bob's ability and readiness to provide a financially secure future, her reluctance to set a date and their physically and emotionally distant marriage will illustrate their incompatibility.

The singularly upbeat tone of the early part of the film is set by Doris Day as the unfailingly cheerful Laurie. *Young at Heart* was Day's final film under her Warner Bros. contract and trades on the vivacious persona built by Day in musicals such as *On Moonlight Bay* (1951) and *By the Light of the Silvery Moon* (1953). Day's image would develop in more complex ways through films such as the dark Ruth Etting biopic *Love Me or Leave Me* (1955) and the romantic comedies *Pillow Talk* (1959) and *Lover Come Back* (1962), in which Day created a progressive screen image of the modern career woman. In 1954, however, Day brings with her a general enthusiasm and an association with depictions of harmonious middle-class family life to contribute to the air of stability and cheerfulness otherwise constructed by the bright sunshine and family concord evident in *Young at Heart*'s early scenes.

The arrival of Alex Burke (Gig Young) points to the two contrasting male identities that will become the focus of the film. Laurie meets Alex when he assists in the birth of a litter of puppies on her neighbor's front lawn. A ninth puppy exceeds its mother's feeding abilities, and Alex advises Laurie's neighbor that the puppy will need to be either bottlefed or drowned. Horrified at Alex's callous suggestion, Laurie rescues the runt of the litter, foregoing the prime puppy she had been promised. "Number Nine" is clearly a symbolic reference to Sinatra's Barney Sloan, who is yet to appear. Barney's experience of underprivilege and exclusion from the family will mirror the frustrated beginnings of his canine counterpart, and Alex's approach to Barney will be just as dismissive. While Laurie will initially be attracted by the able but ruthless qualities Alex displays here, she will ultimately be compelled by Barney's need for her nurturing response.

Alex initially provokes an undercurrent of disquiet in the Tuttle household as each of the sisters is instantly attracted to his good looks and exuberant confidence. However, it soon becomes obvious that Alex is marked as the natural successor to the Tuttle patriarch. Gig Young would forge a screen identity through the 1950s as a fantasy male in films such as *Desk Set* (1957), *Teacher's Pet* (1958), and *Ask Any Girl* (1959).[43] In *Young at Heart,* too, his confident, ambitious composer conforms to the ideal of an attractive, upwardly mobile, middle-class male. Alex's background matches that of the Tuttle family, ensuring he fits neatly into his new environment. His father and Tuttle senior are old school friends, and Alex trades on this family connection to gain entry to both the Tuttle home and the financial opportunities it offers. Alex invites himself to dinner and blithely assumes command at the dinner table, issuing orders about where each member of the family should be seated. He additionally secures lodgings in the house, creating a central place for himself in this familiar family environment where he is perfectly positioned to eventually take on the patriarchal role.

Alex exemplifies the 1950s professional male, wearing his gray flannel uniform throughout the film. He has an advance to compose music for a stage musical but achieves a further subsidy for his work by winning a teaching post at the Music Foundation with Gregory's assistance. Alex is an obvious exponent of a networking approach to professional success identified by C. Wright Mills in his 1951 book *White Collar*. Mills examines an increasing emphasis on personal relations and self-image in place of expertise, arguing: "Now the stress is on agility rather than ability . . . on who you know rather than what you know; on techniques of self-display and the generalized knack of handling people, rather than on moral integrity, substantive accomplishments, and solidity of person."[44] Mills detects the type of business culture Tom Rath refers to as "a very tricky business with a lot of tricky angles." While Rath is instinctively wary of negotiating his way around this culture of manipulation, Alex comfortably employs orchestrated strategies to achieve his goals. As Gregory relates to his family how Alex quickly charmed the usually implacable president of the foundation into offering him a position, he provides further evidence of the brash composer's cynical methods. Despite the minimal talent frequently noted by Gregory, therefore—Alex is rarely seen near the piano—Alex's ambition, unwavering confidence, and interpersonal skills will yield a successful and profitable career as a composer in the musical theater.

In the light of the air of familial harmony and confident middle-class masculinity established during the first thirty minutes of the film, the disruption caused by the arrival of Sinatra as Barney Sloan is substantial. The only reference to Barney comes moments earlier in Alex's description of the man who arranges his music as "a little unpredictable." When Alex opens the front door of the Tuttle home to his work colleague, Barney is facing away from the house and toward the street, suggesting the indifference toward suburban domesticity that will soon become apparent. This delay in the visual presentation of Sinatra, who is billed as Day's costar in the film, highlights the impact of his star image on characterization. With Sinatra's face hidden, attention is forced on the fedora, which had been loosely associated with Sinatra since the 1940s in films such as *Step Lively* but which by the 1950s was becoming a staple part of Sinatra's iconography, appearing on early Capitol albums *Songs for Young Lovers* (1954) and *Swing Easy* (1954). The character is, therefore, immediately invested with all the complexities of Sinatra's star image. In his *New York Herald Tribune* review, Bill Zinsser suggested the overwhelming impact Sinatra's building image has on Barney, commenting: "He walks into a home which is so relentlessly happy and American that it's almost a parody . . . Then enter Sinatra. Good old Frankie. That morose face, that crooked smile, that sloppy posture, those hollow eyes—all are a pleasure to behold."[45] Sinatra's star image brings associations of embittered alienation to the film, constructed through biography and recent films such as *From Here to Eternity* and *Suddenly.* His entrance therefore immediately alters the prevailing tone, introducing into the narrative a dark negativity that increases as Barney's character unfolds.

Ignoring Alex's attempts at polite small talk, Barney casts his eye suspiciously around the house and quickly sums up its traditional American appeal, remarking sarcastically: "Figures. Rug on the floor, piano, smell of cookin' from the kitchen. It's homes like these that are the backbone of the nation. Where's the spinning wheel?" Rather than embracing this picture of middle-class domesticity as a comfortably familiar environment, as Alex has done, Barney demonstrates his inexperience in suburbia through his description of the Tuttle home as a cliché from a mythological past. Barney gravitates immediately toward the piano and harp, his sites of comfort, and the discussion between the two men reveals their contrasting social positions. While Alex is en route to teach a class at the Music Foundation, he has secured for Barney a job playing piano and singing at a down town "joint" where his meager salary will be supplemented by "tips on a plate." Barney is resigned to this unsatisfying form of employment. Even though Alex suggests he may experience a "different class of people" than those he played to in New York, Barney sees only parallels, commenting wryly, "Yeah, suburban drunks. They don't listen, either." Unlike Alex, who commands the attention of both professional colleagues and the Tuttle family from his very arrival on the scene, Barney is accustomed to society's lack of attention to him as a musician or an individual. Alex's treatment of him illustrates the social boundaries that consistently exclude Barney. While Alex works and lives alongside Gregory and makes use of Barney's superior talent to assist his own professional achievements, he isolates Barney in a career wilderness and boardinghouse lodgings.

When Laurie introduces herself to this interloper, the contrast between her middle-class suburban environment and Barney's working-class urban experience is at its most stark. Day's and Sinatra's star images are invoked as Laurie's sunny optimism is challenged by Barney's dark cynicism. Laurie encourages Barney to complete the song he is composing, suggesting the possibility of a hit record. Barney's reluctance, however, is a result of his experience, which leads him to predict future failure. He describes himself as "a glove man," explaining, "You shag flies in the hot sun all your life, but you never go to bat." As he moves around the couches, bookcases, and lace curtains of this comfortable middle-class home, Barney relates a tale of opportunities denied and ambitions thwarted. Beginning life as an orphan and receiving a limited education, Barney has spent six years of the Depression unemployed and served as a private during World War II without being rewarded for any noted heroism. He is convinced his unlucky life will culminate in his being killed by a strike of lightning. Much of the misfortune Barney attributes to the workings of "the fates" or "Lady Luck" is, in fact, evidence of the class alienation that defines his existence. His admission that he changed his name from something "a little more Italian" in an effort to "throw them off the track" recognizes the social factors that have impacted on Barney as a working-class Italian American male.

Barney displays a male identity unfamiliar to Laurie. Her father's professional status and Alex's rising career uphold her belief that courage and ambition overcome all obstacles to success. Further examples of male achievement are all around Laurie. As a brash self-made man—the "'I sold newspapers as a kid but look at me now' type," as Barney terms him—Bob implicitly refutes Barney's claims of dispossession. Even Amy's suitor Ernie (Lonny Chapman), who undertakes plumbing work in the Tuttle home, owns the company, as the sisters are at pains to point out. Amy, in fact, berates Ernie for performing manual labor when he employs and pays "men in overalls." Suburban men are professional and successful, and their sociable demeanor reflects their contented self-assurance.

Barney's distinction from this model is striking. His negative feelings about his chances of musical success, and his "insulting" directness in his early conversation with Laurie, differentiate him from the positive depictions of advancing careers and social niceties normally on display in middle-class suburbia. While Alex charms his way into a teaching position using family contacts, Barney's interaction with the assistant manager at the "joint" where he is to perform reveals a mutual lack of respect. Bartell belittles Barney, issuing orders and calling him "boy." Barney's response is to make fun of his boss's self-importance, displaying anti-authority behavior that almost results in his dismissal. Barney has no professional power, and it therefore takes Laurie to rescue the situation by playing on her schoolgirl friendship with Bartell's daughter. Only when he can associate Barney with this middle-class world does Bartell afford him due respect and address Barney as "Mr. Sloan."

Laurie continues to draw Barney into her middle-class arena, which is largely defined by domesticity. The Music Foundation remains unseen through the film; instead, the Tuttle home is the locus of all events, from everyday life to family celebrations. When the family ventures outside the home prior to Barney's arrival, they recreate the domestic atmosphere on the beach with a record player, a sewing basket, and steel cooking drums. Women plainly control the domestic sphere and the men who exist within it. As Barbara Ehrenreich suggests, commentators were often critical of feminine control of the home environment, identifying a process of emasculation. *Look* magazine, for example, asserted that controlling women were responsible for creating the corporate conformist: "Female dominance . . . may, in fact, be one of the several causes of the 'organization man' who is so deplored today. What he is doing is just building his own masculine world. His office is *his* castle."[46] In *Young at Heart,* the middle-class male characters conform to this image of emasculated maleness. Gregory is patronized as an absentminded father and brother, and his daughters fail to submit to his professional authority when he conducts their musical performances. Amy issues orders to Ernie even prior to their commencing a relationship, and, following his initially dominant behavior, Alex becomes a useful parcel carrier for Laurie on her shopping expedition.

Laurie's attempts to "make a human being" out of Barney by molding him into a typical middle-class male are just as domineering, even though presented as a component of her nurturing role in their building relationship. She persists in urging Barney to complete his song, and her aim to domesticate him translates into a curtailment of his independence as Laurie surreptitiously fits curtains at his lodgings, encourages him to press creases into his ill-fitting suit, and secretly purchases a birthday present for her father on Barney's behalf (Figure 1). However, Barney remains physically and culturally alienated from the suburban domestic

Figure 1: With the aid of Aunt Jessie, Laurie begins her attempt to domesticate Barney in the middle-class suburban setting of the Tuttle family home. (*Young at Heart*)

sphere, thoroughly resisting emasculation. The image of Barney/Sinatra polishing spoons in the Tuttle kitchen is perhaps the most incongruous of the film. Barney experiences each family gathering at a distance, often remaining in quiet solitude at the piano while the festivities occur. Rather than being incorporated into her domestic sphere, he removes Laurie from the home when they elope on the day she was due to marry Alex in the Tuttle living room.

Through their marriage, Barney brings Laurie into his world. He exposes Laurie to a working-class existence in the urban nightspots where his work is conducted and through their married life in a dark and dingy two-room apartment. Despite his talent, Barney struggles in his career, unable to employ the manipulative tactics adopted by Alex that have projected him forward to a hit show. Barney is able to provide none of the financial security enjoyed by Fran, and Laurie loses the sunny disposition that was a sign of her protected suburban family life. By resisting suburban conformity, Barney is characterized as a figure of heightened masculinity. Rather than Barney, it is Laurie who is transformed in this environment. The yellows and pinks she wore previously make way for the navy blues and blacks that reflect her changing mood. Her disrupted contentment is equally a result of the powerful emotions exhibited by Barney, which contrast with the subdued self-control of Alex. The passion Barney displays when attempting to dissuade Laurie from marrying Alex—which causes her only tears in the film—and the violence of his anger that she is still wearing the bracelet Alex gave her, demonstrate a powerful masculinity that is limited to Barney alone.

Despite this shift in emphasis toward the depiction of a working-class male identity, the idealization of the American middle class that underpins the narrative necessitates Barney's ultimate assimilation. Viewing the comfortable interaction between Laurie and Alex at the Tuttle family's Christmas celebrations, and humiliated by a financial handout from Alex, Barney attempts suicide. In *Four Daughters,* Mickey's suicide attempt is successful, leaving Ann (Laurie) and Felix (Alex) to be reunited. This conclusion, together with Garfield's more resigned playing of the role, points to an acceptance of class boundaries during the era of the Depression and a narrative implication that crossing the social divide has inevitably destructive consequences. In *Young at Heart,* Barney survives and is incorporated into the suburban family success story. The bars of music introduced earlier have been transformed into a hit song, and the couple have a new son named Lightning—a positive twist on Barney's negativity—suggesting Barney now conforms to the middle-class male ideal. Laurie is returned to her pastel shades and smiling demeanor, and the family gathers around Barney at the piano, making him a central player in the domestic sphere. This improbable ending most distinguishes *Young at Heart* from *Four Daughters* and indicates a cultural shift in attitudes toward class. Postwar notions of a classless society, and the consequent depiction of the middle-class lifestyle as normality, require that Barney's exclusion is ultimately challenged. Having been redefined as a successful husband and father, therefore, Barney is fully integrated into the suburban family.[47] In *The Man with the Golden Arm,* the depiction of a disenfranchised urban environment denies the possibility of this kind of comprehensive integration and further strengthens Sinatra's working-class screen image.

"Here We Go, Down and Dirty": Working-Class Survival and Alternative Values in *The Man with the Golden Arm*

The Man with the Golden Arm was originally a project of John Garfield, who purchased the film rights to Nelson Algren's 1949 novel in the early 1950s and planned to produce the film through his company, Roberts Productions. When Garfield died in 1952 at the age of thirty-nine, the rights were secured from the star's estate by director Otto Preminger. As in the case of *On the Waterfront* (1954), Sinatra competed for the starring role with Marlon Brando. Although Sinatra was initially chosen for the role of Terry Molloy by director Elia Kazan, the agreement culminated in a lawsuit and out-of-court settlement when producer Sam Spiegel opted instead for the box office appeal of Brando.[48] Sinatra's eager response to the first seventy pages of script for *The Man with the Golden Arm,* which had been sent simultaneously to Brando, ensured he beat his rival to the role of heroin addict Frankie Machine.[49]

Following Billy Wilder's representation of alcoholism in *The Lost Weekend* (1945), and Preminger's use of words such as *virgin* and *pregnant,* which still shocked the censors, in *The Moon Is Blue* (1953), drug addiction was Hollywood's last moral taboo. The Production Code disallowed cinematic depictions of illegal drug taking, and on its release, *The Man with the Golden Arm* failed to receive a Motion Picture Association of America (MPAA) seal of approval. United Artists responded by resigning their membership and requesting that state censors each make an individual decision on whether to allow the film to be screened. *The Man with the Golden Arm* was exhibited in the majority of states and went on to receive Academy Award nominations for Sinatra's performance and Elmer Bernstein's jazz score. Sinatra repeatedly expressed his opinion that his portrayal of Frankie Machine was his finest film performance. His characterization also met with the approval of Algren, who told screenwriter Budd Schulberg: "I was afraid nobody out there could play it and that Preminger . . . would crap it up. But Sinatra was Frankie Machine, just the way I wrote him in the book."[50]

The Man with the Golden Arm clearly addresses drug addiction in an explicit manner unfamiliar to cinema audiences in 1955. Scenes showing Frankie being injected with heroin by dealer Louie (Darren McGavin) or suffering the effects of withdrawal make plain the importance of the drugs theme to the film's narrative. However, of equally central significance is the film's examination of an American underclass, which the working class has become in the context of images of postwar prosperity. Frankie Machine represents the pathetic hopelessness of the working-class male, alienated from the postwar American success story and trapped by the inevitability of his social status. Frankie opens the film, arriving home by bus, having spent six months in a drug rehabilitation center. When the poker game where he worked as dealer was raided by the police, Frankie surrendered himself for arrest on behalf of boss Schwiefka (Robert Strauss), exemplifying his consistent positioning at the bottom of the social ladder.

Frankie returns to an environment marked by its physical and emotional darkness. Preminger's original intention was to shoot *The Man with the Golden Arm* on location in Chicago. Cost restraints forced filming to move to an old RKO backlot, however, creating an increased air of claustrophobia around Frankie's home streets. Dark buildings housing pool halls, bars, and pawnbrokers highlight the stifled ambition in this stagnant urban wasteland, where men stand around on rubbish-strewn streets or use alcohol or drugs as a temporary means of escape (Figure 2). As Frankie's girlfriend Molly (Kim Novak) retorts when he dismisses her current companion Johnny as "a hundred per cent habitual drunk": "Look, everybody's a habitual something. With him, it's liquor is all." In Algren's novel, Frankie is addicted to the morphine he takes to ease the pain of a war injury. In Preminger's film, the heroin Frankie began taking "only for kicks" becomes a way of coping with the despair of his unfortunate existence, replacing an earlier fondness for alcohol.

On his return, Frankie is determined to remove himself from this immobility. Having learned to play the drums in rehab, Frankie expresses his intent to find a position with a big band, telling his admiring sidekick Sparrow (Arnold Stang), "I'm the kinda guy, boy, when I move, watch my smoke." Despite this assertion of active self-determination, however, there is an inevitability that Frankie will be drawn back into the circles that feed his addiction. His moniker, "the man with the golden arm," relates to his skill as a poker dealer. This is the arena where he enjoys a measure of respect, being the main draw for highrolling players, and also a level of control. As he pointedly tells one player: "I decide when we need a fresh deck at this table." Yet the financial beneficiaries of the games are Schwiefka and Louie, who use contrasting methods to maintain their grip on Frankie. Physically aggressive and gauche, Schwiefka has Frankie arrested, ensuring he misses his appointment with a showbusiness agent and returns to work as a dealer. Louie is first seen taunting a one-armed alcoholic with a drink, demonstrating his sadistic streak. He employs subtler methods with Frankie, however, persuading him to return to dealing for economic reasons and seductively drawing Frankie

Figure 2: The dispirited expressions worn by Frankie and Molly as they discuss their doomed relationship reflect the mood of the local nightclub where Molly works as a hostess. (*The Man with the Golden Arm*)

back to heroin, repeatedly suggesting, "Come over my place." Louie is a working-class model of the cold American capitalist, as persuasive as corporate advertising, his threepiece suit, hat, and cane positioning him as a dandified version of a middle-class business executive.

Meanwhile, Frankie's idea to adopt the name Jack Duval—a name with "real class," as Molly notes—signals his need to remake his male identity to achieve his distant goal. The film draws Sinatra's star image into the text with Frankie's fanciful talk of bobbysoxers and the bow tie Algren refers to as "a regular Sinatra jazzbow."[51] However, Frankie's ill-fitting pinstriped suit has been stolen from a department store by Sparrow and fails to transform him into a candidate for success. Random acts of assistance from a doctor and show-business agent suggest a window of opportunity.

Yet Frankie's attempts at upward mobility are continually frustrated as Schwiefka sets up the arrest for the theft of the suit and the agent loses his phone number. When he eventually gets the opportunity to audition before Shorty Rogers and Shelly Manne (playing themselves), Frankie is humiliated by the physical effects of his addiction that make his hand shake. He exits the room speechless, with his head bowed, embarrassed by his inability to move beyond his social position. This failure to grasp his singular chance for advancement prompts Frankie's withdrawal from drug use. With Molly's assistance, he begins the process, declaring, "Here we go, down and dirty." This line, which Frankie also uses to open the poker games at which he deals, makes the overt connection between his social arena and the drug addiction intended to assist his survival but that ensures he remains tied to this disenfranchised class.

The women with whom Frankie is involved are equally imprisoned by their environment. Frankie's wife Sophia (Eleanor Parker), or Zosh as he calls her, feigns disability to maintain a hold on Frankie. Zosh stays in her wheelchair in their one-room apartment, occupying her time with a scrapbook of newspaper reports of the car accident caused by Frankie's drunk driving. Zosh is psychologically confined to the small world she occupies with Frankie and fearful of the romantic and career opportunities for her husband that might lie beyond it. She therefore encourages Frankie to return to dealing and obstructs his efforts at self-advancement, banning him from practicing his drumming in the apartment and unwittingly forcing him downstairs to Molly's room. Zosh's emotional blackmail is accompanied by her attempts to physically limit Frankie. Each time he moves to keep an appointment that will assist his musical ambitions, Zosh grasps at Frankie, pulling him toward her in an attempt to prevent him from leaving.

In contrast, Molly acts as a nurturing presence in Frankie's life. She encourages his unrealistic dreams of fame, assuring him, "You was always whistling and drumming on tables and things. Real good, too." When Frankie's dreams are abruptly extinguished, Molly provides the location and emotional support for his withdrawal from drugs. Her experiences, however, dictate her pessimism regarding her own life. When Frankie suggests their relationship will eventually work out, Molly's response reveals that she is conditioned to disappointment: "All my life has been one day—on and on and on." Although the film trades on the sexual imaging already developing around Novak through films such as *Phffft!* (1954) and *Picnic* (1955), her attractiveness fails to glamorize her character. Novak's hunched shoulders, and the slouched posture she adopts as she moves between the bar, one-room apartment, and club that define her world, instead point to Molly's resignation to her social position. Her use of her good looks in a burlesque joint is one more indicator of her lack of opportunity rather than an avenue for change.

When confronted simultaneously by Johnny's demands for money and Frankie's renewed addiction, Molly feels pressured enough to throw her few belongings in a suitcase and leave her apartment. Prior to this, however, the relationship between Frankie and Molly has provided them both with an emotional oasis. The joking and laughter that occur between the characters when together contrasts sharply with their otherwise morose dispositions. The positive warmth evident in their relationship is best depicted in a scene that, at the same time, illustrates their alienation from middle-class values and opportunities. Having collected his membership card from the Musicians Union, Frankie—in his stolen suit—strolls with Molly around Chicago's commercial district. This area of the metropolis projects an air of bustling activity and limitless opportunities through its skyscrapers, its bright and airy streets, and the sound of car horns, which distinguish it from the dismal stagnancy of Frankie and Molly's home environment. Their temporary exposure to this arena of middle-class opportunity and success only highlights their exclusion from it. Their alienation is made plain as Frankie and Molly gaze into the shop windows that speak of the postwar consumerist agenda. Frankie's elation at commencing his route out of the underclass prompts a momentary desire to reconstruct himself as a middle-class male, as he jokingly offers to buy Molly a Chrysler car or a television set, the favored consumer items of the 1950s. When they reach the shop window displaying the kind of suburban kitchen lauded by Nixon, however, Frankie reasserts the values that separate them from the middle-class family ethos represented by this image.

In his discussion of the novel and film, Robert C. Rosen argues this scene is "emblematic of Preminger's conformist vision." Rosen interprets the film as an endorsement of the postwar success story, contending that Preminger presents Frankie's dream of becoming a jazz drummer as an achievable goal. He therefore suggests that when Frankie and Molly look into the shop window, "Visually they are absorbed into this immaculately clean, glass-enclosed dream of consumer happiness."[52] On the contrary, however, Frankie views the setup as an illustration of materialistic excess, commenting to Molly: "Would you look at this production? And only for cookin'. Now, who would want a thing like that?" Considering the "wife" alone at the sink while her "husband" ignores her in favor of reading a magazine, Frankie criticizes the emotional coldness of this fictional relationship in which the couple fail to communicate. Through the film, Frankie demonstrates his inadequacy in the role of male provider, and the success he now craves is not for its own sake, but to enable him to secure a hospital place for Zosh, move Sparrow away from dealing in stolen dogs to a job with a band, and formalize his relationship with Molly. Frankie demonstrates a paternal sensitivity in his relationships, massaging Zosh's legs or back to ease the pains she fakes and lovingly putting Molly to bed on her return from a night working at the club. Therefore, as Frankie and Molly imagine themselves into the scene destined to remain fictional for them, they imagine their own ideal of family life, consisting of inquiries about their day, a steak supper, and a cozy evening listening to music. The scene thus moves away from a detached materialism and instead is translated into a simple picture of emotional warmth and marital intimacy.

The conclusion of the film suggests that Frankie and Molly can look forward to a more optimistic future together. Frankie has rid himself of his heroin addiction, and Zosh has committed suicide after her feigned injuries and her murder of Louie are discovered, leaving Frankie and Molly free to pursue their relationship. As Sinatra and Novak walk toward and past the camera, however, pointing to their departure from their previous existence, the camera tellingly lingers on what is left behind. Moving in the opposite direction, Sparrow returns to the same dark, littered streets that remain unchanged from the beginning of the film, and there is little to indicate that the circumstances for Frankie's social advancement have fundamentally altered beyond his improved health.

Sinatra's working-class image highlights America's shifting attitudes toward class. The symbolic value Sinatra initially holds among the working class as a story of success reinforces the positive tone of the culture's standardization of working-class masculinity during World War II. The West Enders' sense of identification with the extremes of his career failure and ambition in the 1950s evidence his continuous association with this class identity. Images of Sinatra as a resentful nonconformist illuminate the dominance of the middle-class male identity in postwar America and its narrow definition in relation to corporate middle management and suburban living. Sinatra's film roles of the 1950s, in turn, dramatize the class conflicts denied by the cultural primacy of the middle class. Stressing a poverty of opportunity and distinct values, *Young at Heart* and *The Man with the Golden Arm* illustrate a working-class alienation from postwar prosperity and the suburban dream and present an alternative class identity for the 1950s cinematic male.

2 Ethnic Stereotyping and Italian American Cultural Identity

> In the summer of 1951, when Skinny [D'Amato] found out just how bad things had gotten for Sinatra, he called and offered him a ten-day run at the 500 Club . . . He offered his friend a chance to return to his roots—New Jersey—to a city that had a congenital weakness for outcasts, troublemakers, and antiheroes, especially if they were Italian. . . . The night of Frank's first show that August, there were so many people on the street in front of the club that, for the rest of Frank's run, Skinny had to hire a dozen cops to control the crowds. "It was like you were seeing the Messiah come to town," said a waitress who worked down the street from the club. "That's how he was to the Italians. They went crazy."
>
> —Jonathan Van Meter, *The Last Good Time*

The exuberant welcome Sinatra received in 1951 at Atlantic City's famous 500 Club highlights how closely Sinatra was identified with an Italian American identity. While most of the American public stayed away from his movies and failed to buy his records, and the press focused on his questionable friendships and stormy private life, the residents of New Jersey greeted Hoboken's famous son as a returning hero. Owned by Paul "Skinny" D'Amato, with whom Sinatra developed a close, lifelong friendship, the 500 Club played host to every successful nightclub star of the 1950s, from Nat King Cole to Dean Martin and Jerry Lewis, whose act originated on the 500 Club stage.[1] However, audiences saved their most enthusiastic welcome for Sinatra. The sense of loyalty they exhibited toward the falling star was driven by Sinatra's aggressive assertion of his Italian American identity. While much of the Anglo-Saxon population balked at Sinatra's unassimilated image, New Jersey Italians appreciated Sinatra's conspicuous expression of his Italian roots.

This chapter examines Sinatra's Italian American persona as a fundamental component of his male identity. Sinatra's family background incorporates the diversity of Italian culture. Born in the port of Genoa, Natalia "Dolly" Garaventes, represented the irrepressible pride of the northern birthplace of Christopher Columbus. Anthony Martin "Marty" Sinatra, carried with him to the United States the loyalty codes and aversion to authority that were firmly established as part of the Sicilian character. Each of these traits is evident in the ethnic image that builds around Sinatra and provokes varied reactions in the changing climate of the 1940s and 1950s. The air of inclusiveness circulating in World War II brings Sinatra's ethnic identity under the cover of American unity. Postwar stereotypes, however, complicate this positive imagery. Cast as the excessively grateful immigrant, or a representative of organized crime, the Italian American male is condemned by Anglo-Saxon culture to an unflattering definition. As Robert Connolly and Pellegrino D'Acierno explain, Sinatra's determined machismo is frequently viewed negatively in the light of existing stereotypes: "'*Sinatraism,*' understood as a generic second-generation self-affirming aggressive sensibility . . . is perceived by the majority culture as 'Little Caesarism': 'Doing it my way' is deemed a dangerous way of organizing the signs of one's personality because it rejects the Other-induced self, the self authorized by the dominant culture, which, in the Italian American case, is the benign, conformist 'Pinocchio-self,' the self that accommodates itself to the other's negative fantasy by constructing itself according to an equally fantastic positive formula."[2] While allegations of Mafia friendships consistently infect Sinatra's postwar ethnic image, Sinatra's readiness to reference this strong male image highlights the Italian American male's reaction against the alternative patronizing and emasculated stereotype. At the same time, commentary frequently interprets Sinatra's focus on his appearance and bonds of friendship in direct relation to ethnic crime. A cultural reading of these characteristics illustrates the historical and contemporary stereotyping of the Italian American male.

Sinatra's screen roles often incorporate an ethnic dimension and utilize the star's noted Italian American identity.[3] In *Young at Heart* and *A Hole in the Head,* the Italian American backgrounds of Barney Sloan and Tony Manetta are a feature of the characters drawn by the film. In *From Here to Eternity,* ethnicity is at the core of the male identity expressed by Private Angelo Maggio. Sinatra's identification with the role is reiterated by commentary that stresses similarities between character and actor. Walter Cronkite noted in 1965: "There were those who said he not only played Maggio, he was Maggio. Gum-chewing, fast-talking, pat on the back of the head wise guy."[4] Sinatra's performance as Maggio draws on and accentuates the star's potent Italian American image. As Maggio challenges authority and resists negative definitions of his ethnicity, he counters the passivity and conformity that dominates the film. The prioritization of family, friendship, and loyalty emphasizes the cultural basis of Sinatra's ethnic identity and contests the stereotyping of the Italian American male.

"I'm American": Ethnic Diversity and Grateful Assimilation

The image drawn of Sinatra as an Italian American during World War II was largely benign, reflecting positive attitudes toward ethnicity in relation to American identity in the mid-1940s. In a published interview with Sinatra in 1943, the famous columnist Louella Parsons described the lifestyle of "the American-Italian boy," telling readers: "Frankie sets great store by his wardrobe. . . . His favorite dish: Spaghetti. He will get up in the middle of the night to eat it." Parsons added that Sinatra spent "most of his time with pals of his entourage who accompanied him from New York."[5] In February 1945, an article published in *Screen Romance* gave readers a tour of the Sinatras' new Hollywood home. In "Dining Alla Sinatra," a fondness for home-cooked spaghetti prepared by wife Nancy was provided as evidence that the couple remained "as unpretentious a pair as ever." The welcoming informality of evenings spent in the "rumpus room" playing cards with colleagues and old friends, and the revelation that "Frankie's loyalty to his friends is proverbial," traded on familiar Italian myths of family, hospitality, and loyalty. Explaining that "in Italian parlance it's 'alla' just as in French it's 'à la,'" and including Nancy's recipes for spaghetti and meatballs and lasagna, the article gave readers the chance to experience this image of Italian American family life.[6]

While both these articles celebrate America's ethnic diversity, they equally draw on stereotypical imagery surrounding the Italian American, making safe aspects of Sinatra's ethnic identity that in the 1950s become highly problematic. Sinatra's close male friendships, heightened sense of loyalty, and focus on his appearance cause no more disquiet here than his preference for Italian food. Yet Italian Americans occupied an ambiguous position during World War II. Unlike the largely assimilated Irish, and the Germans and Japanese, alienated by their homelands' continuous fight against the Allies, Italian Americans were simultaneously mistrusted and dismissed as an irrelevance. The commanding position taken by Mussolini on the world stage in the 1920s and 1930s, before he was ousted from power in 1943, was a source of pride for many Italian Americans, encouraged in their support for Il Duce by much of the popular Italian-speaking press, the fraternal association Sons of Italy, and the anticommunist Catholic Church.[7] Although most had rejected fascism by the onset of war, a lingering suspicion of the political allegiances of Italian Americans remained, reinforced by Italy's initial alliance with Germany and invasion of France in 1940. At the same time, Italians were deemed a far less threatening force than their Nazi counterparts. When FDR decided in October 1942 that Italians should no longer be considered aliens of "enemy nationality," while restrictions on German citizens were kept in place, he explained his reasoning to Attorney General Francis Biddle: "I don't care so much about the Italians. They are a lot of opera singers, but the Germans are different, they may be dangerous."[8] Battlefield reports also belittled the Italian male. As Thomas Doherty notes, Darryl F. Zanuck's *At the Front in North Africa* (March 1943) included an intertitle that read: "Captured Italian paratroopers seem very depressed at being safely out of the war." This was followed by a cut to "shots of joyous Italian POWs, thrilled to be out of the battle and secure in American hands, turning somersaults in the desert sand."[9]

The prevailing perception of Italian Americans as a harmless distraction allowed space for their incorporation into the culture of tolerance promoted in World War II. Just as the elevation of the working man acted to demonstrate the "ordinary" American's dedication to the fight for democracy, the country celebrated its ethnic diversity, embracing a sense of difference and distinguishing America from the intolerance of European fascism. The 1944 novel *A Bell for Adano* followed an Italian American soldier from the New York Bronx around Europe. In his foreword, John Hersey claimed: "America is the international country. . . . Our army has Yugoslavs and Frenchmen and Austrians and Czechs and Norwegians in it, and everywhere our Army goes in Europe, a man can turn to the private beside him and say: 'Hey, Mac, what's this furriner saying?'. . . And Mac will be able to translate."[10] Festivals held around the country also promoted the United States as a nation constructed through ethnic difference. The Festival of Nations held in St. Paul, Minnesota, in May 1942 involved approximately two thousand people and thirty-two nationalities in a mass demonstration of American unity.[11]

The cultural acceptance of Italians as legitimate Americans occurred in this climate of tolerance. Their inclusion, despite a history of fascist sympathy and an initial alliance with the Axis powers, gave rise to the stereotype of the excessively grateful Italian immigrant. When FDR's decision to declassify Italians as "enemy" aliens was announced by Attorney General Biddle at a Carnegie Hall rally, a report was released claiming that famed conductor Arturo Toscanini, listening to the radio broadcast, "threw his arms round the machine . . . held it close while he took in the roar of applause . . . kissed it, turned it off and burst into tears."[12] Publicity of this sort created a demeaning image of the Italian American as the immigrant who most desperately craved acceptance as a fully fledged American.

The radio show *Life with Luigi,* which aired on CBS between September 1948 and March 1953, drew on this stereotype for its protagonist Luigi Basco.[13] Played by New York Irish character actor J. Carrol Naish, Italian immigrant Luigi was part owner of an antiques shop in Chicago and sent weekly letters home to "mama" that formed the basis of the show. The U.S. citizenship classes he attended at night school with a variety of European immigrants combined with sponsor Wrigley's Spearmint's description of *Life with Luigi* as "a friendly, enjoyable show that sort of symbolizes the American spirit of tolerance and good will" to highlight the series's promotion of American democratic ideals. Sinatra's appearance on an edition broadcast in October 1950 draws attention to the show's emphasis on the Italian immigrant's grateful assimilation.[14] Having correctly identified Sinatra as the mystery voice in a radio contest, Luigi wins a trip to New York to spend the day with the star. Sinatra plans to introduce Luigi to urban nightlife in Toots Shor, 21, and El Morocco. However, Luigi persuades Sinatra instead to accompany him on a tour of the Statue of Liberty, Empire State Building, and Museum of History, where the visitor reminds Sinatra of the country's inclusive traditions. When the pair visit Luigi's friends in New York's Little Italy, Sinatra reassures his companion about his own roots, telling him, "I come from a neighborhood like this," and goes on to perform the popular Italian song "O, Marie" ("Maria, Mari"). Having been warned earlier that Sinatra may wish to forget his Italian background, Luigi nervously asks him, "What are you?" Sinatra's reply, "I'm American," is followed by Luigi's delighted comment, "That's the perfect answer," reemphasizing the extent to which American tolerance relies on willing assimilation.

Naish's portrayal of the simple, heavily accented, grateful Luigi presents an unflattering stereotype of the mother-obsessed, conformist Italian American male. Sinatra articulated his distaste for the characterization to journalist Pete Hamill some years later, omitting mention of his appearance on the show: "You know what radio show I hated the most? . . . It was called *Life with Luigi,* with J. Carrol Naish—there's a good Italian name for you—and it was all about Italians who spoke like-a-dis, and worried about ladies who squeeze-a da tomatoes on-a da fruit stand. The terrible thing was, it made me laugh. Because it *did* have some truth to it. We all knew guys like that growing up. But then I would hate myself for laughing at the goddamned thing."[15] Sinatra distances himself from the character Hamill likens to the caricature of "the organ grinder, the fruit peddler, a Mediterranean variation on the earlier role of the Stage Irishman." As Hamill suggests, this persona avoids a more threatening stereotype of Italian American masculinity based around violent criminality.[16] Despite FDR's patronizing assurance that the Italians represented little menace in 1942, his earlier choice of words to describe the country's invasion of France referenced a more disturbing image. Rudolph J. Vecoli points to the offense taken by Italian Americans at the president's description of Italy's actions as a "stab in the back," noting, "their dismay was heightened by the figure of speech which brought to mind the stereotype of the Italian-with-a-stiletto."[17] This violent stereotype emerged from the criminal activities of the precursors to the Mafia, the Black Handers, in Italian American urban communities in the early part of the twentieth century. FDR's unfortunate turn of phrase highlights the two distinct stereotypes with which Anglo-Saxon culture defined the Italian American male: one emasculated and beholden, the other dangerously violent.

"Our Hoodlum Singer": Resisting and Reclaiming the Negative Stereotype

While Sinatra's Italian American image was incorporated into World War II's celebration of ethnic diversity and co-opted into *Life with Luigi's* assimilationist agenda, his postwar ethnic persona was often much more problematic. Commentary frequently associated Sinatra with violent gangster imagery through oblique cultural references and, more directly, by suggesting connections with infamous Mafia figures. The first such accusation followed an incident in Havana in 1947. On February 20, the Scripps-Howard journalist Robert Ruark headlined his column in the *Washington News,* "Sinatra Is Playing with the Strangest People These Days." Ruark reported that Sinatra had traveled to Havana in the company of Joe and Rocco Fischetti, associates of Al Capone, and had been spotted socializing with the deported mobster Charlie "Lucky" Luciano.

In subsequent editions, Ruark referred to Luciano as "Sinatra's boyfriend" and "Sinatra's buddy."[18] Hearst columnist Lee Mortimer periodically made similar allegations and in August 1951 published an attack on Sinatra in an article published in *American Mercury*. Among Mortimer's claims were the assertions that Sinatra's early career had been sponsored by New Jersey racketeer Willie Moretti, that the Fischetti brothers had persuaded Tommy Dorsey to release Sinatra from his egregious personal contract, and that Sinatra had traveled to Havana for the purpose of delivering two million dollars in cash to Luciano.[19] In April 1960, Mortimer declared: "Sinatra . . . has been chosen by certain interests to take over the entire amusement industry."[20] Mortimer's allegations followed an altercation between the two in Hollywood nightclub Ciro's on April 8, 1947, during which Sinatra physically assaulted Mortimer. After his arrest, Sinatra gave his reasons for the attack: "For two years, he's been riding me. . . . He called me a dago and I saw red."[21] Although he later withdrew the accusation of an ethnic slur, and the matter was settled out of court, Sinatra drew attention to the prejudices underlying the negative stereotype of the Italian American male.

Sinatra consistently denied any involvement with Mafia figures. Responding to the accusations regarding his Havana trip, he argued it would be physically impossible for a man of his weight to carry two million dollars in cash, adding: "I was brought up to shake a man's hand when I am introduced to him without first investigating his past. Any report that I fraternised with goons or racketeers is a vicious lie."[22] When Walter Cronkite asked Sinatra in 1965 about his alleged connection to Chicago mobster Sam Giancana, Sinatra replied that it was due to "a legitimate business reason; we built a hotel in Las Vegas."[23] However, when called to testify in January 1967 before a Las Vegas grand jury investigating mob control of the casinos, he denied any financial dealings with Giancana.[24] Sinatra equally objected publicly to the general stereotyping of Italian Americans as violent criminals. In May 1967 he took on the role of chairman of the American Italian Anti-Defamation League, leading a campaign to eliminate negative depictions of Italian Americans in films and televisions shows such as the FBI drama *The Untouchables,* until the controversy aroused by his appointment provoked his resignation the same year. Nevertheless, Sinatra's willingness to draw on this tough male persona indicates a sense of identification with this powerful Italian image. Considering Italian American audiences' problematic engagement with negative stereotyping in *The Godfather* (1972), Pellegrino D'Acierno suggests that perceptions of Italian American identity place the community in a "double bind": "damned if you do identify yourself with the negative stereotype, for that is to be an accomplice to those who have caused your tribe to be stigmatized; damned if you don't, for that cultural stereotype is the only one through which the 'grandiose self' is displayed . . . this 'double bind' situation is the normal condition—dilemmatic, to say the least—of the Italian American within the majority culture."[25] Rather than adopt an assimilated, emasculated persona in the style of Luigi Basco, the Italian American male opts to identify with the alternative stereotype through which a strong ethnic male identity might be expressed, even with the disapproval of the dominant Anglo-Saxon culture. Despite protesting the accusations against him and his community, Sinatra frequently referenced this violent persona, distancing himself thoroughly from its weaker counterpart. Suggesting, "If it hadn't been for my interest in music. . . . I'd probably have ended in a life of crime," or allowing Johnny Carson to introduce him on stage as "our hoodlum singer," Sinatra characterized himself as a tough working-class Italian American male.[26] The star indicated that by claiming this identity he was, in part, responding to ethnic stereotyping: "Sometimes with me it was a case of if-you-got-the-name-you-might-as-well-have-the-game. . . . You think I'm just some wop wise guy off the street? All right, I'll *be* a wop wise guy off the street and break your fucking head."[27] At the same time, these direct references to violent criminality and their often humorous context make safe this potentially dangerous image. Dean Martin's "roast" of Frank Sinatra in 1978 featured numerous jokes about the star's alleged Mafia connections and violent nature.[28] Similarly, although *The Godfather* drew a thinly disguised characterization of Sinatra through the role of singing star Johnny Fontane (Al Martino), Sinatra's impersonations of Brando's Don Corleone making an offer "you can never refuse" while performing "Mack the Knife" drew attention to his male image while mocking its credibility.[29]

"A Mysterious Ethnic Conspiracy": Italian American Otherness and the Kefauver Hearings

Italians have historically held an ambiguous status in American society. Racially defined by their whiteness, they were nevertheless viewed as the ethnic group least able to assimilate to Anglo-Saxon norms by virtue of their dark skin and cultural differences. Pellegrino D'Acierno describes Italian Americans occupying a position of "inbetweenness," making them "the minority . . . that authentic, or more codified, minorities

. . . regard as part of the White, European, Christian majority, and that the majority culture regards as the most alien, the most Other."[30] Though clearly not subjected to the divisive injustices inflicted on African Americans, elements of similar treatment illustrate Italians' insecure status as white Americans. In 1911 the U.S. House Committee on Immigration debated whether they should regard "the south Italian as a full-blooded Caucasian."[31] The various lynchings of Italians also reflected this distinct attitude toward their ethnicity. In 1899, five Sicilian men described as "black dagoes" were lynched for socializing with African Americans with whom they worked in the sugar fields of Louisiana.[32] One of the most infamous cases involved the assassination of New Orleans Police Chief David Hennessy in October 1890 in the midst of a trial involving rival Sicilian factions. Before dying, Hennessy proclaimed: "The Dagoes did it." When the eleven accused Italians were acquitted, they were lynched by locals, who also suspected that the trial had been rigged by a Mafia conspiracy of silence. Most American newspapers expressed approval of the lynchings, and Theodore Roosevelt, at the time a rising politician, described the unprosecuted murders as "a rather good thing."[33]

This differentiation of Italians as the most "other" of European immigrants continued in the twentieth century. The 1924 Immigration Act placed restrictions on the number of immigrants from southern and eastern Europe, and the quota system was reaffirmed by the 1952 McCarran-Walter Act. In the 1950s, the low status afforded Italian Americans combined with suspicions regarding ethnic crime in an updating of the negative stereotype of the violent Italian American male. The Kefauver Committee, formally the Senate Special Committee to Investigate Organized Crime in Interstate Commerce, made a direct connection between the Italian American community and violent criminality, announcing the existence of a nationwide crime syndicate termed *the Mafia*. The hearings of the committee, initiated by Democratic Senator for Tennessee Estes Kefauver, were given local television coverage as they took place in New Orleans, Detroit, and St. Louis, and on the West Coast. When they moved to New York in March 1951, *Time* magazine sponsored national broadcasts of the hearings that were watched by 80 percent of the television audience. While the Black Handers were limited to a small-scale urban myth and Prohibition activities were spread among Italian, Irish, and Jewish gangsters, the appearance on American television screens of Frank Costello and other characters with names ending in a vowel made real the imaginary Italian American stereotype. As William Howard Moore argues, by ignoring the social and economic factors that allowed organized crime to flourish, the committee suggested it was central to Italian American culture. The investigations "implied that it essentially originated outside of American society and was imposed upon the public by a group of immoral men, bound together by a mysterious ethnic conspiracy."[34] The message given to Middle America by the Kefauver Committee hearings was that violent criminal behavior was embedded in Italian American culture.[35]

"For Me, a Tuxedo Is a Way of Life": Cultural Distinctions and Self-Display

In a climate in which the image of the Italian American male is dissolved into a violent negative stereotype, Sinatra's attitudes and personal style become an active assertion of his distinct cultural identity. Sinatra's determination to retain his surname is the clearest indication of his unwillingness to conceal his ethnic identity. The 1940s and 1950s produced numerous Italian singers in the field of popular music, most of whom adopted Americanized names. Dean Martin (Dino Crocetti), Vic Damone (Vito Farinola), and Tony Bennett (Antonio Di Benedetto) all reinvented themselves for a wide American audience by ridding themselves of their most obvious Italian marker. Sinatra's disinclination to take the name suggested by Harry James, "Frankie Satin," was an early indicator of what would be a trend of cultural nonconformity. Sinatra explained to Pete Hamill: "Of course, it meant something to me to be the son of immigrants. How could it not? How the hell could it not? I grew up for a few years thinking I was just another American kid. Then I discovered at—what? Five? Six?—I discovered that some people thought I was a dago. A wop. A guinea. You know, like I didn't have a fucking *name.* That's why years later, when Harry . . . wanted me to change my name, I said no way, baby. The name is Sinatra. Frank fucking Sinatra."[36] Sinatra's remarks illustrate a male persona that can be contrasted markedly with the Italian American identity of Dean Martin, the star with whom he often presented a united Italian front. Appearing together in the 1950s and 1960s, Sinatra and Martin emphasized their common background. On *The Frank Sinatra Show* in November 1957, the host introduced his guest as "a fellow paisano, Mr. Dino Martin," and the stars went on to stage a mock dice game and play with stereotypical imagery. Sipping drinks and sharing cigarettes at a makeshift bar, the pair traded Italian parlance, commenting on Martin's performance of "O, Marie," "That's a nice-a song." In Rat Pack performances, Sinatra and Martin defined themselves in opposition to Sammy Davis Jr.'s African American Judaism in shows that made a feature of the stars' racial and ethnic diversity.[37]

Yet Martin's Italian American identity provides a compliant, inoffensive contrast to Sinatra's more disruptive male image. Sinatra recorded a small number of Italian songs, such as "I Have but One Heart" ("O Marenariello") (1945) and "Come Back to Sorrento" (1950), in the early part of his career, but they were not among his best sellers, and he declined to perform them in concert appearances.[38] In contrast, Martin openly traded on the romantic image of the Italian troubadour, making his singing career with songs such as "That's Amore," his first hit record from the soundtrack of *The Caddy* (1953), and "Volare" ("Nel Blu Dipinto di Blu"), a hit in 1958. Martin's easygoing style, which differentiated him from Sinatra's edgy unpredictability, presented an unproblematic version of Italian American masculinity for Anglo-Saxon consumption. Nick Tosches places this nonchalance at the heart of Martin's Italian identity, suggesting: "Deep down, that, as much as anything, was what he was, a *menefreghista*—one who simply did not give a fuck."[39] In performance, this translates into a relaxed congeniality that submerges any negative ethnic connotations. Sinatra's unapologetic ethnic identity, however, resists such accommodations and is revealed in far less superficial ways.

Sinatra's heightened concentration on his appearance and close male friendships are the frequent subject of comment. The gangster-style imagery consistently invoked misreads Sinatra's male identity in relation to a familiar stereotype. *Time* magazine's 1955 synopsis of the Sinatra story, as well as defining the star in strict class terms, paints a vivid picture of Sinatra's brimming "Polo Grounds"–sized closet and colorful male companions: "The man looks, in fact, like the popular conception of a gangster, model 1929. . . . He dresses with a glaring, George Raft kind of snazziness—rich, dark shirts and white figured ties, with ring and cuff links that almost always match. . . . Frankie has his gang. He is rarely to be seen without a few, and sometimes as many as ten of 'the boys' around him, and some look indeed like unfortunate passport photographs."[40] *Time*'s references to veteran of the gangster genre George Raft, Sinatra's distinctive styling, and the beat-up characters with whom he surrounds himself reiterate the casting of Sinatra in the mold of a modern-day urban criminal. In 1956, Adela Rogers St. Johns constructed a similar image in a *Cosmopolitan* article. Suggesting Edward G. Robinson and Paul Muni as Sinatra's early movie heroes, Rogers St. Johns reflects on their influence on Sinatra's behavior and his apparent desire to style his male identity in similar ways: "To this day, the way he wears his elegant and expensive clothes, the way he moves about at the head of an entourage composed of those who serve him plus hangers-on and friends, his long stride with its hint of swagger and menace, the angle of his hats—all testify to the accuracy of a remark his friend Bing Crosby once made about him. 'I think that he's always nurtured a secret desire to be a "hood,"' Crosby said, but he added, 'But, of course, he's got too much class, too much sense, to go that route—so he gets his kicks out of barking at newsmen and so forth.'"[41] Both these articles make the connection, with little subtlety, between Sinatra's antidote to gray flannel and coterie of male friends, and ethnic criminality. Comparing Sinatra to the screen gangsters, whose dapper style and masculine environment signified their power and male aggression, the authors give Sinatra's new successful image an air of threatening illegality.

This leap between Sinatra's male styling and Mafia imagery demonstrates the potency of this negative Italian American stereotype in 1950s culture. Choosing to interpret Sinatra's male identity as an illustration of Mafia machismo, commentary fails to consider Sinatra's image as a guide to cultural differences intrinsic to the star's ethnicity, implying a narrowly defined cultural acceptability. Sinatra cultivated a distinctive visual image in the 1940s with the bow ties that became an established part of his style. In the 1950s, Sinatra creates a highly stylized image of sophisticated urban masculinity with the suit, fedora, and raincoat that become his staple look on Capitol album covers, in films such as *Pal Joey,* and in television appearances. The high premium Sinatra places on an elegant style is evident in his remarks about the appropriate way to wear a tuxedo: "For me, a tuxedo is a way of life. When an invitation says black tie optional, it is always safer to wear black tie. My basic rules are to have shirt cuffs extended half an inch from the jacket sleeve. Trousers should break just above the shoe. Try not to sit down because it wrinkles the pants. If you have to sit, don't cross your legs. Pocket handkerchiefs are optional, but I always wear one, usually orange, since orange is my favorite color. Shine your Mary Janes on the underside of a couch cushion."[42] In the context of a postwar Anglo-Saxon culture bent on the submergence of individual style, the intensity with which Sinatra approaches his appearance differentiates him from accepted norms. Rather than providing evidence of the star's organized crime connections, the attention Sinatra pays to dressing up ties him to his cultural identity through the Italian notion of *la bella figura,* defined here by Pellegrino D'Acierno:

At the level of social interaction, it designates proper or improper public behavior and thus activates all those protocols that pertain to maintaining and augmenting "face.". . . . At the second level, *la bella figura* represents the aesthetic principle governing the presentation of self—looking one's best at all times and coming off well in whatever situation. Here we are speaking of image management that is, in effect, a mode of self-fashioning, one that is governed by aesthetic considerations that are for Italians and Italian Americans in no way superficial: The *figura* is the woman or the man. . . . It is essentially a formula of self-respect and respect for others in that it requires one's best effort.[43]

Sinatra's considered visual appearance is part of a concern with self-presentation fundamental to Italian culture. Herbert Gans noted similar characteristics in the West Enders. Making clear distinctions between what he termed the practice of "individual display" among Italian Americans and the kind of "consumption competition" evident among the "*nouveau riche,*" Gans concluded that Italian singers exemplified the community's tendency toward self-display and personal style, suggesting: "It is no accident that they are as much creators of a distinctive personal image as they are purveyors of songs. Italians have done well in contemporary popular music because it emphasizes the development of an individual image and style more than technical musical skill."[44] Sinatra's visual image combines with his distinctive musical style in a feast of ethnically inspired self-display. In a 1965 interview with *Life* magazine, Sinatra revealed that the blend of American popular music and Italian bel canto tradition through which he created his vocal style was rooted in his desire to distinguish himself from the mode of singing developed by Crosby and emulated by most male popular singers of the late 1930s and early 1940s. He explained: "When I started singing in the mid-1930s everybody was trying to copy the Crosby style. . . . It occurred to me that maybe the world didn't need another Crosby. I decided to experiment a little and come up with something different."[45] As Henry Pleasants clarifies, by employing techniques such as the *portamento* or *glissando* (the slur), and introducing codas (tails) to familiar songs, Sinatra consciously identified himself as a singer with an individually defined style.[46]

The essential Italian principle of *la bella figura* relates equally to ideas of appropriate public behavior. The determination to present one's best self to the world requires a display of proper conduct among company. D'Acierno suggests the example of a family laying out its best crystal for a dinner party, a guest accidentally breaking a glass, and the family, in order to minimize embarrassment, offering the guest another glass to smash. In his famous 1966 *Esquire* article, Gay Talese relates a tale remarkably similar to this indicator of Italian self-respect. An old school friend of Sinatra's daughter Nancy reports that, as a child, she attended a party hosted by Sinatra at his ex-wife's home. When the girl accidentally knocked over and smashed one of a pair of alabaster birds, Nancy started to bemoan the fate of one of her mother's favorite ornaments. Cutting her off sharply, Sinatra immediately smashed the other bird and reassured the girl.[47] While Talese reports this incident as a pointer to Sinatra's unpredictable nature, it openly demonstrates the extent to which his behavior is rooted in his marked ethnic identity.

"All the Way": *Uomini Rispettati* and Mutual Obligations

Talese's article also considers the imagery surrounding Sinatra in relation to close male friendships and the codes of loyalty by which they are purported to be bound. In 1955, *Time* drew a troublesome image of Sinatra and "the boys," adding: "As they march in bristling phalanx along Sunset Strip, Frank walks lordly at the head of them."[48] Sinatra as the powerful leader of a menacing male group is typical of imagery that consistently hints at an Italian American stereotype. Talese's approach defines Sinatra's male persona largely in relation to a maintained ethnic identity. In an interview with *Redbook* in 1959, Sinatra recalled an incident from his youth that reveals his developing attitude toward friendships. When swimming with friends at a local pool, Sinatra would allow the other boys to use his pass so that they could gain entry without paying. When he was caught passing his permit through the fence, Sinatra alleges he was beaten up by the attendant. He recalls: "I was hurt all right, but I was hurting from something more. All those times I got those guys into that swimming pool, but when I was getting clobbered not one of them came over to help me. They just—scramsville."[49] Talese discusses the high premium Sinatra places on loyalty in relation to his ethnicity, drawing a distinction between Sinatra's attitude toward relationships and the norms of Anglo-Saxon culture. Relaying actor Brad Dexter's proclamation "I'd kill for him," Talese remarks: "It is a characteristic that Sinatra, without admission, seems to prefer: *All the Way; All or Nothing at All.* This is the Sicilian in Sinatra; he permits his friends, if they wish to remain that, none of the easy Anglo-Saxon outs. But if they remain loyal, then there is nothing Sinatra will not do in turn—fabulous gifts, personal kindnesses, encouragement when they're down, adulation when they're up. They are wise to remember, however, one thing. He is Sinatra. The boss. *Il Padrone.*"[50] Talese's reading draws out the cultural basis for the enormous importance Sinatra attaches to loyalty, which most postwar commentary fails to acknowledge. Yet by introducing the notion of Sicilian male power relationships, his analysis reverts to a familiar stereotype. This ambiguity is reiterated in Talese's description of a scene he observes in a New York bar. In an episode akin to the opening scenes of *The Godfather,* Sinatra holds court in a secluded spot at the back of the bar, while various men attempt to gain access to pay their respects. Witnessing the deference shown to Sinatra, Talese terms him *"Il Padrone.* Or better still, he is what in traditional Sicily have long been called *uomini rispettati*—men of respect: men who are both majestic and humble, men who are loved by all and are very generous by nature, men whose hands are kissed as they walk from village to village, men who would *personally* go out of their way to redress a wrong."[51] Although Talese steers clear of direct references to organized crime, drawing instead on Sinatra's ethnic heritage, the air of violence and vengeance evoked by references to Sicilian power figures again associates Sinatra's image with a negative Italian American stereotype.

When these connections are unraveled, however, Talese finds Sinatra's basic ethnic identity in the behavior and attitudes he transports into the successful Anglo-Saxon world he inhabits: "When Sinatra sits to dine, his trusted friends are close; and no matter where he is, no matter how elegant the place may be, there is something of the neighborhood showing because Sinatra, no matter how far he has come, is still something of the boy from the neighborhood—only now he can take his neighborhood with him."[52] The male identity that 1950s commentary obliquely attributes to a proximity to organized crime is as much a product of the working-class Italian American neighborhood of Sinatra's Hoboken upbringing. Herbert Gans describes Sinatra and his Rat Pack friends as "a group of Hollywood corner boys,"[53] and William F. Whyte's study of the type of community in which Sinatra's ethnic identity evolves demonstrates these connections. Whyte's examination of an eastern city slum populated by Italian immigrants and their descendants was published in 1943. Whyte places the male inhabitants of "Cornerville" in two categories, as either upwardly mobile college boys bent on self-advancement through education, or "corner boys" whose lives revolve around the social activities in which they engage on local street corners. Among these second-generation Italian men, issues of loyalty and power form the basis on which relationships are built. The "corner boys" are differentiated from their college counterparts by the priority they give to the function of the group over a desire for individual achievement. This dominant concern for the group results in relationships bound by loyalty at their core. Whyte explains: "The code of the corner boy requires him to help his friends when he can and to refrain from doing anything to harm them. . . . Actions which were performed explicitly for the sake of friendship were revealed as being part of a system of mutual obligations."[54] Whyte notes that by demonstrating loyalty as part of this reciprocal network, "corner boys" maintain their cultural identity; those who move outside the Italian American community and relinquish such values are viewed negatively as having succumbed to Americanization.[55] As Herbert Gans identifies, Sinatra's perceived retention of his working-class Italian American identity makes him a particular object of admiration for the West Enders. The close male friendships he sustains, and the sense of loyalty he demands, illustrate his unwillingness to discard the ethnic traits that bind him to his immigrant community, even as he distances himself from it through a successful career. By failing to acknowledge this cultural basis for Sinatra's attitudes, shifting readings instead to images of power and ethnic crime, postwar commentary exposes the consistent negative stereotyping of the Italian American male.

"I Just Hate to See a Good Guy Get It in the Gut": Power and Frustration in *From Here to Eternity*

The most noted cinematic depiction of Italian American masculinity in the 1950s came in the 1955 film *Marty*. Ernest Borgnine's Academy Award–winning performance as thirty-three-year-old New York butcher Marty Piletti presented a comforting picture of the Italian American male. Culturally defined by his bonds to family, friends, and the Roman Catholic Church, Marty is berated by family and customers about his unmarried status. His frustrating search for a bride demonstrates the central position held by the family in Italian American culture. The film equally examines the loosening of traditional ties. The wisdom of a widowed mother-in-law residing with a young married couple is an ongoing debate. Similarly, while Marty's close male friendships are a feature of his experience, when they threaten to impede the possibility of marriage to Brooklyn schoolteacher Clara Snyder (Betsy Blair), whom his friends dismiss as a "dog," Marty makes plain his willingness to detach himself. With the prospect of marriage to a non-Italian, Marty conveys the progressive assimilation of the Italian American male.

As Private Angelo Maggio in *From Here to Eternity,* Sinatra challenges this benign image of inclusion. The ethnic traits displayed by Maggio and his sense of alienation illustrate the cultural differences and stereotypes that exclude the Italian American. Sinatra ferociously sought the role, having read James Jones's novel and identifying closely with the Italian American character. He later remarked: "I knew that if a picture was ever made, I was the only actor to play Private Maggio, the funny and sour Italo-American. I knew Maggio. I went to high school with him in Hoboken. I was beaten up with him. I might have been Maggio."[56] Sinatra lobbied Columbia studio head Harry Cohn for the part and bombarded director Fred Zinneman with telegrams signed "Maggio." According to Cohn's wife, Joan, the mogul regarded Sinatra as "a washed up song-and-dance-man," only reluctantly granting him a screen test.[57] Various rumors exist as to how Sinatra eventually won the part. The most infamous is the notion of organized crime intervention suggested by *The Godfather* and Johnny Fontane's appeal for Don Corleone's assistance in securing the war movie role that will resurrect his career. Less fanciful, however, is the fact that Sinatra's main rival, Eli Wallach, was contracted to appear in a Broadway version of Tennessee Williams's *El Camino Real,* directed by Elia Kazan, and his agents were engaged in protracted salary negotiations with Cohn. Sinatra's impressive screen test, his availability, and his offer to play the part for a paltry eight thousand dollars won him the role. Coached extensively during filming by Montgomery Clift, Sinatra gave an Academy Award–winning performance that rejuvenated his acting career and led to the kind of dramatic roles he had previously been denied. *Variety* described Sinatra's performance as "the greatest comeback in theater history."[58]

From Here to Eternity is set in the United States Army's Schofield Barracks in Hawaii immediately prior to the Japanese invasion of Pearl Harbor in 1941. Private Robert E. Lee Prewitt, played by Clift, arrives on a requested transfer from the Bugle Corps, upset at being passed over for promotion because of some in-house favoritism. Captain Dana Holmes (Philip Ober) is the regimental boxing coach and has pulled similar strings to bring Prewitt to "G" Company. Knowing Prewitt's reputation as a middleweight, Holmes intends to use his new recruit to win the year's boxing championship and put himself in line for the rank of major. Prewitt, however, has pledged to abandon boxing, having blinded opponent and friend Dixie Wells. Despite Holmes's promises of swift promotion and his offer of the position of company bugler, Prewitt remains steadfast in his refusal to box. His individualism is an immediate cause for concern.

Holmes warns him against building notoriety as a "lone wolf" and counsels him: "You should know that in the army it's not the individual that
counts." The captain's ethos of advancement through conformity is the
prevailing culture, disrupted by Prewitt's stance. Sergeant Warden (Burt
Lancaster), who, in practice, runs the company as a result of Holmes's
absence and disinterest, makes the demand for conformity clear to Prewitt. Resistant to Warden's pressure to ease both their positions, Prewitt
declares: "A man don't go his own way, he's nothing." Warden's response
highlights America's shifting attitude toward independence of spirit:
"Maybe back in the days of the pioneers a man could go his own way.
But today, you gotta play ball." Peter Biskind argues: "It is Warden, not
Prewitt, who emerges as the hero of the film. He's an organization man like
Holmes, and an individualist like Prewitt; he combines the best of both
worlds. Warden is ready to cut through army red tape when he has to, but
he's not about to go AWOL."[59] While Warden is the least self-destructive
of the film's male characters and described variously as "the best soldier
I ever saw" and "a good man," he is not rewarded for his combination of
individualism and establishment conformity. When he embarks on an
affair with Holmes's wife, Karen (Deborah Kerr), she suggests that he
become an officer so that he can transfer out of her husband's company
while she gains a divorce. Warden's reluctance is based partly on his
lack of respect for superiors such as Holmes. Equally, though, Warden's
attitude is characteristic of the postwar corporate male who has little
ambition for advancement. He tells Karen: "I don't want to be an officer.
I'm happy where I am." When another sergeant complains, "I'm getting
sick and tired watching you being a stooge for Holmes," Warden vehemently protests, stating his intention to make a change. However, his
unwillingness to risk the position he has negotiated for himself means
that his career is stalled and his relationship doomed.

Termed by Warden a "hardhead," Prewitt is the film's individualist.
When he refuses to accede to Holmes's pressure, the boxing team sets
about inflicting a measure of "the treatment" in an attempt to force
conformity. The ditch digging and mountain hikes to which Prewitt is
subjected, however, fail to break his resolve, and he remains stridently
independent. At the same time, Prewitt maintains a strong belief in the
established order. Named after the Southern general, he stays devoted
to the army, declaring himself "a thirty-year man." Despite demands
for him to conform to a corrupt system, Prewitt reveres the institution,
which he views as merely tarnished by individuals. When he develops
a relationship with Lorene (Donna Reed), a "hostess" he meets at the

New Congress Club, she finds his respect for the army inexplicable. Yet Lorene, too, is determined to become part of a system she recognizes as unjust. Lorene arrived in Hawaii having been jilted by her rich boyfriend because of her low social status. Her plan to make enough money to return home and buy her way into respectable society is based in her desire to become "a proper wife, who can run a proper home and raise proper children . . . because when you're proper, you're safe." By failing to confront the system, both Prewitt and Lorene limit their challenge to a temporary bout of individualism.

As "tough monkey" Angelo Maggio, Sinatra presents an alternative male identity, alienated from the establishment and with values that are markedly different from the corporate submissiveness of Warden and Prewitt. Prewitt passively accepts "the treatment," pushed to defy orders only when one of the boxing team, at Holmes's behest, kicks a bucket of dirty water into his path. Maggio's fearlessness in confronting authority and the significance he attaches to personal relationships indicate the cultural differences that define him. Maggio's first scenes reveal the powerlessness and sense of loyalty that underpin his persona. As Prewitt arrives at Schofield Barracks, he comes across Maggio crouched in front of the officers' quarters, broom in hand, clearing stones from the path. Maggio's lowly position in relation to authority is immediately made clear. His lack of power and essential vulnerability are equally emphasized by the loose-fitting vest that exposes Sinatra's thin frame. Screenwriter Daniel Taradash confirms that Sinatra's physical inadequacies contributed to the decision to cast him in the role: "One crucial difference in Frank's favor was his size. . . . Eli was a pretty muscular guy with a great physique. He did not look like a schnook. He looked like he could take two MPs with no trouble at all. Frank, on the other hand, looked so thin and woeful and so pitifully small that the audience would cry when they saw this poor little guy get beaten up."[60] The visual impact of Sinatra's slight build heightens the physical vulnerability and lack of social power around which Maggio's persona is constructed. While Prewitt waits to be seen by Holmes, Maggio hovers outside the office with his broom, communicating with his friend through the window. Physically excluded, he recognizes his lowly position in the organization's hierarchy. At the same time, he demonstrates the allegiance to Prewitt that will be evidenced through the film: "I feel for ya, pal, but from my position I can't quite reach."

The sense of loyalty Maggio shows toward his "buddy boy" makes theirs the only authentic male friendship in the film. Undeterred by Prewitt's quiet stoicism, Maggio draws him into a warm friendship, prefacing the close buddy relationships Sinatra develops on screen in *Not as a Stranger, Some Came Running,* and *Never So Few.* While Holmes ingratiates himself with superiors and Warden maintains loose ties to other servicemen, Maggio values his friendship with Prewitt. As soon as "the treatment" commences during a game of pool, Maggio comes to his friend's aid, confronting the aggressors: "Look, the guy don't have to fight if he don't want to without getting kicked around. . . . Why don't you take off?" The threatening response he receives from one of the boxing team points to his alienation from power: "You want busted head, Maggio? . . . Keep your big nose out, altogether." However, Maggio maintains a sense of fair play: "I just hate to see a good guy get it in the gut." As he continues to intercede on Prewitt's behalf, Maggio is subjected to the same punishments inflicted on his friend.

Family and friendships assume the highest importance for Maggio and illustrate his cultural difference. He passes around family photos, proudly pointing out his father, "Mr. Maggio," and loans Prewitt the oversized shirt his sister has sent him. Unlike Prewitt, Maggio has little respect for institutional authority. His initial remarks to the new arrival demonstrate his lack of awe: "This outfit they can give back to General Custer." Pete Hamill reports how Sinatra's attitude toward authority was formed by an awareness of systemic corruption: "You know what we all thought growing up? We thought *everybody* was on the take. We *knew* the cops were taking. They were right in front of us. But we thought the priests were on the take, the schoolteachers, the guy in the marriage license bureau, everybody. We thought if God came to New Jersey, he'd get on line to get his envelope."[61] Sinatra's perception of corrupt authority is reiterated by William F. Whyte. The extortion practices permitted by relationships between racketeers and the local police lead the inhabitants of "Cornerville" to view officers as "parasites" or "the dregs of the department."[62] Their disdain for a fundamentally dishonest system, Whyte indicates, frees them from the necessity to submit to authority.

Maggio exhibits a disregard for abusive power in his dealings with Sergeant of the Guard James R. "Fatso" Judson (Ernest Borgnine). The confrontation sparked by Fatso's erratic piano playing at the New Congress Club exposes the prejudices that define Maggio's cultural alienation and highlights his determination to defend his Italian American identity. Maggio's complaint is met with Fatso's taunts of "little Wop" and "little Mussolini." Maggio resists both epithets, which cast him as an illegitimate, undemocratic American. He is unimpressed by both Fatso's physical size and army status. When another soldier attempts to advise him of Fatso's identity, Maggio barks, "What do I care who he is?" and moves once more to physically confront him. On a further occasion, Maggio challenges Fatso when the sergeant whispers an apparently disrespectful comment about his sister. Lunging at Fatso's back with a chair, Maggio begins a fight that is resolved only by Warden's timely intervention. Skinny Private Maggio's readiness to battle with his knife-wielding, heavy-set superior when his family background is disparaged reveals his prioritization of his ethnic identity over submission to authority.

When Maggio defies company orders, walking off guard to reclaim his weekend pass, the frustrations often masked by his amiable air are revealed. Just as he runs through the company kitchens yelling, "Hot, hot, H.O.D!," Maggio makes an amusing drunk, rolling a couple of olives as dice and declaring, "Snake eyes. That's the story of my life." His statement, however, demonstrates his awareness that his alienation is permanent. While Prewitt, who rose to corporal in the Bugle Corps, has the opportunity to advance if he conforms to the group ethos, Maggio's ethnic identity and the values he espouses will continue to affect his fortunes. His sense of fate and disregard for authority make him indifferent to the consequences of his actions. Maggio resists Prewitt's attempts to return him to the base before they "get in trouble," expressing his weariness at the authoritarian conformity required by the army: "What's the matter with you? Can't a man get drunk? Can't a man do nothing? . . . Has a man gotta be hounded all his life? Well, I'm tired. I ain't no criminal. I ain't no coward" (Figure 3). By going absent without leave, Maggio challenges the controls that restrict him. His assertion of his worth directly confronts the prevailing negative stereotypes of Italian American masculinity bound up in ethnic crime and World War II images of cowardice on the battlefront. When two military policemen approach, Maggio baits them, "Come and get me, you guys," and struggles with them until he is battered to the ground. His combative reaction echoes the "corner boys'" disrespect for guardians of the law and highlights his increasing frustration.

When a court-martial lands Maggio in the stockade, he continues to resist authority, immediately vowing to escape. Fatso's campaign of physical beatings is met with Maggio's disdain as he unfailingly spits in the sergeant's eye. Finally escaping, and before dying in his friend's arms, Maggio urges Prewitt to take a similarly defiant stand against authority. Maggio's impact on his "paisan" is seen in the extent to which Prewitt adopts the values exhibited by his Italian American friend. By challenging

Figure 3: Maggio rails at Prewitt's attempts to return him to the base, expressing his frustration at the restrictions and prejudices to which he is subjected. (*From Here to Eternity*)

"the treatment" meted out against Prewitt, Maggio places loyalty at the core of their relationship, setting up the same system of mutual obligations viewed by Whyte in Cornerville and evident in Sinatra's expression of his ethnic identity. Murdering Fatso in a backalley knife fight, Prewitt demonstrates his loyalty by avenging Maggio's death. Even in this act, however, Prewitt illustrates his ultimate faith in the system, telling Fatso: "The army's gonna get you sooner or later, Fatso, but before they do, I want a piece of you myself." The film vindicates Prewitt's confidence in the justice of the system when Holmes's corrupt culture is discovered and he is removed from his post. By allowing him to retire and avoid court-martial, however, the film shows the inequities of the hierarchical structure Prewitt supports. The circumstances in which the two friends meet their deaths best relay their basic cultural differences. While Maggio dies escaping his oppression and vowing continual resistance, Prewitt is killed by an American soldier following the Japanese invasion as he desperately attempts to rejoin the company where his passive conformity is demanded.

Time magazine's review of *From Here to Eternity* remarked of Sinatra's performance: "His face wears the calm of a man who is completely sure of what he is doing as he plays it straight from Little Italy."[63] Sinatra's affinity with feisty underdog Maggio, who challenges authority and proudly asserts his ethnicity, originates in the star's crucial Italian American identity. Sinatra's ethnic image develops in the context of the country's celebration of diversity in World War II and the prominent reemergence of the organized crime stereotype in the 1950s. Misreadings of Sinatra's male styling occur as Senator Kefauver's hearings and the desire for innocuous Italian imagery mark Sinatra's star persona as distinctively threatening. Simultaneously resisting and reclaiming the negative stereotype, and exhibiting the values and attitudes fundamental to his ethnicity, Sinatra assertively expresses a potent Italian American cultural identity, which challenges conventional definitions and emphasizes the differences and ties that bind ethnic masculinity to the American character.

3 Anticommunist Witch Hunts and Civil Rights

> Those of you who know me . . . feel pretty secure about the
> way I think, the way I am. As far as anyone else is concerned,
> if my lifetime—more than half a century lived in the spot-
> light of public life—if those 50-plus years are not enough to
> show my covenant on the issue of civil rights, I am not going
> to waste my time . . . defending the obvious or itemizing a
> laundry list of my deeds to benefit the brotherhood of man.
> . . . Even saying this much embarrasses me.
>
> —Frank Sinatra

The controversy sparked in 1987 by the decision of the Los Angeles branch of the National Association for the Advancement of Colored
People (NAACP) to bestow on Sinatra a Lifetime Achievement Award is a
measure of how far political perceptions of the star had shifted since the
postwar years. While the president of the L.A. chapter commended Sinatra as "an individual who has been pushing and championing the rights
of minorities for over fifty years," demonstrators outside the ceremony
condemned Sinatra for his 1981 performance at South Africa's Sun City
resort, which put Sinatra on a United Nations blacklist. Angry protesters
carried placards describing the star as "Botha's Ambassador," and the
anti-apartheid group TransAfrica published fullpage advertisements in
the *New York Times* labeling Sinatra "one of the faces behind apartheid."
In his acceptance speech, Sinatra dismissed the need to justify his actions, termed South African President P. W. Botha "a bum" and railed
against his critics who, he argued, "seek to divide not only blacks and
whites but the blacks themselves."[1] To those actively opposing the South
African regime, Sinatra's concert performance represented the legitimiza-

tion of a foreign racist state by a star of the Hollywood establishment. To the Los Angeles NAACP, Sinatra's record of campaigning for the civil rights of all Americans deserved recognition. The extreme reactions to the star's award reflect the contentions that consistently surround Sinatra's involvement in racial politics.

Sinatra engaged with civil rights continuously through his career. As late as Independence Day 1991, the *Los Angeles Times* published an article in which Sinatra called on readers to "come to grips with this killer disease of hatred, of bigotry and racism and anti-Semitism."[2] Yet the star's association with the race debate has provoked little academic interest. Sinatra's involvement in politics during World War II and the postwar period has not gone unnoticed. Gerald Meyer considers Sinatra's connection to liberal organizations in the 1940s, positioning the star in the history of Hollywood's Popular Front.[3] Ronald Brownstein's examination of Sinatra's involvement with John F. Kennedy's 1960 presidential campaign effectively illustrates an increasingly close and complex relationship between American politics and show business.[4] However, the attention given to Sinatra's broad association with liberal politics has been to the detriment of any analysis of his engagement with civil rights. A consideration of Sinatra's position in relation to racial, ethnic, and religious tolerance usefully demonstrates the problems experienced by Hollywood and its stars in addressing this issue.

Sinatra enters the civil-rights debate through cinematic work and personal statement, insisting on the diversity of America's racial, ethnic, and religious identity. Thomas Cripps's initial verdict on Sinatra's 1945 short film *The House I Live In* was that the film represented "two steps forward and one back" for the civil-rights cause.[5] However, close analysis of the film, in the context of Hollywood's discussion of the country's racial dynamics in the immediate postwar period, reveals the progressive nature of the piece. Criticism of Sinatra's liberal politics occurs in a climate of anticommunist extremism and exposes the role played by sections of the press in cultivating the atmosphere of witch hunts promoted by the House Un-American Activities Committee (HUAC). A shift toward explicit yet still limited depictions of America's racial inequalities in the 1950s illustrates the problems still experienced by Hollywood as politicians expressed their reluctance to address the growing problem of civil rights. The indictment of racism evident in the 1958 film *Kings Go Forth* serves to demonstrate this readiness to promote social change and the constraints that hindered industry attempts to progress the civil-rights cause.

An American Dilemma: Corner Boy Politics and the "Good War"

Sinatra identified himself as a staunch supporter of the Democrats by endorsing a succession of liberal leaders through World War II and the postwar period. In 1944 he campaigned extensively for a fourth term for Franklin Delano Roosevelt, recording radio programs for the Democratic National Committee, donating funds to the president's election campaign, and telling his fans: "This peace will depend on your parents' votes on November seventh."[6] In 1952, Sinatra came out in favor of the Democratic candidate Adlai Stevenson, performing at the "Hollywood for Stevenson" rally at the Palladium in Los Angeles, and again supporting Stevenson in the 1956 campaign, singing the national anthem at the opening session of the Democratic National Convention. Sinatra also famously led the Hollywood contingent championing Senator John F. Kennedy in 1960. He performed at numerous fund-raising events and provided the campaign with its theme song, a specially adapted version of the Sammy Cahn/Jimmy Van Heusen hit "High Hopes" from Sinatra's 1959 film *A Hole in the Head.*

Sinatra commented on his involvement in Democratic Party politics: "I've been campaigning for Democrats ever since I marched in a parade for Al Smith when I was a twelve-year-old kid."[7] He was initially drawn into the political arena by his mother, Dolly, who served as a ward leader in Hoboken's Ninth District in the 1920s, using her knowledge of Italian dialects to recruit immigrant support for the Democrats. However, his political perspective has a wider cultural basis. Just as Sinatra's codes of loyalty and individual style illustrate his Italian American cultural identity, as a Democratic Party supporter Sinatra retained the political allegiances indicative of his urban immigrant background. William F. Whyte explains the distinctions made between Democrats and Republicans in "Cornerville":

> To get ahead, the Cornerville man must move either in the world of business and Republican politics or in the world of Democratic politics and the rackets. He cannot move in both worlds at once; they are so far apart that there is hardly any connection between them. If he advances in the first world, he is recognized by society at large as a successful man, but he is recognized in Cornerville only as an alien to the district. If he advances in the second world, he achieves recognition in Cornerville but becomes a social outcast to respectable people elsewhere. The entire course of the corner boy's

training in the social life of his district prepares him for a career in the rackets or in Democratic politics. . . . In effect, the society at large puts a premium on disloyalty to Cornerville.[8]

Through his continuous support for the Democratic Party, Sinatra displays his loyalty toward the working-class Italian American community of his youth and reinforces his strong ethnic identity. Sinatra's cultural experience also prompts his intense involvement with tolerance and civil-rights issues. Sinatra commented in his sixties: "When I was young, people used to ask me why I sent money to the NAACP and, you know, tried to help, in my own small way. I used to say, Because we've been there too, man. It wasn't just black people hanging from the end of those fucking ropes."[9] The ambiguous racial status of Italian Americans and a history of lynchings and discrimination meant that inequality was a feature of the community's experience. When Italian anarchists Nicola Sacco and Bartolomeo Vanzetti were executed in 1927 for the murders of two men killed in a Massachusetts shoe-factory robbery, questions raised about the trial's evidence and its focus on the defendants' political beliefs heightened Italian Americans' perception of America's white Anglo-Saxon bias. Engaging with civil rights in the postwar period, Sinatra draws on his sense of ethnic injustice to address the country's more explicit racial divide.

During World War II, America's racial and ethnic divisions were actively denied as the country concentrated on galvanizing support for what was cast as the "good war" against German fascism and Japanese inhumanity. The Office of War Information (OWI) co-opted Hollywood into an image-building exercise, demanding films that presented an inclusive image of American life. The manual for filmmakers produced by the OWI adopted the theme of Henry Wallace's "Century of the Common Man," terming the war a "people's war" and urging the depiction of multiethnic platoons "using names of foreign extraction" and the occasional inclusion of black officers.[10] This stress on America's acceptance of diversity resulted in films such as the 1943 release *Bataan,* in which the combat unit cobbled together to destroy a bridge in the fight against the Japanese was a uniquely democratic group that included a WASP, a Hispanic, a Filipino boxer, an Irish American, a Jew, and an African American. As Gary Gerstle points out, the World War II image of the multicultural platoon differed from its World War I counterpart in its focus on the preservation of ethnic distinctions rather than the molding of servicemen into the "all American fightin' man," making it a positive representation of American democracy.[11] The inclusion of African American servicemen in this picture, however, presented a false image. While some integrated units existed in World War II, the armed services remained officially segregated until President Truman ordered integration in 1948. Although the navy and air force complied at this stage, the army resisted full desegregation until African American troops were required for the war in Korea in 1950.

Despite being a liberal New Deal agency, the OWI had difficulty squaring its desire to show African Americans as part of the country's diverse identity with the need it felt to censor the reality of segregated armed forces, Jim Crow segregation in the South, and de facto segregation in the North. The version of *Action in the North Atlantic* (1943) that hit the screen illustrates the OWI's dilemma in its omission of the original screenplay's characterization of a black pantryman who questions why he should fight for the Allies. Gerstle explains: "Its censors objected both to the portrayal of a black as subservient and to the screenwriters' determination to have this black character challenge his subservience."[12] The 1944 documentary *The Negro Soldier* represented a limited expression of appreciation for the contribution of African American servicemen but reinforced a misleading image of American tolerance.

The OWI's and Hollywood's denial of American racism occurred despite the fact that World War II highlighted the injustices of the country's racial divisions. As African Americans fought for democracy in Europe but still faced fundamental indignities at home, the call for racial equality gained an increased sense of urgency. Labor leader A. Philip Randolph's threatened March on Washington in 1941, which prompted the Fair Employment Practices Commission, combined with African American newspapers' "Double V" campaign, for victory in war and victory over inequality at home, to demonstrate a growing impatience. In 1944, Swedish economist Gunnar Myrdal published *An American Dilemma,* which examined racist practices in the South and called on Americans to live up to the "American Creed," a belief in equality, freedom, and opportunity. The substantial increase in the NAACP's membership during the war years, from 50,000 to 400,000, added to the mood that sought a resolution to the country's social divisions.

"I Can Lick Any Son of a Bitch in This Joint": Preaching Equality and Racial Integration

Hollywood was a prominent indicator of the shifting postwar cultural climate. While conservative organizations existed in Hollywood, such as the Motion Picture Alliance for the Preservation of American Ideals, formed in 1943 by filmmakers including Walt Disney and King Vidor, the industry was dominated by a liberal sensibility. The film capital's liberal streak dated back to 1930s Popular Front organizations such as the Hollywood Anti-Nazi League, the Motion Picture Artists' Committee, and the Motion Picture Democratic Committee. The Popular Front was a broad coalition of radicals and liberals formed in 1935 to fight fascism at home and abroad and to work with the unions toward social reform.[13] Diverted from more radical filmmaking by the war effort, liberal screenwriters, directors, and actors returned their attention to America's social divisions as World War II concluded.

Sinatra inserted himself into Hollywood's race debate in a number of significant ways. He was the first white star to perform on *Jubilee,* a program produced for African American GIs, breaking the Armed Forces Radio Services' color bar.[14] In 1945, Sinatra published several articles calling for racial, ethnic, and religious tolerance. In "What's This about Races?" Sinatra compared American discrimination to the evils of the Nazi regime. Positioning himself as a typical second-generation immigrant, he recalled the taunts of "little Dago" he suffered as a child, while friends were labeled "Kikes" or "Niggers." Sinatra went on to remind readers that "all men are *created* equal" and that "*everybody* in the United States is a foreigner," and he encouraged them to "stamp out prejudices that are separating one group of United States citizens from another."[15]

Again directing his message at the nation's youth, Sinatra also intervened in two school disputes. On October 23, 1945, he attended the Benjamin Franklin High School in Harlem, where disturbances had broken out between Italian American and African American students. At the integrated school, recognized as an exemplary model of tolerance and intercultural education, Sinatra encouraged the students to "act as neighborhood emissaries of racial good will."[16] The following month he visited Froebel High School in Gary, Indiana, where white students had staged walkouts when the school board attempted to fully integrate its African American students in school activities. Sinatra confronted the initially unfriendly crowd, declaring: "I can lick any son of a bitch in this joint." Accusing local politicians of inciting the strike action, Sinatra urged the students to rethink their actions and reject the influences of those opposed to racial integration.[17] Sinatra's appearance in Indiana failed to resolve the dispute but added further to his image as a star active in racial politics. Columnists began writing about Sinatra as a performer with "a deep sense of his brother's wrong and a social conscience that hasn't been atrophied by money or fame."[18] He was also honored with a number of awards, such as the first scroll presented by New York's Bureau of Intercultural Education, and his name was added to the 1945 Honor Roll of Race Relations by the curator of the Schomburg Collection of Negro Literature of the New York Public Library.[19]

"Don't Let Anybody Make Suckers Out of Ya": The House I Live In and the Postwar Push for Tolerance

Sinatra's role in *The House I Live In* was his most high-profile association with the political issue of tolerance and was an important contribution to Hollywood attempts to stimulate a debate around race. Released in September 1945, *The House I Live In* was a ten-minute short put together by a Hollywood team loaded with liberal credentials. The project was overseen by Dore Schary at RKO, who, along with Samuel Goldwyn, would later become one of the two lone voices opposing the Hollywood studios' decision to dispense with the services of the "Hollywood Ten." Production was handled by Frank Ross with direction by Mervyn LeRoy, who had been involved in a number of Warner Bros.' social-critique movies of the 1930s, among them *I Am a Fugitive from a Chain Gang* (1932) and *Gold Diggers of 1933* (1933). The soon to be blacklisted Albert Maltz provided the screenplay. The title song was written in 1942 by lyricist Lewis Allan, who penned the Billie Holiday ode against lynching, "Strange Fruit," and composer Earl Robinson, whose "Ballad for Americans," written in 1940, was a fifteen-minute work that claimed freedom as a basic American value. The song "The House I Live In" had its first airing in the USO morale booster *Follow the Boys* (1944), before being appropriated for Sinatra's 1945 intolerance short. All of the contributors to the production gave their services gratis, Sinatra and his musical director Axel Stordahl included, with Schary providing RKO facilities for shooting free of charge. All proceeds from the film went to organizations involved in social work for adolescents.

The House I Live In stresses the significance of tolerance for a nation of immigrants, asserting the need for postwar America to address its social divisions. Establishing a semidocumentary style, the film opens with Sinatra in a recording studio performing his hit of the previous year, "If You Are but a Dream." Exiting into an alleyway for a break, Sinatra is confronted by a group of boys chasing another boy into a corner. As Sinatra breaks up the scene, he attempts to establish the reason for the "gang war" and is eventually told by one of the boys: "We don't like his religion." (The particular religion is not made explicit, but the suggestion is that the boy is Jewish.) Sinatra's response is to label the protagonists "Nazis," reasoning that "Religion makes no difference, except maybe to a Nazi or somebody as stupid." To illustrate the possibility of positive cooperation between the religions, against a backdrop of documentary-style footage, Sinatra relays the tale of Colin Kelly, "an American and a Presbyterian," and Meyer Levin, "an American and a Jew," who worked together to sink the Japanese battleship the *Haruna* a few days after Pearl Harbor.[20] The short concludes with Sinatra singing the title song to the boys with orchestral accompaniment, after which the boys depart, bringing the former outcast along with them.

Appealing to Sinatra's core youth market with classic star close-ups, *The House I Live In* tackles its subject matter at a necessarily basic level. More problematically, the decision to focus on religious prejudice has led to criticism that the film falls short of addressing the more explosive issues of ethnic and particularly racial intolerance and that it additionally avoids the notion of American culpability through its allusions to Nazism. Thomas Cripps, for instance, suggests that the film "missed its mark, preferring the relatively safe ground of religious bigotry rather than the emerging national issue of racism."[21] While anti-Semitism is most prominent in the film, America's problematic relationship with ethnic and racial diversity is also quite clearly confronted, as *The House I Live In* utilizes the context of World War II to reinforce the relevance of its message. Positioning himself as a part of both immigrant and American culture, Sinatra challenges the boys' intolerance by relating it to their ethnic differences, telling them: "My dad came from Italy, but I'm an American. But should I hate your father because he came from Ireland or France or Russia?" There is significance, of course, in the choice of the neutral Irish and the French and Russian Allies. The uncritical inclusion of Russia in the immediate aftermath of the war contrasts with later postwar representations of the communist state and is typical of the period. Three melodramas from 1943, for example—*Mission to Moscow, Song of Russia,* and *The North Star*—gave Russia a positive, democratic image, and each was retroactively condemned by HUAC in 1947.[22] Conspicuously excluded from *The House I Live In*'s expressions of tolerance are the Japanese, Sinatra referring to them throughout the film as "Japs" and, in so doing, demonstrating the vitriol directed toward an enemy who had attacked American soil. A 1942 government decree had enabled the forced internment of 100,000 native Japanese Americans and resident Japanese aliens on America's West Coast, and American attitudes toward the Japanese became particularly hardened following news reports of the torture of American prisoners on

Bataan in the same year.[23] Reflecting these sentiments, an advertisement for the 1943 film *Behind the Rising Sun* asked audiences to "See why the villainous Japs have simply got to be exterminated!" Though by the end of the war Hollywood was beginning to consider the Japanese in more complex terms, with films such as *First Yank into Tokyo* (1945), remnants of wartime intolerance certainly remained.[24]

While *The House I Live In* was able to argue the absurdity of other varieties of ethnic intolerance in a direct manner, the difficulties involved in Hollywood attempts to address the more controversial topic of race discrimination had not abated, despite concerted efforts to make some headway. These difficulties are exemplified by Thomas Doherty's comparison of two episodes of the *March of Time,* a twenty-minute independent feature released every four weeks during the war under Twentieth Century Fox distribution, each film devoted to a specific topic. Their January 1941 release, the proclamatory *Americans All!,* took as its subject the European refugee fleeing German anti-Semitism and failed to make any reference to race. In contrast, *Americans All,* released in July 1944 with a noticeable loss of exclamation mark, showed black and white Americans mixing socially, and black troops serving in the jungles of the Pacific, and pointed out "the injustice of denying to the Negro the rights of American citizenship while expecting him to shoulder its ultimate responsibility—that of defending his country with his life."[25] While this shift illustrates a move toward an open discussion of the country's racial dynamics, the intransigence of southern distributors made alternative methods of addressing the issue often more productive. *Americans All,* for example, was denied a release in the South, therefore failing to reach a large section of the audience to whom its message was addressed.[26]

The decision to concentrate attention on religious rather than racial intolerance in *The House I Live In* is, therefore, unsurprising and made it one of a number of films that took a similar route. The 1946 Warner Bros. short *It Happened in Springfield* had been intended as a representation of more enlightened attitudes toward race that were being promoted in a public school following local race riots. However, a decision to use outtakes from the *March of Time* sequence, which showed black and white Americans socializing, was abandoned once those involved discovered the fate of *Americans All* in the South. The film consequently turned into a discussion of ethnic pluralism that excluded all African American presence.[27] *Down Beat*'s review of *The House I Live In* certainly suggested that the current political climate was significant in restricting the expression of the film's theme: "There is not a single allusion to the Negro problem in the picture. . . . It was Sinatra himself who insisted that if the Negro factor could not be dealt with frankly, it should be eliminated entirely, that a complete and conspicuous omission would be a more honest way to deal with the matter than the usual run-around tactics."[28] A similar omission is apparent in Sinatra's rendition of the title song. Robinson and Allan's hymn to American democracy, or "the dream that's been a-growin' for a hundred and fifty years," is a celebration of diversity that, in its 1944 cinema appearance, was performed by a black gospel group, the Golden Gate Quartet, and included a reference to the War of Independence in the line "The little church at Concord/Where freedom's fight began."[29] By 1945, the sole reference to race comes in the declaration: "All races and religions/That's America to me."

It would, however, be inaccurate to suggest that the film is completely devoid of any reference to racial inequality. In a later reassessment of *The House I Live In,* Thomas Cripps praised the film as the best of a series of shorts, including *Don't Be a Sucker* (1943) and *The American Creed* (1947), that "displayed a coy eagerness to proceed—eagerness because they loaded their plots with indictments of racism, coy because each found a way to blame evil foreign agents for the spread of it."[30] Cripps points to Sinatra's parting shot to the boys, "Don't let anybody make suckers out of ya," as evidence of an allusion to foreign infiltration, although, as in the case of Sinatra's plea to students in Indiana, the reference is as likely to be to the unhealthy influence of bigoted Americans. In his ambivalence, however, Cripps acknowledges the assault on racism that lies in the text and that is illustrated in various ways. *The House I Live In* is comparable to a number of Hollywood features made during the immediate postwar period that adopted the theme of anti-Semitism as shorthand for intolerance in general, using World War II as a timely indicator of the dangers of undemocratic attitudes. As well as *Crossfire* (1947) and *Gentleman's Agreement* (1947), which made additional allusions to race through the notion of "passing," these included Maltz's own *The Pride of the Marines,* a film particularly notable for its combination of attacks on anti-Semitism and ethnic intolerance and its dignified representation of an African American male. While it presents a positive picture of various religions working together, *The Pride of the Marines* does not shy away from suggesting that the war has failed to expunge intolerance. Jewish and Irish soldiers fear returning home to the same prejudices, and another exhibits prejudice toward a Mexican soldier alongside whom he has previously fought. Sinatra was particularly affected by the film, expressing his support in a letter to Maltz: "I have never been so emotionally moved by anything. . . . I know you *do* understand that my anxiety and interest in our social and discrimination (or what have you) problems have been hungrily awaiting such valuable assistance. . . . You've got to hit 'em right in the kisser with it and, baby, you really did."[31] The 1948 film *The Boy with Green Hair* took another indirect route to the subject as an allegorical tale of intolerance. The story of a war orphan who suffers prejudice and alienation when his hair turns green overnight, the film reminds its audience that America's involvement in the war was dictated by the requirement to rid the world of this kind of intolerance. The film's color metaphor alludes further to the specifics of racial prejudice.

In addition to the use of religious intolerance as an all-encompassing method of confronting discrimination, Sinatra's reference to blood in *The House I Live In* suggests a more direct targeting of the issue of race. When one of the boys balks at being labeled a Nazi, since his father was wounded in the army, Sinatra asks if his father received "some of that blood plasma." Having discovered that both parents of the Jewish child have donated blood that could conceivably have been used to save the life of the boy's father, Sinatra uses the point to stress equality as a basic truism, telling them: "God created everybody. He didn't create one people better than another. Your blood's the same as mine; mine's the same as his [pointing to the Jewish boy]." The social consequences of racial bloodlines for inhabitants of the South make this reference highly significant. By specifically addressing the subject of blood plasma, the film goes to the root of the philosophy of a fundamental inequality between the races that the war had failed to resolve and had even perpetuated. Beyond the racial separation of the armed forces, such beliefs extended as far as the segregation of blood meant for the treatment of servicemen. The practice of classifying blood plasma by race as well as type, adopted by the Red Cross and the armed forces, was carried out for reasons the surgeon general deemed "not biologically convincing" but "psychologically important in America."[32] As government officials legitimized existing attitudes at their very root, cinema challenged this wartime inconsistency in films such as *Somewhere I'll Find You* (1942). Clark Gable's war correspondent reports back from the front line in Bataan that black and white soldiers fought together "and when they bled, their blood was the same color." Similarly, Sinatra's assertion of the sameness of blood directly challenges racism at its core and reveals the message of *The House I Live In* as an appeal for tolerance that incorporates religion, ethnicity, and race.

The House I Live In was of central importance in establishing Sinatra's political image, and the film's life extended far beyond its original release. Sinatra's FBI file, for example, notes a report in the *People's Daily World* that the film was to be shown at the Bret Harte School in November 1947, and Jon Wiener recalls watching the annual showing of the film at Sunday school in St. Paul, Minnesota, in the early 1950s.[33] Sinatra's reenactment of the piece on a 1951 edition of *The Frank Sinatra Show* illustrates some subtle shifts in the political context in the intervening six years. World War II continues to be a point of reference. Guest Jack Benny notes in his introduction the passing of Armistice Day, which has come to represent "a symbol of the things this country's always fought for: freedom, equality, and our way of life," and presents *The House I Live In* as "a picture that pretty well expresses all of these things." In his updated version, Sinatra moves from labeling the boys "Nazis," to terming them, ironically, "one of those Rat Pack gangs." One of the boys now has a father who has been wounded in Korea, and Sinatra's immigrant references no longer include Russia but are restricted to the uncomplicated Ireland, Sweden, and Holland. Most significant is the inclusion of an African American boy among the group of children.[34]

Sinatra continued to perform the title song at a variety of concerts and events, with the song taking on varying meanings as Sinatra's political image evolved. In 1952 he performed "The House I Live In" at the Los Angeles "Hollywood for Stevenson" rally, indicating that equality was still central to the concerns of liberal Hollywood. In 1964 he recorded the theme as part of a post-Kennedy album of patriotic songs, which also included performances by Bing Crosby and Fred Waring. As producer Sonny Burke's cover notes acknowledge, the album brought together three performers "whose political viewpoints may well be degrees apart." Burke suggests the combined motivation behind the album is America's "need to instill among its people the true feeling of brotherhood and the real meaning of its Constitution."[35] By the time Sinatra performed the song during *The Main Event* at New York's Madison Square Garden in 1974, his political shift to the right, suggested by his support for Richard Nixon's 1972 presidential campaign, had turned "The House I Live In" into an anthem for conservative patriotism.[36]

"Sinatra, Commie Playboy": Government Witch Hunts and the Hearst Press

At the time of the film's release, the progressive tone of *The House I Live In* was embraced by Hollywood. At the 1946 Oscar ceremony, Sinatra, Mervyn LeRoy, and Frank Ross were each presented with a special Academy Award, and Sinatra expressed his wish that "very soon we can make more pictures like *The House I Live In* which will bring the same message."[37] Reactions from other quarters were indicative of the growing tide of antiliberal feeling that manifested itself in the years of communist witch hunting that followed. Albert Maltz was blacklisted by HUAC and jailed for six months in 1950 as a result of what the committee considered to be the communist influence in his screenplays. Although he worked sporadically thereafter, Maltz remained uncredited until the late 1960s.[38] Sinatra, too, was subjected to continuous criticism during the 1940s as a result of his politics. Projects such as *The House I Live In* positioned Sinatra as a Hollywood liberal. This image was reinforced by his involvement with organizations such as Paul Robeson's American Crusade to End Lynchings, American Youth for Democracy, and the Independent Citizens' Committee of the Arts, Sciences, and Professions, on which Sinatra served as vice president in 1946. He also received awards from the journal *New Masses* for "greater interracial understanding" and the "contribution made to promote democracy and interracial unity."[39]

Sinatra also declared his support for the forward-thinking Henry Wallace. Wallace served as vice president to Roosevelt between 1940 and 1944 and was dismissed from President Truman's government because of his public opposition to the administration's policy toward the Soviet Union. He went on to form the short-lived Progressive Party in 1948, and his resolute determination to effect social change captured the imagination of liberal Hollywood, as Ronald Brownstein suggests: "His unyielding, undiluted expression of the true faith—cooperation with the Soviets abroad, social justice at home—made Wallace a hero to liberals everywhere, and nowhere more than in Hollywood."[40] Sinatra aligned himself with Wallace, suggesting to reporters: "Poverty. That's the biggest thorn. It comes down to what Henry Wallace said, to what he meant when he said every kid in the world should have his quart of milk a day."[41] In 1947, Sinatra wrote to Wallace, who was then editor of the liberal weekly the *New Republic,* calling for "mutual respect, whether it's on the slum level of one kid for another or at the top of the ladder where it's one government for another, one race for another or one belief for another."[42] In what reads as an appeal to Wallace to reconstruct Roosevelt's legacy, Sinatra warns: "Until another leader we can trust, as we trusted him, takes up the fight we like to think of as ours—the fight for tolerance, which is the basis of any fight for peace—it's going to be tough to be a liberal."[43] Sinatra again signals tolerance as his main concern and points to the problems posed for those involved in liberal politics.

Criticism of Sinatra's association with liberal organizations and causes came from various sources. The Federal Bureau of Investigation initially opened a file on the star in 1943 following a bizarre letter that suggested Sinatra's singing was a vehicle for right-wing political extremism.[44] The FBI continued to record his alleged affiliations through the postwar period, with the result that Sinatra was denied clearance to entertain the troops in Korea in 1954.[45] When Sinatra was invited to have tea with President Roosevelt at the White House in September 1944, the Republican senator from Nebraska, Kenneth Wherry, complained: "That crooner! Mr. Roosevelt could spend his time better conferring with members of the Senate."[46] Westbrook Pegler, a political writer for the Hearst publication *The New York Journal-American,* took to calling Sinatra the "New Dealing crooner."[47] During the eight years following the release of *The House I Live In,* Sinatra was named as a communist twelve times to the House Un-American Activities Committee by, among others, Jack B. Tenney, a California state senator, and Gerald L. K. Smith, the right-wing leader of the America First Party.[48]

Sinatra avoided being called to testify before HUAC's televised Hollywood hearings, which commenced in October 1947. However, he expressed his support for the "Unfriendly Ten," who included Maltz, Edward Dmytryk, and Dalton Trumbo, as part of the Committee for the First Amendment.[49] This organization was formed in October 1947 as a response to what members viewed as HUAC's unconstitutional activities. Alongside several United States senators, its most vocal members included John Huston, William Wyler, Humphrey Bogart, and Lauren Bacall. On October 26, Sinatra appeared on the First Amendment Committee's *Hollywood Fights Back* radio broadcast to warn of the dangers to democracy posed by HUAC's hearings: "Once they get the movies throttled, how long will it be before the Committee goes to work on freedom of the air? How long will it be before we're told what we can and cannot say into a radio microphone? If you make a pitch on a nation-wide network for a square deal for the underdog, will they call you a Commie? . . . Are they gonna scare us into silence? I wonder."[50] Sinatra's direct challenge to HUAC's actions was one more factor giving rise to the type of communist smear his broadcast predicted. Among the more extreme publications condemning Sinatra as a communist sympathizer was the

Red Scare pamphlet *Red Betrayal of Youth,* in which the following diatribe appeared in 1948 under the title "Sinatra, Commie Playboy":

> One of the outstanding young Reds in Hollywood is Frankie Sina-tra. . . . Of late this young Red punk has been touring the country swooning bobby soxers with his baritone voice while he tells their parents how to vote. He appeared before 16,000 left-wingers in Mad-ison Square Gardens [sic] last year at the opening of a nationwide campaign by the Communist Party and the New Deal's "Russian Firsters" to capture the veteran's [sic] votes. Frank Sinatra, defiant in bow tie, demanded freedom for the Chinese; a campaign against the Spanish government; and public recognition of the political pos-sibilities of radio crooners. While Sinatra and others demanded the overthrowing of Franco, Red Fascists passed out handbills in the crowd which read, "Veterans—Join the Communist Party. . . . Our party stands for the ownership and control of the nation's economy by the workers and farmers." Through this one performance alone any intelligent person ought to be able to see how "Red Frankie," with his gentle purring voice is swooning the youth of America into the arms of atheistic Communism.[51]

Similar accusations appeared in the popular press. Dissenting voices on rival journals and subsequent analysis suggest that Sinatra's treatment at the hands of, in particular, the Hearst press, was indicative of a deter-mined crusade against the Left by a section of the media. Jim Tuck argues: "In the late forties New York's Hearst papers faced communism as if they were preparing for Armageddon. . . . Given this total war mentality, one can understand the Hearst policy that redbaiting should not be limited to political columnists, editorialists, and news writers."[52] Sinatra's political activities, therefore, were denounced by not only political writers such as Westbrook Pegler but also showbusiness columnists such as Jack Lait and Lee Mortimer, both of whom Tuck describes as "xenophobic, homophobic, and invincibly bigoted."[53]

Sinatra's reported associations with underworld figures were often the channel through which criticisms of his politicking were made. Following his sojourn in Havana in September 1947, during which he was photo-graphed in the company of Charlie "Lucky" Luciano, the Scripps-Howard columnist Robert Ruark remarked: "Mr. Sinatra, the self-confessed savior of the country's small fry, by virtue of his lectures on clean living and love-thy-neighbor, his movie shorts on tolerance, and his frequent dab-blings into the do-good department of politics, seems to be setting a most peculiar example for his hordes of pimply, shrieking slaves, who are alleged to regard him with the same awe as a practicing Moham-medan for the Prophet."[54] Ruark exhibits a clear repulsion for Sinatra's perspective on racial politics that was echoed by Lee Mortimer and his superior, Jack Lait. Stereotyping Sinatra's ethnic identity by tying the star to violent crime imagery, the Hearst reporters made Sinatra's liberal politics appear dangerously un-American. Their preoccupation with Sinatra's involvement with the cause of equality intensified follow-ing his altercation with Lee Mortimer at Ciro's nightclub in April 1947. Lait used the incident to ask: "Who qualified Sinatra to clean up juvenile delinquency, plead for the underprivileged and assail discrimination?"[55] As various Hearst papers featured stories on Sinatra five days running, *Daily Variety* commented: "It looks as though Frankie Boy has taken on the whole Hearst organization."[56] In his 1951 article, Mortimer insinuated corruption of the Kefauver Committee hearings as an introduction to an assault on Sinatra. The journalist casually established a link between the way in which, he suggested, Sinatra had been "adopted" by organized crime to glamorize their narcotics enterprises, and the methods used by communists to promote their cause. Mortimer indicated that a gov-ernment dossier on Sinatra revealed "many well-known entertainment figures had been 'captured,' either with or without their knowledge, by the underworld, the Communists, or both. The Communists and the gangsters both have the same motive, acquiring respectability by as-sociation with prestige names. Frankie's contacts with both groups are numerous."[57] Mortimer's attempt to associate Sinatra with both ethnic crime and communist activity suggests a political motivation behind his negative stereotyping.

"We Must Proceed Gradually": Hollywood Anxiety and Moderate Political Progress

Like many Hollywood stars, Sinatra exhibited some apprehension about the political attacks to which he was subjected, which his subsequent actions revealed. Following his attendance at the 1947 HUAC hearings, Humphrey Bogart backtracked: "I went to Washington because I thought fellow Americans were being deprived of their Constitutional rights. . . . I see now that my trip was ill-advised, foolish, and impetuous."[58] In April 1948, Sinatra, alongside Joe DiMaggio and Jimmy Durante, took part in a radio broadcast to the people of Italy's new republic, attempting to persuade them to vote against the Communist Party in the forthcoming national election.[59] Sinatra's FBI file records that an intermediary approached the bureau in September 1950 with the star's offer to assist in identifying "subversives," an offer curtly rejected by J. Edgar Hoover's top aide Clyde Tolson in a handwritten memo to his boss stating: "We want nothing to do with him."[60] In 1951, Sinatra attended a Central Park rally of the Stop Communism Committee, which aimed to combat "Red influences in the entertainment world."[61]

As Ronald Brownstein suggests, Sinatra's activities were indicative of reactions to the shifting political climate in Hollywood: "With conservatives questioning the patriotism of almost anyone who had marched against Hitler or for civil rights in the company of Communists, the Hollywood liberals felt as if a new ice age had descended."[62] Both rounds of HUAC hearings combined with the demise of radical liberalism in the wider political arena to create an atmosphere of fear on the West Coast. Former government attorney Alger Hiss was put on trial and imprisoned in 1951 when found guilty of working as a Soviet agent. Richard Nixon, then Republican senator for California, attempted to discredit the politics of the New Deal further in 1952, telling the *Kansas City Star:* "There's one difference between Reds and Pinks. The Pinks want to socialize America. The Reds want to socialize the world and make Moscow the world capital. Their paths are similar; they have the same bible—the teachings of Karl Marx."[63] Nixon included in his definition of "Pinks" those who supported the New Deal or the progressive wing of the Democratic Party.

Despite this antiliberal culture, Sinatra remained engaged in racial politics through the 1950s as Hollywood attempted to address civil rights in a more direct manner. The pressing need to forcefully promote social change was evident from the slow progress of political moves across the postwar period. In 1947, Truman commissioned a study of racism titled *To Secure These Rights,* which called for an end to segregation and became part of his platform for the presidency. In the case of *Shelley vs. Kraemer* the following year, the Supreme Court ruled that it was unconstitutional for states to place restrictions on the sale, rental, or leasing of property to nonwhites.[64] In 1949, Truman urged Congress to create a permanent Fair Employment Practices Committee, establish penalties for members of lynch mobs, and outlaw segregation in interstate transportation. This climate of limited advances continued in the 1950s. In the 1954 case of *Brown vs. Board of Education of Topeka,* the Supreme Court overturned the policy of "separate but equal" public school education in the South sanctioned by the 1896 *Plessy vs. Ferguson* decision. In its direction to states to progress toward school desegregation with "all deliberate speed," the Supreme Court enabled states to individually interpret how immediate was the requirement for change. The remarks made during the case by President Eisenhower to Chief Justice Earl Warren with regard to those resisting integration indicate the administration's indifference to civil rights: "[They] are not bad people. All they are concerned about is to see that their sweet little girls are not required to sit in schools alongside some big black bucks."[65]

The Democratic leadership was no more committed to a civil-rights agenda. While asserting his support for equality issues, Adlai Stevenson chose as his running mate for his 1952 presidential campaign an Alabama senator who was vehemently opposed to desegregation. In 1956, Stevenson was booed off stage by a Los Angeles audience when he suggested: "We must proceed gradually, not upsetting habits or traditions that are older than the Republic."[66] Satirist Mort Sahl accurately caught the political mood, remarking: "Eisenhower says he's for integration but gradually; Stevenson says he's for integration but moderately. It should be possible to compromise between those extremes."[67] The Civil Rights Acts of 1957 and 1960 were limited in both their aims and effects. Creating a Civil Rights Commission and a Civil Rights Division of the Justice Department, and introducing legal measures to prevent the infringement of voting rights, the acts relied on modest measures that would prove insufficient.[68]

In the midst of this political caution, African Americans were beginning to assert through direct action their right to full acceptance as part of the American identity. In December 1955, NAACP worker Rosa Parks instigated the Montgomery Bus Boycott, which resulted in a federal court ruling that bus segregation in Alabama was unconstitutional. When black students attempted to enroll at Central High School in Little Rock, Arkansas, in September 1957, President Eisenhower was compelled to use U.S. paratroopers and federalize the National Guard to quash the obstructions enabled by Governor Orval Faubus. Newsreel footage of white southerners protesting violently as black schoolchildren attempted to enroll brought the issue of American equality to national and international attention. Following his involvement in the Montgomery campaign, Martin Luther King Jr. founded the Southern Christian Leadership Conference (SCLC) in 1957 and activated the Civil Rights Movement, which progressed quickly in the 1960s.

Sinatra reentered America's race debate in the late 1950s via articles and films that drew attention to the country's racial prejudices and inequities. In July 1958, Sinatra's article "The Way I Look at Race" appeared in the African American magazine *Ebony*. Making reference to recent events and legislation, as well as his background in relation to racial politics, Sinatra discussed his hopes that the "national disease" of bigotry would be eradicated by the education of future generations, and that moves toward desegregation would herald a new era of racial equality. He expressed support for Louis Armstrong in his criticism of government reticence to act to protect the black schoolchildren at Little Rock and applauded Sammy Davis Jr.'s fund-raising work for the Chicago Urban League. Referring to the curiosity provoked by his close relationships with black performers, Sinatra asserted: "A friend to me has no race, no class, and belongs to no minority. My friendships were formed out of affection, mutual respect, and a feeling of having something strong in common. These are eternal values that cannot be racially classified. This is the way I look at race."[69] Sinatra acknowledged the huge influence a variety of black artists had on him as a performer, citing, among others, Billie Holiday, Ethel Waters, Lester Young, and Miles Davis. He went on to deplore the assault on Nat Cole that occurred during his performance in Birmingham, Alabama, in April 1956 and expressed his disappointment that Cole's television variety show had failed to find a national sponsor.[70] In 1986 the African American magazine *Jet* described Sinatra's article as "the most significant stand taken by a famous white person since Mrs. Eleanor Roosevelt. . . . [It] gave support to the cause of racial justice and equality."[71]

"It Was Like a New Kick for Me": American Racism in *Kings Go Forth*

In "The Way I Look at Race," Sinatra also discussed his performance in the 1958 release *Kings Go Forth,* a film that exemplifies Hollywood's attempts to directly confront American bigotry. A shifting culture is apparent in the late 1940s and early 1950s, when films progress beyond using anti-Semitism to address prejudice, to a more open discussion of inequality. The narrative of *No Way Out* (1950) deals with race riots and overt racism, as Sidney Poitier's newly qualified doctor is called "nigger" and "coon" by Richard Widmark's bigoted criminal. A number of films also examine racial "passing." Mel Ferrer's African American doctor in *Lost Boundaries* (1949) encounters intolerance on both sides of the racial divide, as his concealment of his racial identity is discovered, and his son is rejected by Harlem's African American community. In Elia Kazan's *Pinky* (1949), Jeanne Crain's light-skinned African American "passes" for white in Boston and returns home to the South and old prejudices. She ultimately reasserts her black identity and dismisses her white partner, telling him: "I'm a Negro. I can't forget it and I can't deny it. I can't pretend to be anything else. I don't want to be anything else."[72]

Kings Go Forth, which reunited Sinatra with *The House I Live In* producer Frank Ross, incorporates the notion of "passing" in its treatment of the country's difficulties with racial identity and examines racism as a specifically American problem. When American troops reach the French Riviera toward the end of World War II, their arrival is greeted by grateful crowds cheering in the streets. By the close of the "champagne campaign," however, they have transported their bigotry to this integrated European community. Sinatra plays Lieutenant Sam Loggins, an officer who develops a friendship with local girl Monique Blair (Natalie Wood). When Monique reveals that her late father was an African American, Sam is temporarily disturbed but soon resumes his relationship with her, having conquered his prejudices. Monique subsequently becomes involved with Sergeant Britt Harris (Tony Curtis), a manipulative charmer who proposes marriage, but, when confronted by Sam, admits: "It was like a new kick for me." Monique attempts suicide, and Britt is killed by German gunfire on a last mission. Following a spell in an army hospital, Sam returns to France wounded and newly promoted to captain and finds Monique running a school for orphans of the war.

Sam Loggins is another of Sinatra's working-class, emotionally sensitive characters. The son of a Harlem candy store owner, he was moved to tears when the owner of the construction firm for whom he worked made him a partner. Not standard officer material because of his limited education and sense of independence, he has Britt demoted for disobeying orders but concedes he responded harshly, "partly because I didn't trust him, and partly because he was born rich and handsome, and I was born poor and not handsome." In his sincere expression of his feelings for Monique, Sam displays a modesty that draws on Sinatra's vulnerable persona, as Sam admits: "I'm not much of a catch. As a matter of fact, nobody ever tried to catch me." In contrast, Britt exudes self-confidence and duplicity. He has attended four colleges in a fruitless effort to prove his worth before he inherits a New Jersey mill fortune, and a rumor circulates about his attempt to bribe a member of the local draft board. His worthless promise of marriage is simply another act of deceit, as he reveals to Monique's mother: "Mrs. Blair, on several occasions I've been engaged to marry, and on several occasions I've been not engaged to marry, if you follow me. And a lot of these girls I wouldn't take to a country club, but, with the exception of your daughter, Mrs. Blair, all of them were white." Allison Graham notes that Britt's admission brings variation to the standard scene in which the African American identity of a character "passing" as white is revealed: "*Kings Go Forth* reconceived the discovery scene as a revelation of *white* deception"[73] (Figure 4). African Americans who mask their identities in *Showboat* (1951) and *Imitation of Life* (1959) are led to self-destruction and humiliation when the lie is unveiled. In *Kings Go Forth,* Monique feels no need to conceal her parentage prior to the Americans' arrival. She delays telling Sam about her African American father only because, she explains: "I know how Americans feel about some things." Her dalliance with "passing" is, therefore, short-lived, and it is Britt's artifice that is punished. Sam pledges to kill him for his betrayal of Monique but is denied his revenge when Britt is shot behind enemy lines.

Monique's actions are prompted by her certainty that bigotry is a standard American trait. While Hollywood frequently depicted racism as an affliction of the South, *Kings Go Forth* shows prejudice to be a feature of the American experience. Immediately prior to filming with Sinatra, Tony Curtis appeared with Sidney Poitier in one of the best-known cinematic parables of racial equality, *The Defiant Ones.* As escaped convicts, chained together because, as one character puts it, "the warden's got a sense of humor," their relationship develops over the course of the film into one of friendship and mutual respect. The characters begin, however, as two representatives of a bigoted American South: one white, working class, uneducated, and economically disenfranchised, and the other an African American advised by his ex-wife to "be nice" but who is unwilling to acquiesce to the racism that defines and restricts him.

Joe David Brown's novel also isolates racial prejudice in the South. Britt hails from Mississippi and carries the history of American racism for the narrative. Sam distinguishes himself from Britt, making the attitudes displayed a product of Britt's class and southern background: "With me it wouldn't have made any difference. But I didn't come from Mississippi. I didn't get letters on crested stationery. I didn't have a Southern mother and two Southern sisters who lived in a mansion with tall white columns. I didn't own a mill. I didn't have social position. I wasn't rich. And I wasn't proud of my family tree."[74] The film version of *Kings Go Forth* departs from this picture of racial inequality as bound up in the culture of the South. By extending its depiction of racism to the North and across the social classes, the 1958 film more forcefully attacks American bigotry. Monique's white American mother explains to Sam that she and her husband retreated to France in the sure belief

Figure 4: Sam initiates the revelation scene in which Britt admits his duplicity and the racism behind his behavior. (*Kings Go Forth*)

that "in France they have a beautiful blindness to color." When Sam turns away from her as she tells of her devotion to "a rare man" and tries to show him a photograph of her late husband, he reminds Mrs. Blair of the racism she left behind. Monique's revelation forces Sam to confront his prejudices. She contends, "*Nigger* is one of the first words you learn in America, isn't it?" In the light of this indictment of American culture, Sam examines his own attitudes in the film's most direct attack on the country's racial divisions: "Monique was wrong. It's not the first one you learn at all. And some kids never learn it at all. Some learn it and never use it. I learned it early and used it often. It showed just how tough I was. And that wasn't all. Where I was brought up—Harlem, near 125th—they were on one side and we were on the other. Why? I don't know why. Except a lot of people need somebody to look down on. Or they think they do." Sam's admission of intolerance learned in the melting pot of New York makes racism commonplace in American society. Both characters' East Coast urban origins shift the focus away from the rural South, and Sam's likable persona illustrates the pervasive quality of discriminatory views.

The two versions of *Kings Go Forth* that still exist indicate the immediacy of its message and the difficulties still experienced by filmmakers addressing the subject of race. One version of the film excludes both Monique's comment about everyday usage of the word *nigger,* and Sam's confession of his prejudices. These omissions hugely diminish the film's assault on racism and suggest a climate of censorship that still restricts Hollywood discussions of inequality in the late 1950s. At the same time, the casting of Natalie Wood in the role of Monique Blair reflects industry caution. In his autobiography, Tony Curtis remarked: "Natalie, of course, didn't look remotely Negro. But in those days a black girl could not have played that part. You could never have hired Dorothy Dandridge."[75] Curtis's comments draw attention to the frequent use of white American actresses in mixed-race roles. Performances by Jeanne Crain in *Pinky* and Ava Gardner in *Showboat* testify to Hollywood's reticence to consider African Americans in lead roles, even in films with such an apt subject matter. Gardner recalls that her choice for the part of Julie Laverne would have been Lena Horne, but the other actresses on MGM's list of possible performers were Judy Garland and Dinah Shore.[76]

The varied critical reactions to *Kings Go Forth* speak of America's diverse attitudes toward race in the late 1950s. The *Films and Filming* reviewer was offended by the film's progressive tone: "*Kings Go Forth,* glib, happy ending and all, really is the limit. It is time someone debunked this kind of specious, hysterical liberalism. It went out years ago—or should have done."[77] In the opinion of the *Los Angeles Mirror-News,* the film failed to go far enough: "The movie *Kings Go Forth* doesn't come close to having the guts of the book by Joe David Brown and the result is a film which is all surface and little depth."[78] These polarized judgments equally demonstrate the inevitable difficulties still involved in bringing effective debates on racism to the screen. *Kings Go Forth* represents Sinatra's last cinematic attempt to discuss discrimination against African Americans. However, Sinatra continued to address intolerance in films that featured alternative races and nationalities. In the 1959 film *Never So Few,* set in North Burma, Sinatra's Captain Tom Reynolds confronts prejudice directed toward both Native Americans and Kachin guerrillas and calls for a bigoted American colonel to respect the culture of his host country. *None but the Brave's* 1965 narrative of American and Japanese soldiers, who form friendships on a Pacific island during World War II, also upholds the notion of a fundamental racial equality. In this first ever American-Japanese coproduction and Sinatra's sole directorial credit, Sinatra reverses the anti-Japanese sentiments expressed in *The House I Live In* and celebrates the differences and similarities between two distinct cultural identities in an antiwar film that concludes with the on-screen message "Nobody Ever Wins."

By continuously engaging with civil rights across the postwar period, Sinatra promoted the notion of a diverse American identity that incorporated all races, ethnicities, and religions and attributed equal value to each. As part of Hollywood's liberal community in the 1940s, Sinatra pressed for social change in the immediate aftermath of World War II. The circuitous ways in which *The House I Live In* addresses American intolerance are indicative of the film industry's attempts to tackle prejudice in an unreceptive political climate. Negative reactions to Sinatra's campaigning locate the star in the midst of the anticommunist extremism of the postwar era and illustrate the impact of the right-wing press on his political image. In the 1950s, the beginnings of the Civil Rights Movement and the reticence of politicians are reflected in *Kings Go Forth*, a film that directly confronts American racism, providing evidence of Sinatra's consistent association with the cause of civil rights and at the same time demonstrating the limits still imposed on Hollywood depictions of America's problematic attitudes toward race.

4 Vulnerable Masculinity and Damaged Veterans

Modern man is not for me
The movie star and dapper Dan
Give me the healthy Joe from ages ago
A prehistoric man.

What has Gable got for me?
Or Mrs. Johnson's blond boy, Van
I want a happy ape with no English drape
A prehistoric man.

When Ann Miller sang of her yen for an old-style man in *On the Town*'s "Prehistoric Man" number, her routine was as much a gentle dig at Hollywood's male icons as a tribute to caveman masculinity. Expressing her distaste for emotionally repressed career-obsessed men driven to psychoanalysis and ulcers, Miller's society girl, Claire Huddesen, puts to good use her interest in the changing nature of masculinity by undertaking research for a museum study titled "Modern Man: What Is It?" Miller's lighthearted critique of male movie stardom and modern masculinity in general illustrates the extent to which questions about the redefinition of masculinity permeate postwar culture. As one of the stars in Miller's expensive chorus line, Sinatra makes a fitting appearance as a male star whose emotionally vulnerable persona has a central place in the renegotiation of traditional male imaging.

The postwar era has increasingly been recognized as a period of noticeable change in relation to Hollywood representations of masculine character. Alongside traditional screen depictions of male confidence and strength, frequent displays of emotional vulnerability indicate a newly broadening definition of the American male in film. In her periodized discussion of screen masculinity, Joan Mellen traces a trajectory of change, from the anxieties of 1940s film noir that destabilized traditional male imagery, to 1950s Hollywood, wherein "the vulnerability of the ideal screen male became the experience of all, and on the screen it was now not merely acceptable but desirable, an indispensable aspect of male sexuality."[1] Like most assessments of this period, Mellen's discussion attributes this trend of adjustment to a generation of young male stars, led by Marlon Brando and Montgomery Clift. While both are central to the development of the postwar screen male beyond traditional imagery, the issues of maturity and sexuality introduced around their screen personas complicate their identities as newly constructed versions of adult heterosexual masculinity. As Steven Cohan's illuminating study of Montgomery Clift reveals, a fan discourse stressing Clift's intense approach to acting combines with the star's homosocial bonding and subordinate positioning in films such as *Red River* (1948) to imbue Clift with an image packed with "feminine, neurotic, bisexual qualities [that] connote the boyishness of Clift's persona on screen."[2] Cohan concludes that the idea of a star such as Clift or Brando as "the boy who is not a man," produced through associations of immaturity, bisexuality, or both, results in a "transvestite effect," which breaks down the opposing categories of male and female and disrupts the direct connection made between gender and sexuality.[3] While issues of maturity and sexuality are equally at play around Sinatra's image, the disruptive effect of his image emerges through the assertion of emotional vulnerability as integral to the American male's identity. By ultimately resisting definition in terms that suggest a compromise of maturity or sexuality, Sinatra's postwar male persona introduces a rarely considered version of adult heterosexual masculinity for the 1950s.

Sinatra's image of emotionally vulnerable masculinity is considered here as it develops through the postwar period. As a singer during World War II, Sinatra's association with a particular musical style and the largely female home front feminizes his male identity. Sinatra's early screen persona draws on this feminized image, evolving in the 1950s into a masculine persona that incorporates vulnerability into the star's representation of the American male. The intertextuality of this male image is highlighted by Sinatra's mood albums with Capitol Records. Their narrative style combines with the cinematic quality of the album covers to illustrate the construction of an emotionally frail character echoed in Sinatra's screen performances. Sinatra's serviceman persona develops further through his various portrayals of World War II veterans. Close analysis of *Suddenly* and *Some Came Running* considers Sinatra's image of emotionally vulnerable masculinity in relation to anxieties over displays of emotional damage and machismo that inhibit assimilation in America's postwar society.

"I Got a Feeling That There's Something Wrong with Me": Female Identification and Emotional Dependence in World War II

Discussions of the reasons for Sinatra's popularity as a singer during World War II often settle on the conclusion that in a country bereft of its young men, Sinatra stood as a figure of desire for American womanhood. One contemporary psychologist explained the Sinatra phenomenon as "a simple and familiar combination of escapism and substitution, to be expected in times of high emotional stress."[4] However, the suggestion that in the female imagination Sinatra served as a comforting replacement for the men serving overseas fails as a complete explanation. Though Sinatra provides a site toward which young women's sexual desires can be directed, his performances also become an expression of feminine vulnerability in the context of war. Lewis Erenberg comes closest to recognizing this phenomenon when suggesting the complexities of Sinatra's persona as a male singer in wartime, arguing: "In an era of loneliness he gave young girls a vulnerable, dark boy next door as a sex object who expressed their desires."[5] Erenberg accurately identifies the emotional ("vulnerable"), ethnic ("dark"), class ("boy next door"), and sexual ("sex object") aspects of Sinatra's image, as well as the unusual position he takes as a male star who conveys the feelings of his female audience. Women's emotional identification with Sinatra, brought about by his musical expressions of vulnerability, has a feminizing effect on his image at a time when representations of heightened masculinity seem more expected or appropriate.

Popular music played a significant role during World War II in boosting morale both at home and overseas. As Kathleen Smith's comprehensive study of the subject demonstrates, World War II was distinguished from its predecessor by the American public's demand for the popular music of the day, rather than the specially penned expressions of patriotic fervor that had defined the popular response to World War I. Despite the efforts of the OWI to find a song with the potential for a level of popularity similar to that achieved by George M. Cohan's "Over There" in World War I, the public responded overwhelmingly to Tin Pan Alley's ballads and swing tunes over songs that made explicit reference to the events in Europe and the Pacific.[6]

The desire to hear popular music as the soundtrack to war was common to both men serving abroad and women on the homefront but was differentiated by the specific musical preference of each group. For American servicemen, big band swing was the music of choice and served a dual purpose. As David Stowe explains, a racially and ethnically diverse music form since its beginnings in the 1930s, when it broke racial and class boundaries for both performers and audiences, swing served firstly as a "galvanizing symbol of national purpose" in the fight against fascism, representing the democratic culture from which it had sprung.[7] In addition, swing provided a measure of escapism for servicemen, returning their thoughts to their home culture and reminding them of the pleasures of civilian life. The significant role played by big band music in raising morale among the troops is evidenced by Glenn Miller's recruitment of serving musicians to transform his army band into an orchestra that would gratify American servicemen's nostalgia for home. When in 1944 *Metronome* published an article by a serviceman criticizing the Glenn Miller army band as bland, the comments were rebuffed by another serviceman who argued that Miller's band, which often played songs popular before the GIs had gone overseas, provided servicemen with an essential tonic, an "avenue of escape . . . things that remind them of home, that bring back something of those days when we were all happy and free and when we used to be able to put on a Miller record or listen to a Miller broadcast or even hear the band play 'In the Mood' in person."[8]

In contrast, female audiences looked less toward music as an affirmation of the democratic way or a retreat from wartime anxieties. Instead, the popularity of ballads on the homefront during America's involvement in World War II suggests that women were drawn to songs and singers who seemed to be in empathy with their emotional state. Among the bestselling songs of 1943 were titles including "You'll Never Know," "Sunday, Monday or Always" and "Don't Get Around Much Anymore," which made no direct reference to the war but spoke of the severing of relationships.[9] Just as films such as *Since You Went Away* (1944) depicted women's wartime lives, for women who were experiencing the ordeal of separation from lovers and husbands, the popular ballads of the day represented a lyrical expression of their feelings of loss and separation.

These songs were most often interpreted by female performers, either those who sang with the big bands, such as Helen Forrest and Jo

Stafford, or by solo artists such as Dinah Shore. As Lewis Erenberg explains: "Women singers and sentimental ballads rose in popularity during the war as they personalized American civilization and the anguish that lay behind the war—enforced separation of the sexes. Women dominated the music audience at home, and they wanted ballads that expressed the pain of waiting for their men to return or the normal life of boys and dating to begin."[10] As a male singer performing ballads that openly expressed feelings of vulnerability from a female perspective, Sinatra was therefore immediately associated with the feminine in ways that went beyond his physically weak appearance and his status as sexual object. By taking up a prominent position in a style of music signified as female in terms of both performers and audience, and through his interpretation of specific songs conveying the emotions of those left behind in the separation of war, Sinatra spent the war years representing not the men on the frontline but the women on the homefront.[11]

Sinatra's stated preference for ballads dates back to his comments in an interview that appeared in *Metronome* in 1943 in which he admitted, "I'm crazy about strings for a vocal background. Tell you the truth, if [Harry] James had had strings at the time I was with the band, maybe I'd never have left."[12] Sinatra's natural inclination toward music arranged around strings rather than the more uptempo swing arrangements was evident in the songs with which he became closely associated during his tenure with the Tommy Dorsey Orchestra, which coincided with the early years of World War II. Songs such as the number one hit "I'll Never Smile Again," recorded with the Pied Pipers vocal group, and "I'll Be Seeing You," another Sinatra/Dorsey hit, resonated with the country's sense of anxiety about the onset of war. Though both songs were first recorded by Sinatra in 1940, his return to them as a solo artist in the following years in radio shows and stage performances connected them more specifically to the context of America's involvement in the war, and also to women's perspective on war as those left behind on the home front. The Jule Styne/Sammy Cahn ballad "I'll Walk Alone," which Kathleen Smith terms "one of the definitive love songs of World War II," was performed by Sinatra throughout the mid-1940s and is perhaps the best illustration of his association with the female experience.[13] Like the title song to *The House I Live In*, "I'll Walk Alone" was first introduced in the 1944 film *Follow the Boys*, this time by Dinah Shore. Its lyrical message of loneliness and faithfulness suggests a woman's reaction to wartime separation:

I'll walk alone
Because to tell you the truth
I'll be lonely.
I don't mind being lonely
When my heart tells me you
Are lonely too.

Please walk alone
And send your love and your kisses
To guide me.
Till you're walking beside me
I'll walk alone.

Sinatra's expression of a female sensibility based around the home-front war immediately establishes the unconventional male identity that develops across the postwar period.

The vulnerability that feminizes Sinatra in relation to World War II masculinity continues on screen through his roles as servicemen. Unlike stars such as Jimmy Stewart and Clark Gable, whose service during the war lent an air of authenticity to their screen performances as brave servicemen, Sinatra's frequent film forays into uniform as servicemen and veterans were in stark contrast with the reality of his war experience. Classified 4F by his local draft board because of a punctured eardrum acquired at birth, Sinatra spent World War II achieving success, fame, and wealth rather than risking his life on the frontline. His failure to serve provoked some resentment among drafted servicemen, who reacted with cynicism to his performances for the troops. To counteract this negative star image, *Modern Screen* reported that while on tour overseas, Sinatra allowed Phil Silvers to use him as a foil for his jokes, with the result, the magazine suggested, that "at last he'd smashed to smithereens the old ghost of absent GI scorn."[14] Appropriately, therefore, Sinatra's early screen roles represent a sanitized version of war that provides a suitable environment for his already feminized star image. In both *Anchors Aweigh* and *On the Town,* Sinatra's sailors on shore leave are far removed from any combat situation in which displays of masculine strength would be required and are, in any case, represented as physically and emotionally vulnerable characters. In *On the Town,* the ship represents a place of safety and comfort rather than danger to the sailors, who sing about their "Shore Leave Blues" while out on a date in New York. In the opening scenes of *Anchors Aweigh,* Sinatra's Clarence Doolittle and Gene Kelly's

Joe Brady are each awarded the Silver Star by their commanding officer, connecting them to traditional ideas of masculine bravery. Such links are soon made spurious, however, by the explanation that the medals have been earned as a result of Clarence being blown overboard from his station and Joe diving into the sea to rescue him.

In his discussion of masculinity in World War II combat films, Robert Eberwein notes the perception articulated in a report in *Time* in 1942 that "The Mama Boys" often chose to serve in the American navy rather than the army, believing it to be a softer option.[15] While Eberwein applies a reading of homosexuality to *Time*'s use of the term "Mama Boys," it may also indicate a level of emotional vulnerability that suggests an unsuitability for intense physical combat. The 1943 film *Bataan* suggests this link between the navy and male weakness through Robert Walker's character, Leonard Purckett. The naval and entertainment imagery that surrounds Purckett as an ex–movie usher who entered the navy as a musician makes him a particularly vulnerable male character within the unit. In one scene, Purckett looks on "like a child lovingly admiring his mother" as a colleague, Todd (Lloyd Nolan), applies a tourniquet to Purckett's wounds.[16] Todd's response to Purckett's admiration is to tie the binding tighter, which is read by Robert Eberwein as a need to disavow maternal behavior between naval men that could be interpreted as representative of homosexuality.

In *Anchors Aweigh,* the instances of maternalism involving Sinatra's Clarence Doolittle are frequent, from the scene in which his lullaby puts both young Donald (Dean Stockwell) and Joe to sleep, to the scene in which Clarence rocks in his chair watching over Joe as he sleeps. These instances of maternal behavior from Clarence are counteracted by his overwhelming emotional dependence on both male and female characters. In a scene in which Clarence finally realizes his affection for the nameless waitress from Brooklyn (Pamela Britton) who has been coaching him in his pursuit of Susan (Kathryn Grayson), their embrace sees Clarence resting his head on the shoulder of his new girlfriend, producing an image of childhood. To an even greater extent, Clarence's relationship with Joe is one of emotional dependence. Like Donald, who seeks Joe's assistance to get him into the navy, Clarence trails after Joe hoping for tips on how to get a girl. One scene in Susan's home makes this comparison clear as both Clarence and Donald peek through the bars of the banister, pleading with Joe, "You promised!" The fear Clarence displays in most situations, from approaching Susan for a date, to getting past the guards at the MGM studios, leads him to admit to Joe: "Sometimes when I watch you, I got a feeling that there's something wrong with me." Clarence's naïveté and vulnerability are viewed as problematic, undermining his masculinity through their feminizing effect. Yet there are indications in Sinatra's musical expression of Clarence's vulnerability of the shift that will take place in relation to Sinatra's male identity. Realizing his faltering relationship with Susan is doomed, Clarence sits alone at a piano on the stage of a deserted Hollywood Bowl and taps out the first few notes of "I Fall in Love Too Easily." Sinatra's performance of this confession of emotional weakness, coupled with the visual imagery of a solitary Sinatra at a piano, is evocative of the saloon song imaging that will soon occur around the star. In this way, the performance represents the cinematic beginning of the adjustment in Sinatra's star image, moving him away from feminine associations to male expressions of emotional vulnerability.

"A Little Lamb Who's Lost in the Wood": From Broadway Convention to the Saloon Song

Sinatra's musical positioning as a point of identification for women, and his physically and emotionally weak screen persona in the context of war, results in his being well placed to represent an adjusted image of masculinity in the postwar period. As screen roles and visual imagery add masculine strength and machismo to his image, Sinatra's varied expressions of emotional weakness suggest vulnerability to be integral to postwar male identity. This hybrid image of postwar masculinity is evident in Sinatra's 1950s mood albums with Capitol Records as much as in the screen performances to which they can be readily linked. The narrative quality of Sinatra's "saloon songs" and corresponding albums, and the visual imagery of the album covers make this music highly cinematic and connect the brand of masculinity expressed therein to Sinatra's cinematic persona as a vulnerable postwar male.

The complexity of Sinatra's emerging masculine image means that associations marked out as feminine linger around the edges. A song such as "P.S. I Love You" on the 1956 album *Close to You,* for example, revisits the female positioning of Sinatra's earlier music, as the domestic imagery of dishes in the sink and a hole burned in the dining room table dominates his letter to the lover from whom he is separated. Yet many lyrical expressions of vulnerability become invested with a strong sense of masculinity, despite the original intent of the songwriters. Sinatra often cited female performers such as Mabel Mercer and Billie Holiday as musical influences,[17] and Philip Furia notes that many of the songs with which Sinatra has become closely associated through their appearance on his Capitol mood albums were originally written to be performed by female actresses in Broadway musical shows of the 1930s. As Furia explains, this was due to the prevailing notion that expressions of vulnerability were the domain of female characters: "In the formulaic boy-meets-loses-then-regains-girl plots of the day, romantic ballads of longing or lament were assigned to female characters, on the conventional assumption that women were more given to wistful or melancholy effusions, while male characters were more often given songs of romantic importunity."[18] Sinatra's adoption of emotionally expressive songs, each with its own "self-contained lyrical drama," therefore represents a shift toward the depiction of vulnerability as part of the male experience. These songs were often so lyrically oriented toward performance by a female singer that the lyrics had to undergo substantial adjustments. In the case of the Rodgers and Hart song "It Never Entered My Mind," for example, written for the 1938 musical *Higher and Higher,* lines about the singer powdering her nose and putting mudpacks on her face were removed when Sinatra recorded his version for the 1955 album *In the Wee Small Hours.*[19]

In opting, at times, to retain the female lyric, Sinatra seems only to intensify the sense of vulnerability expressed in the song just as he claims it for the 1950s male. In "Someone to Watch Over Me" from Sinatra's first Capitol album, *Songs for Young Lovers,* he adds to the sense of powerlessness felt by his "little lamb who's lost in the wood" by keeping a line usually replaced by Ira Gershwin for male performers, and simply inverting the subject/object positions so that it reads:

> Although *I* may not be the man some
> Girls think of as handsome[20]

Sinatra's rendition of the song in *Young at Heart* illustrates this increased sense of vulnerability as the yearning style of his performance combines with the masculine imagery of its context. The performance by Barney Sloan in a dimly lit bar is prefaced by a heated discussion that the confrontational character has with the bar's assistant manager. Seated at an upright piano and bathed in the smoke from his cigarette, he glances frequently toward Doris Day's Laurie as though addressing the song's pleas directly to her. Sinatra's performance style adds to the emotional pull of the song as he extends the "Oh" of "Oh, how I need" across three beats, increasing the sense of yearning in the lyric. As the camera focuses on Laurie's reaction at the end of the performance, her intrigued expression suggests Barney's display of vulnerability has attracted her attention, as a contrast to the supreme confidence exuded by her current love interest, Alex Burke.

Beyond these connections with female-oriented lyrics and performers, many of the, in Sinatra's terminology, "saloon songs" with which he is most closely associated express emotional loss from a specifically male perspective. By labeling these songs "saloon songs" rather than "ballads," Sinatra distinguishes them from his earlier emotionally expressive performances, and places them firmly in the male domain. Their narrative style means that Sinatra's performances have a cinematic quality even outside a film setting, and they often connect Sinatra to a sense of modern urban anxiety. Both "Angel Eyes" and "One for My Baby," which appear on the 1958 album *Frank Sinatra Sings for Only the Lonely,* function as male laments to the loss of a relationship.[21] Both place Sinatra in a barroom setting as he relates his tale to a lone bartender or his fellow drinkers. In live performances, Sinatra often emphasized the narrative style of such songs by explaining their context as part of his introduction and going on to physically act out the narrative. During a concert at London's Royal Festival Hall in 1962, for example, Sinatra introduced "One for My Baby" as a song usually sung in an "out-of-the-way bar" by "a young man who's been sopping up the sauce for about four or five hours . . . this man has the troubles of the world on his shoulders . . . girls . . . I know! . . . he has this tale to tell." As Sinatra goes on to perform the song with a slouched stance, rubbing his forehead and frequently drawing on his cigarette, the rendition resembles less a stage performance than a character-based film scene.[22]

Similarly, "Angel Eyes," which Will Friedwald describes as having a "James M. Caine–like [*sic*] libretto,"[23] goes further in connecting Sinatra's persona to a postwar film noir style of masculinity. Romantic disillusionment at the hands of a femme fatale and hints of jealousy and revenge propel this song's narrative forward with lines such as:

> Angel eyes that ol' devil sent
> They glow unbearably bright.
> Need I say that my love's misspent
> Misspent with angel eyes tonight.

Like Philip Furia, Robert Connolly and Pellegrino D'Acierno note Sinatra's choice of the elevated songs of Broadway as significant. They stress the effects that Sinatra's image and performance have on songs of this type, arguing: "Sinatra appropriates these songs, makes them his own by personalizing and eroticizing them, especially those involving the amorous catastrophe, infusing them with the Sinatran *tenebroso,* an urban and mass-media version of that dark sound that comes from what the poet Federico Garcia Lorca calls the *duende* (mysterious power)."[24] By substantially altering the style of older ballads and "acting out" their narratives, Sinatra brings an emotional darkness to the songs that reconstructs their tone and context. Will Friedwald comments, for example, on the impact that Sinatra's performance style has on "It's a Lonesome Old Town." The song, which had previously served as the theme for a pre-radio bandleader, was transformed by Sinatra's rendition on *Only the Lonely* into "a bona fide exercise in musical drama."[25] Through the connections he makes between ethnicity and an urban popular culture, and the effective expression of dark emotions, Sinatra inflects the standard saloon song with the same sense of anxiety that surrounds the postwar city and its inhabitants as depicted in film noir. The sense of anxiety and alienation represented in this trend of films draws on the image of the city as the milieu of the working-class immigrant reignited by the postwar decampment of much of the white Anglo-Saxon population to the suburbs. Sinatra's emotionally dark performances, then, often combine with visual imagery suggestive of male urban alienation. On an edition of *The Dean Martin Show* in 1958, Sinatra's somber rendition of "Last Night When We Were Young" from *In the Wee Small Hours* is echoed by the positioning of Sinatra, in dress suit and cape, in an urban night scene with accompanying shadows and wintry snow.[26]

This narrative of emotional despondency is extended on the Capitol albums on which a single mood is conveyed through Sinatra's protagonist. On albums such as *In the Wee Small Hours, Only the Lonely,* and *No One Cares,* the songs travel along a structured path, reinforcing a sense of character, narrative, and performance. On the 1957 album *Where Are You?,* a narrative can be traced from the raw disbelief of "Where Are You?," to the helpless searching of "I Cover the Waterfront," the despair and bitterness of "I'm a Fool to Want You," and the desperate pleadings of "Baby, Won't You Please Come Home." Sinatra confirms this narrative approach in his comments concerning the planning of an album:

> First I decide on the mood for an album, and perhaps pick a title. Or sometimes it might be that I had the title, and then picked the mood to fit it. But it's most important that there should be a strong creative idea for the whole package. Like Only the Lonely, or No One Cares, for instance. Then I get a short list of maybe sixty possible songs, and out of these I pick twelve to record. Next comes the pac-

ing of the album, which is vitally important. I put the titles of the songs on twelve bits of paper, and juggle them around like a jigsaw puzzle until the album is telling a complete story, lyric-wise. For example, the album is in the mood of "No One Cares"—track one. Why does no one care? Because there's a "Cottage for Sale"—track two. And so on, until the last track . . . the end of the episode.[27]

The stress on male vulnerability expressed in narrative form in both songs and albums confirms the idea of a particular male persona being developed through characterization.

Much has been made of the extent to which Sinatra's biography authenticates this persona. Sinatra's publicist in the 1940s, George Evans, suggested that the stress caused by the star's extramarital affairs could be detected in Sinatra's performances: "Hard work and extended play, I mean after hours, never hurt Frank. But emotional tension absolutely destroyed him. You could always tell when he was troubled. He came down with a bad throat. Germs were never the cause unless there are guilt germs."[28] More notably, arranger Nelson Riddle, with whom Sinatra collaborated on the majority of his Capitol albums, made a direct connection between Sinatra's troubled marriage to Ava Gardner and the success of his saloon song recordings, suggesting: "It was Ava who did that, who taught him how to sing a torch song. That's how he learned. She was the greatest love of his life and he lost her."[29] This kind of deduction about the impact of life on art is less relevant than the way in which press reports contributed to Sinatra's star image as an emotionally vulnerable male. A variety of articles over the course of his high-profile relationship with Gardner provided details of their numerous separations and rapprochements. In her column "The Voice of Broadway," *New York Journal-American* writer Dorothy Kilgallen devoted several issues in 1952 to one well-documented spat between the couple during which Sinatra reportedly threw Gardner and Lana Turner out of his Palm Springs home. In one October issue, Kilgallen claimed: "Frank Sinatra is frightening his friends by telephoning in a gloomy voice, 'Please see that the children are taken care of' and then hanging up. He called the next day to apologize, blaming it on The Glass."[30] As in this case, many press reports positioned Sinatra as the dependent partner in the relationship, stressing either *his* inability to cope with their separation or *his* desire for a reconciliation. Following the same incident detailed by Dorothy Kilgallen in 1952, journalist Earl Wilson's column carried the headline "Frankie Ready to Surrender; Wants Ava Back, Any Terms."[31] While marriage to one of Hollywood's most celebrated beauties invested Sinatra's star image with an air of successful virility, the cumulative effect of these press reports was to heighten the sense of emotional dependence around him. This circulating image impacts on readings of Sinatra's musical persona and screen performances.

"Album Cover Moments": Cinematic Imagery and Urban Anxiety

One of the features of film noir is its ambivalence with regard to core definitions of male identity. Few leading-male characters of the genre represent masculinity in traditional and positive terms, suggesting instead that American masculine identity veers between capable but uninspiring male figures, and nontraditional and heavily flawed individuals. The choice of companion open to Phyllis Dietrichson (Barbara Stanwyck) in the film noir archetype *Double Indemnity* (1944) illustrates the negative associations attached to masculinity through her financially capable but controlling husband and her weak and malleable partner in crime, insurance salesman Walter Neff (Fred MacMurray). Through his musical style and visual imagery, Sinatra carries the film noir sensibility of unstable masculinity into 1950s culture, translating its negative associations into a positive broadening of masculine definitions. Richard Dyer suggests that Humphrey Bogart and Robert Mitchum work as exceptions to film noir's negative male imagery and that "it would be interesting to analyse whether it is these characters as written or only as played that makes them seem to be positive assertions of masculine norms."[32] While Mitchum's performance in, for example, *Out of the Past* (1947) brings a self-assuredness and physical strength to his screen character, who has been duped by the schemings of a woman, the overpowering sensibility brought by Sinatra to his male characters is an emotional weakness that defines his male identity. The bruised masculinity represented by Sinatra's musical persona forms the basis for his screen roles, often affecting readings of roles that may appear unsympathetic. This brand of masculinity is adjusted in the context of new debates around issues of ideal male identity and the resettlement of war veterans.

The cinematic connections to be drawn from Sinatra's musical persona of damaged masculinity are most clearly effected by the album cover artwork. Robert Horton's description of the Capitol album covers as "little movies"[33] draws on the evocation of character and scene in the visual imagery of a tearful harlequin on *Only the Lonely* or a jet-setting swinger on *Come Fly with Me* (1957). Unlike Sinatra's earlier albums with Columbia Records, which often featured a standard photograph of Sinatra on their cover, the highly stylized Capitol album covers represent Sinatra as a character within a scene, illustrating the album's mood and narrative as though a publicity poster for a film. Color becomes an indicator of mood, so that the bright orange background of *Songs for Swingin' Lovers!* (1956) and the rich blue sky of *Come Fly with Me* contrast with the blacks and browns of Sinatra's saloon song albums, where Sinatra is depicted as a solitary figure in an afterdark urban environment. While Sinatra's upbeat albums invariably picture the singer in an open stance, facing the viewer directly, on the saloon song album covers, his face is often partially obscured. The face half bathed in darkness on *Only the Lonely*, or partly hidden by the hand on which Sinatra is resting on *Where Are You?*, suggests a character emotionally withdrawing from the world. Often, his loneliness within a crowd illustrates the extent of his emotional vulnerability, as on the cover of *No One Cares*. Recalling his "One for My Baby" male with a "tale to tell," Sinatra is photographed seated at a bar, staring at the drink in his glass and with a cigarette in his other hand while smiling couples make conversation in the room behind him.

The cover artwork of *In the Wee Small Hours* draws most effectively on film noir imagery. Sinatra is positioned as a character at the corner of an empty city street in the dark of night. Again, his face is partially obscured by his sideways stance and suggests an introspective mood as he gazes downward. Dressed in dark suit and tie, with a pocket handkerchief and fedora, and holding a cigarette from which smoke trails upward, the character presented here would become familiar through films such as *Young at Heart* and *Some Came Running,* in which similar imagery suggests the protagonists' masculine anxiety. Pushed to the side of the frame in the *Wee Small Hours* scene, Sinatra is flanked by tall, flat buildings and the streetlamp that also appears on the cover of *Songs for Young Lovers.* As a site that reveals the surveillance tactics of a private eye or the locale for an easy pickup, the streetlamp finds a frequent place in cinema's urban landscape. It can work also as an iconographic reference to urban loneliness, as in Edgar Ulmer's dark 1945 film *Detour.* Ulmer's cuts back and forth from nightclub singer Sue (Claudia Drake) and musician Al (Tom Neal) to a streetlamp bathed in fog, as Sue tells her fiancé she is leaving to try her luck in Los Angeles, make this piece of urban scenery a feature of his male character's sense of loss. The streetlamp is highlighted again when Al's story of blackmail and murder has been told and the lonely character leans against a lamp to light his cigarette, a scene particularly reminiscent of Sinatra's album cover imagery.

In their analysis of film noir's visual motifs, Janey Place and Lowell Peterson explain: "Claustrophobic framing devices such as doors, windows, stairways, metal bed frames, or simply shadows separate the character from other characters, from his world, or from his own emotions. And objects seem to push their way into the foreground of the frame to assume more power than the people."[34] Though Sinatra is foregrounded in the *Wee Small Hours* scene, the streetlamp beside him and the imposing buildings that surround him suggest both a loss of power and a physical and emotional disconnection from the human world. It appears as though Sinatra has been transplanted into one of Edward Hopper's metropolitan settings such as *Approaching a City,* with its similarly angular urban landscape. Many noir directors were directly influenced by Hopper's modern urban style. In preparation for *Force of Evil* (1948), for example, Abraham Polonsky took his cinematographer to an exhibition of Hopper's work in order to guide him toward the look he required for the film, in effect, as Nicholas Christopher notes, "full of black windows, looming shadows, and rich pools of light pouring from recessed doorways and deep stairwells."[35] As with Hopper's paintings, this noir sensibility may be achieved cinematically through the effective use of color, as well as through the low-key lighting and contrast expressionist photography of black and white. Nicholas Christopher and James Naremore both point to *Leave Her to Heaven* (1945), in which hot and cold colors are used to represent different emotional states. A scene in which Gene Tierney, dressed in a pale blue nightgown, falls purposefully down the stairs in an effort to abort her character's unborn child, for example, dissolves to an image of her walking out of the sea in a blood red swimsuit.[36] Green hues and shadows permeate the cover scene of *In the Wee Small Hours,* highlighting the "black windows" and "recessed doorways" so suggestive of a film noir style. The effect of both is to visually illustrate the emotional condition of Sinatra's character in the cold urban environment he inhabits, just as Sinatra's performances of songs such as "Mood Indigo" and "Ill Wind" on the album musically evoke the same urban loneliness.

The visual imagery of film noir litters Sinatra's screen roles, even where the films would not be generically categorized as such. His musical performances on film often reinforce connections with the male persona evident in the songs and imagery of his saloon song albums. In the 1957 biopic *The Joker Is Wild,* Sinatra plays Joe E. Lewis, the singer who transformed himself into a nightclub comic after Chicago gangsters cut his vocal cords when he attempted to leave their employ and move to an alternative Prohibition club. Lewis moves from cocky exuberance to extremes of vulnerability, expressed first through his loss of confidence and wariness of relationships, and later through a reinvigorated Lewis's self-destructive alcoholism. When Lewis is reduced to playing "second banana" in a burlesque show, he performs at a benefit and, after the show, tries to avoid the crowds by exiting behind a cyclorama pitched backstage. From the other side of the screen he can hear the sounds of the after-show party and Bing Crosby's live accompaniment.[37] Just as on the cover of *No One Cares,* Sinatra appears distanced from a more contented world, as those on the other side are projected as shadows onto the scrim. Lewis has separated himself from his friends and from the image he had of himself as a successful performer. Hiding behind a fright wig in a burlesque show, or behind a backstage curtain, he has become one of the "untouchables" mentioned when socialite Letty Page (Jeanne Crain) joins him. Having been coaxed reluctantly into dancing, Lewis explains to Letty that the strange effect of the cyclorama is that "we're the only real people here. The rest of them, they're only shadows." "Real" masculinity is represented by the mix of self-assurance and bravado exhibited by Lewis at the start of the narrative, and the physical damage and depleted confidence he now displays. Though dressed in an ill-fitting suit and without a pocket handkerchief, Lewis's sporting of a fedora and Sinatra's own visible scars, which add to those of his character, draw Sinatra's star image into the text to heighten the complexity of this male persona.

As discussed in relation to the notion of *la bella figura,* style of dress is an integral part of Sinatra's image, from the bow ties of his bobby-soxer days onward. The Capitol album covers on which Sinatra appeared in dark suits and fedoras, with accompanying pocket handkerchiefs and raincoats, helped to establish an iconographic image and, at the same time, reinforced a sense of modern urban masculinity. The centrality of the fedora to this image is clear, with significance often being attached to the angle at which the hat is worn as an indicator of a particular mood. Bill Zehme, for instance, suggests, "The higher he pushed it back, the more vulnerable he became. The lower he pulled it, the more debonair and intimidating."[38] In reality, the difference from one album cover to another is imperceptible. Rather, the hat acts to reinforce the specifics of each persona, suggesting the flair of a stylish playboy or the vulnerability of a world-weary loser. *Metronome*'s description of *Songs for Swingin' Lovers!* as a "be-hatted, tie-loosened, almost impeccable set of performances" latches on to this imagery to suggest the freewheeling atmosphere projected through the album's songs.[39] Sinatra's fedora and loosened tie on the cover of *In the Wee Small Hours* indicate instead his character's weary emotional state.

The other accessory essential to this iconic picture of Sinatra is the cigarette. It appears in Sinatra's hand on most of his saloon song albums of the 1950s but is conspicuously absent from their swingin' counterparts. In stage performances, Sinatra's tendency to use a cigarette as a prop when acting out the character of "One for My Baby" or "Angel Eyes," and then discard it, signals further that smoking is an activity associated with this particular brand of masculinity. Sinatra can be seen doing this on numerous occasions, such as for his performance of "One for My Baby" at the Royal Festival Hall in 1962. During a nightclub-style segment of a 1959 edition of *The Frank Sinatra Show,* he follows a fast-paced version of "Just One of Those Things" by picking up a cigarette for his performance of "Angel Eyes," which he discards before moving on to "The Lady Is a Tramp." In another edition of his show, Sinatra brings together the various elements of his vulnerable male persona as he performs "One for My Baby" dressed in raincoat and fedora, with a cigarette in his hand, seated at a bar with a lone bartender. This performance appears to recreate the scene on the cover of *No One Cares,* again emphasizing the intertextuality of this image and its cinematic basis achieved through the establishment of character, narrative, and scene.[40]

The associations made between smoking and ideals of masculinity are long-standing. Smoking had consistently been projected as a male pastime in American culture, and advertisers had directly linked smoking and masculinity since campaigns during World War I made such declarations as "When our boys light up, the Huns will light out!"[41] By the 1950s, the cigarette manufacturer Marlboro was advocating a return to the traditional masculinity of America's western heroes with the tattooed cowboy known as "The Marlboro Man."[42] The confident, active, independent air projected through this image in the natural surroundings of "Marlboro Country" equated smoking in the mid-twentieth century with ideas of male strength and validated this image of masculinity as natural. In contrast, Sinatra's use of the cigarette in specific relation to his saloon songs suggests urban man to be less easily definable in such traditional terms.[43] The associations of loss and vulnerability that surround Sinatra's lone male mean that the cigarette often appears as something of a comfort blanket of masculinity, to which his characters cling in an effort to prevent their vulnerability from descending toward feminization.[44]

For Sinatra, then, the cigarette acts as what Vsevolod Pudovkin has labeled an "expressive object," a term used to describe objects that play an "active" part within a film's narrative through the sheer force of their presence or the ways in which characters or actors use them.[45] James Naremore appropriates the term to explain how objects may be used by actors as "signifiers of feeling," citing examples such as Jack Lemmon's use of a tube of nasal spray in a scene in *The Apartment* (1960), which moves his character, C. C. Baxter, from nervousness to surprise to joy.[46] Sinatra's consistent and specific use of the cigarette in musical performances and imagery that express male weakness means that the cigarette has a powerful effect on Sinatra's masculine image in films that trade on the vulnerability suggested by this persona. Since the early days of cinema, smoking had been used to indicate various aspects of masculinity. From the perverse manliness of the black-hatted villains of 1920s westerns to the bravado of Depression-era gangsters, masculinity could be expressed by the lighting of a cigarette at a well-chosen moment. Michael Starr's analysis of Humphrey Bogart's smoking moments illustrates the extent to which the cigarette can be used to advance the cause of both narrative and character. In *To Have and Have Not* (1944), for instance, Lauren Bacall as Marie introduces herself to Bogart's Harry Morgan by asking, "Anybody got a match?" In *The Big Sleep* (1946), Bogart's line "I lit a cigarette and blew a lungful at him and he sniffed it like a terrier at a rathole!" speaks of Philip Marlowe's tough and cynical attitude toward the world around him.[47]

Sinatra's close association with the cigarette both on screen and through musical imagery means that it becomes an even more effective tool for illustrating his characters' particular vulnerabilities. The point is perhaps best proven by *Young at Heart,* which features a variety of what Robert Horton calls "album cover moments,"[48] highlighting the seamless link between the visual imaging of Sinatra's music and film roles (Figure 5). Like *To Have and Have Not, Young at Heart* has its plot advanced by cigarettes; one of Barney's opening lines to Laurie is "You got a cigarette?," and his pretext for escaping the Tuttle family festivities on Christmas Day—which precipitates his suicide attempt—is to buy some cigarettes.[49] Smoking is also a marker of the male characters' class identities. Real estate operator Bob Neary smokes a cigar as a symbol of his success; patriarch Gregory Tuttle cuts a figure of learned contentment with a pipe; and the streetwise, urban Barney spends a large part of the

Figure 5: A publicity still image of Barney Sloan in an urban barroom with a sole bartender for company, resembling the style of Sinatra's saloon-song Capitol album covers. (*Young at Heart*)

film with a cigarette resting on his lower lip. Critics certainly noticed the extent to which Sinatra is seen smoking in the film and the impact this has on characterization. Lee Rogow of *The Saturday Review* noted that Sinatra "smokes enough cigarettes for six cynics," and Bill Zinsser of *The New York Herald Tribune* suggested, "When he drags on a cigarette, you know he's enjoying it all for its rich, full, injurious flavor."[50]

Cigarettes appear consistently when Barney is at his most vulnerable and help build a character that closely relates to Sinatra's persona on the album covers that follow *Young at Heart*. When Sinatra performs "Someone to Watch Over Me" and "Just One of Those Things" at the piano (the latter scene also including a lone bartender), a cigarette is positioned conspicuously at his side, with smoke trailing up the screen beside him. In the Tuttle home, as Barney watches the easy interaction between Laurie and her ex-fiancé Alex, he leans on the back of his chair, framed by the Christmas tree lights behind him, cigarette in hand. The scene with the most powerful claim to an album cover link comes when Barney pushes his car accelerator to the floor, stops the wipers clearing the snow from the windshield, and looks up at the fates to do their worst. The scene takes place in the dead of night, and Sinatra has a lighted cigarette resting on his lower lip. Like the hat and the turned-up collar on his coat, the cigarette accentuates both the modern urban masculinity of Sinatra's character and his ultimate vulnerability. Feeling as though his temporary respite from emotional obscurity is at an end, the only reply Barney can muster is to bring his life to what he feels is its inevitable conclusion, giving the musical a particularly dark feel, despite its artificially positive ending. Around Sinatra, the cigarette therefore becomes an emblem of a newly diverse brand of male identity, revealing an essential vulnerability without the effect of feminization.

"Haven't You Any Feelings at All?": Male Strength and Damaged Masculinity in *Suddenly*

Sinatra's screen roles of the 1950s carry a film noir sensibility of unstable masculinity into a postwar context in which debates around the resettlement of war veterans and middle-class masculine ideals come to the fore. In *On the Town* and *Anchors Aweigh,* Sinatra's largely feminized persona as a naval man safely located outside the perimeters of physical combat corresponds with his musical image as a female point of identification. Sinatra's frequent portrayals of war veterans again distance him from displays of masculine bravery. Here, however, Sinatra's more complex male image shifts the emotional dependence established through his earlier roles to machismo and emotional damage caused by the war's demands on men. Now located in a changed postwar America, Sinatra's characters are disconnected by their experience from an ideal image of male confidence and security. The image building around Sinatra through music and film performances assists in reading the vulnerabilities of his characters not as evidence of feminized masculinity, but as part of the postwar male experience.

Interest in the 1954 film *Suddenly* often centers on the mythology surrounding the assassination of President John F. Kennedy. A tale of a plot to assassinate an American president, the film is said to have been viewed by Lee Harvey Oswald a few days prior to Kennedy's demise, a rumor that led Sinatra in 1971 to withdraw the film from circulation for over twenty years.[51] However, conflicting representations of masculinity, and the emergence of war as a consistent reference point for the attitudes of each of the characters, make postwar male identity a central theme. Although the narrative sets up a debate around what it means to be an American man, its insistence on reasserting traditional American masculinity as the way forward illustrates the film's denial of the war's effects on the stability of this male image. By reestablishing ideas of male strength, family structure, and religious values by the end of the film, the narrative aims to contain the disruption to male certainty represented by Sinatra's character, John Baron. However, Sinatra brings with him to the role associations of innocence and vulnerability from serviceman characters such as Clarence Doolittle and Angelo Maggio, which counteract this narrative intent. The image of emotionally damaged masculinity evoked through Sinatra's 1950s musical persona impacts further on perceptions of the violent character he portrays.

Before the credits roll, a conversation between a tourist and a policeman reveals that the town of Suddenly derives its name from the violence and chaos of its gold-rush past, a hint of what Sinatra's assassin will bring to this sleepy community. Suddenly is shaken out of its complacency by the news that the president of the United States is to make a brief stopover in the town on his way to his White Springs retreat, an idea suggested by Dwight D. Eisenhower's regular trips to Palm Springs.[52] While Secret Service agents swarm over Suddenly to prepare security, aided by local sheriff Tod Shaw (Sterling Hayden), would-be assassin Baron and his two accomplices invade a home and take its family hostage to secure a vantage point for their mission. This is a family made incomplete by World War II. Ellen Benson (Nancy Gates) lost her husband in the war and now lives with her father-in-law, "Pop" Benson (James Gleason), and her son, "Pidge" (Kim Charney). However, it is also a family built on male traditions, as the name Peter given to three generations of Benson men testifies. Ellen's views on her son's upbringing become the early focus of the film's attention, as she is attacked for her unwillingness to prepare Pidge for his assigned social role.

The film proper opens with a shot of Pidge looking wistfully into the movie theater, where a war film is playing. Joined by Tod, he complains that his mother has forbidden him from going to see war films or buying the toy gun he points to in a toyshop window. In an exchange between the two characters, the film reveals its perspective on male violence.

Tod: "If you had the gun, what would you do with it? Stick up a filling station?"

Pidge: "Heck no. I'd be sheriff. And I'd catch all those rogue agents and cattle rustlers, just like you."

During the course of the film, the narrative asserts that male violence is a positive and necessary force when displayed in correspondence with the law and agreed morality. Ideas of masculinity projected through war and American gun culture provide an arena for debate as Ellen and Baron both contest, in different ways, accepted notions of ideal male identity. However, as the negative associations of male violence are assigned to the psychological disturbance of an individual, the film ultimately reaffirms the validity of masculine strength.

As a representative of the law and a patriarchal role model to Pidge, Tod carries the theme of ideal American masculinity for the narrative. Within the community, Tod assumes a position of power as he strides around town issuing orders. He attempts to claim a similar position in the Benson family, to whom he attaches himself, correcting Pidge on his manners and advising Ellen on her need to move beyond her grief for her late husband. More importantly, he suggests to Ellen that her protectiveness toward Pidge is unhealthy. Ellen's unwillingness to allow her son to watch war films that will teach him "the art of death and destruction; the cruelties, the tortures" is countered by Tod's argument: "He's gotta know that these things exist. Then he can fight against them when it's his turn." Tod's assumption that the death and destruction emanates from the opposing side—a possible reference to American perceptions of Japanese conduct in World War II—clearly refutes any idea that American displays of masculine strength need be viewed negatively. On the contrary, he suggests it is Pidge's birthright to become another example of male strength. Sure in the rightness of his argument, Tod goes against Ellen's wishes and buys the toy gun for Pidge without her knowledge.

The cause of converting Ellen to the male way of thinking is taken up again by her father-in-law. As a veteran of World War I and former presidential bodyguard to Calvin Coolidge, Pop Benson's respect for traditions of honor and heroism strikes a reverential tone. While Ellen sees her husband's death as a murderous waste, Pop is appalled by her attitude, arguing that his son died "in the performance of his duty." Quoting "life, liberty and the pursuit of happiness" at Ellen from the Declaration of Independence, Pop positions displays of masculine violence as central to the very concept of America as prescribed by the founding fathers.

The patriarchal basis for this perspective allows Pop, just like Tod, to assume a sense of superiority so that he feels able to tell Ellen plainly to "stop being a woman." Later, he proudly shows off his bullet wound to Baron, even though it was gained during a shooting trip with the former president rather than in combat, suggesting physical wounding to be a male rite of passage. However, the men's attempts to persuade Ellen of the need to prepare Pidge for his male destiny suggests masculinity as they define it to be a role-playing exercise. Ellen's apparent ability to steer the course of Pidge's male development makes masculinity under this definition a product of nurture rather than nature. As Harry Brod explains in his discussion of theories of masculinity: "To speak of a role is to invoke a distinction between the behavior exhibited and the 'real' person behind or beneath the role, the agent *in* the role."[53] Therefore, while Tod and Pop assert the naturalness of Pidge's attraction to guns and violence, which Ellen's intervention threatens to disrupt, their very language of "duty" and "his turn" suggests a socially directed role.

Pidge's image of Tod as upholding a sense of strong masculinity speaks further of unnatural performance, having been gleaned from the movies. His idea of a sheriff who wages war against cattle rustlers suggests Tod's brand of masculinity to be an anachronism, which trades on America's mythological past and now exists only in a movie theater. Film and television imagery recurs throughout the film as Pidge labels Baron a "gangster"; television repairman Jud (James Lilburn) asks, "Is this a stick-up?"; and Baron comments, regarding Ellen's conversation with a special agent, "She played her part real good. Should be in television." Tod is a believer in marriage, the church, and community spirit, and his confidence in moral absolutes has not been dented by his experience of war. His connection to a traditionally invulnerable male identity therefore remains firm. Sterling Hayden's physicality lends itself to this image of masculine strength. His deep voice reinforces Tod's commanding air, and Hayden's height and stocky build suggest a heightened masculinity denoted by physical and emotional strength. Hayden's most notable film roles up to this point had been as a career criminal in *The Asphalt Jungle* (1950) and opposite Bette Davis in *The Star* (1952). In John Huston's crime caper, while he ultimately succumbs to a gunshot wound in his attempt to escape the city for his backwoods farm, Hayden's Dix Handley acts throughout the film as a physical protector to the slightly built Sam Jaffe as Doc. In *The Star,* Hayden again promotes a positive image of a World War II veteran as the hands-on owner of a shipyard. Having rejected acting as effeminate, and assisted by a GI loan, Jim Johannson spends his time repairing engines and rescuing Davis's aging actress from jail and her attempts to regain her stardom. Hayden's role as Sheriff Tod Shaw builds on this image of physical strength and self-assurance. Nevertheless, Tod at times appears to struggle to live up to the role to which he has appointed himself. Neither a husband nor a father, he is frozen out of the Benson family by Ellen, who tells him, "No one can take Pete's place." Similarly, his role as the town's head law enforcer is usurped by the Secret Service agents who assume control of the day's proceedings, effectively emasculating Tod by his own definition of masculinity.

The impact of Baron, and Sinatra, on *Suddenly*'s narrative is to challenge Tod's, and Hayden's, image of impenetrable masculinity. Baron's revelation of the destructive effects of war, and Sinatra's building persona as a vulnerable male, work against the narrative to argue the invalidity of traditional images of masculinity in the postwar context. Baron's exposure of male power as role playing is demonstrated initially by the ease with which he enters the Benson home posing as an FBI agent. Baron shows his disregard for the foundations of home, family, and country upon which Tod and Pop have argued that the war was fought and through which traditional American masculinity functions. Invading the family arena, Baron tramples through its popular mythology, calling Pidge a "squirt" and threatening to kill the boy if they fail to follow his instructions. His comment to Pidge that "squirts like you are supposed to grow up and be president" is clearly full of irony, since Baron goes on to deride his hostages' professed loyalty to the president by offering to shoot one of them instead. To Baron, the president is the ultimate role player. When even his colleagues question the morality of murdering America's most respected male figure, Baron argues in response: "It's just another man; a man!"

Tod's assumption of command of the hostage group and his "duty look" are viewed by Baron with a similar lack of respect. These attributes of strength and authority have been devalued by Baron's experience of the war when the officer class "big shots" displayed their fear on the frontline while he "chopped." The foundations for his assessments of the masculinity of those around him can all be traced back to the war to which he constantly refers when commenting on the bravery or otherwise of the other male characters. While he declares that Pidge has "lots of guts," his judgment on his fellow assassins is that they would fail to make the grade in a combat situation. When Bart (Christopher Dark) threatens Pidge after being duped by his toy pistol, the assassin's angry reaction provokes amused laughter from Baron who comments: "I'm not sure that he couldn't take ya." Baron takes most pleasure in mocking the sheriff's stature as a hero of the community. As he sneers at Tod, "Your guts are showin' all over the place, brave boy," he makes clear that he views Tod's male bravado as a performance. When Tod is shot in the arm by one of the assassins and asks Baron to straighten out the break, Baron watches with satisfaction Tod's quiet stoicism and his refusal to express his pain, as though aware of the sheriff's need to maintain an image of strength.

Baron forces Tod to remain seated through most of the siege, cutting his opponent down to size. When the two characters stand close to each other, the height differential between them reinforces Tod's sense of self-assuredness and Baron's insecurity, as the sheriff towers over him. Virginia Wright Wexman draws attention to the power relationships in *The Maltese Falcon,* which are illustrated through the various height differences among the actors. Wexman suggests that Bogart's midrange height falls between the shorter villains he will outwit and the taller policemen, who represent social justice in the narrative, highlighting Sam Spade's position in the power structure of that criminal world.[54] In *Suddenly,* the contrasting physicalities of Sinatra and Hayden are marked by the difference in build between Sinatra's thin frame and Hayden's stockiness. The obvious height difference between the two stars also gives added power to Hayden's character, despite the situation in which Baron appears to have control. One midrange shot in particular reveals Baron's vulnerability in this way, as Tod discloses the fact that rather than reaching officer rank, as Baron assumes, he was a corporal in the army. With the two stars moving closer together, Hayden towers over Sinatra as the latter strains to reach his eye level. The childish glee in Sinatra's voice as Baron taunts Tod—"Corporal? I made sergeant!"—compounds the sense that Baron is seeking a place of male superiority over Tod, who, since the war, has attained a position of authority.

Baron's failure to recognize Tod's authority is based, as he explains, on his possession of the gun. America's gun culture, which works its way through the gangster films watched by the television repairman and the westerns viewed by Pidge, has been ratified by the war, making violence for the proper cause an indicator of heroism. The war has made Baron an expert on guns, so that he can inform his colleagues of the relative merits of the tommy gun, revolver, and rifle and even marvel at the realism of Pidge's toy gun. Baron feels an attachment to the guns, stroking them admiringly in appreciation of the power they invest in him. He stresses an awareness that as a symbol of strength in war, the gun creates a false impression of male identity, the gun alone now making him "a sort of god." Baron reveals the fragility of his sense of masculine worth created by his possession of guns and the violent behavior he displayed in World War II, explaining: "Without the gun, I'm nothing. And I never had anything before I got one. First time I got one in my hands and killed a man, I got some self-respect. I was somebody." The machismo demanded of men during the war has allowed Baron to excel at male heroics, providing him with an opportunity to live up to the male "role." His admiration for the nuclear bomb and its ability to simultaneously kill 100,000 people suggests that war places a premium on violent excess. His frequent repetition of the fact that he won a Silver Star for killing twenty-seven men "all by myself" confirms the rewards given for male violence, Baron's reliance on wartime ideals for his masculine image, and his need for reassurance. It contrasts sharply with Tod's quietly self-assured response, "I got by," when Baron comments that he must have been a good soldier. When Pidge scoffs that Baron probably stole the award, and one of his fellow assassins asks, "For the love of Mike, what's a Silver Star?," it suggests that this ideal has become irrelevant and that Baron's failure to recognize this has resulted in his inability to adapt the expression of his masculinity for the postwar world. By swapping his wartime heroism for a career as a "gun for hire," Baron has exposed male violence as negative and so alienated himself from postwar ideals.

In order to live up to the machismo required by war, Baron has learned to deny his emotions. His cold professionalism with regard to the assassination, for which he has no political motive, is the consequence of his army training, enabling him to assert: "I got no feeling against the president. I'm just earning a living." As Michael Kimmel notes, the invulnerability demanded of America's servicemen was questioned in the war's aftermath as investigations exposed the reality that existed behind this image of uncomplicated bravery: "After the war, psychiatrists probed past the military veneer to reveal a trembling terror underneath the soldier's bravado. Many soldiers in the second World War, it turned out, could not fire their rifles and return enemy fire, and about 75 percent of all infantrymen rarely fired their weapons at all. A large number became incontinent in battle, and many men would 'feign emotional disorder' in order to get out of the line of fire."[55] With the American military creating false notions of bravery, and individuals performing a role for which they were often ill equipped, male fear was a hidden feature of the war experience. To move beyond an image of strength to a realization of the heroic ideal therefore required the dulling of emotions through which vulnerabilities might be revealed. As Baron argues: "Feelings are trap. They're a weakness." The 1949 film *Twelve O'Clock High* suggests the denial of emotions to be a routine requirement as American airmen are pushed to what the air force terms "maximum effort," despite the suicides and trauma that result. Brigadier General Frank Savage, played by Gregory Peck, advises his unit to "consider yourself already dead" so that any fears or vulnerabilities will not prevent them from doing their job effectively. By the close of the film, however, Savage has experienced a breakdown as the cumulative result of submerging his own emotions in the service of his duty. Baron's description of his wartime exploits as "choppin'" illustrates the extent to which he has been able to dehumanize the victims of his violence. His assessment that his colleagues, who failed to serve, are inadequate for the task of assassination because of their ability to feel makes the direct connection between the war's demands of machismo and the emotional vacuity that he continues to display. To Ellen's question, "Haven't you any feelings at all?," Baron's reply is, "No, I haven't, lady. They were taken out of me by experts." His admission that he has been trained not to feel makes clear the direct influence the war has had on his behavior.

Despite these connections between Baron's postwar conduct and the demands of war, the narrative intent is clearly to depict his assassination attempt, as well as his recognized heroism, as the result of psychological disturbance. Tod wages a psychological war against Baron, aimed at causing him to reveal his vulnerabilities, a tactic noted by Bart, who counsels, "You're talking too much, Johnny." Baron's constant references to the war illustrate the extent to which his war experience has been a positive affirmation of his masculinity. Yet Tod fails to acknowledge the damaging effects of the war on Baron's emotional state. The narrative sets up Baron as the discarded child of an unmarried mother and an alcoholic father who deposited him in a "home." Disconnection from the norms of society has traditionally been taken as an indicator of disturbed pathology, and Baron's social alienation before the war marks him out as deviant. Ignoring Bart's warning, Baron's talk of his alienation and distressing dreams highlights the disturbed psychology and social abnormality with which the narrative and the other characters associate his male identity. Baron relates: "Why, before the war, I drifted and drifted and ran. Always lost in the great big crowd. I hated that crowd. I used to dream about the crowd once in a while. I used to see all those faces scratching and shoving and biting. And then the mist would clear, and somehow all those faces would be me. All me, and all nothing." Tod's response—"But the war changed everything, eh, Baron?"—suggests his recognition of the war's effects on Baron's psyche. Yet Tod fails to acknowledge the war's positive promotion of violence as a contributing factor to Baron's behavior. Instead, he views the conflict simply as an arena in which Baron's latent disturbance came to fruition, insisting that rather than providing evidence of male heroics, Baron's war record proves him to be "a born killer, that's all" (Figure 6). He goes on to surmise that Baron's discharge from the army came about as a result of a Section 8, "psycho in charge of killing," placing responsibility firmly in Baron's hands.

As a home-invasion narrative, *Suddenly* is one of a number of postwar films that addressed an anxiety that dangerous outside influences could challenge the security of the middle-class American home. As criminals invaded suburban family homes, the films often made psychological disturbance a central factor in the characters' behavior. In *The Dark Past* (1949), William Holden as an escaped convict takes over the mountain retreat owned by a psychology professor and his family. The professor's analysis of the convict's recurring dream reveals his aggression to have been prompted by his guilt at having murdered his violent father, again rooting male aggression in psychosis. In *The Desperate Hours* (1955), Humphrey Bogart, as another escaped convict, Glenn Griffin, invades the home of the respectable Hilliard family, headed by Fredric March. Like *Suddenly,* the narrative of *The Desperate Hours* sets up a competition between the hegemonic masculinity of the mild-mannered Hilliard and the violent psychological disturbance of Griffin. Similar to John Baron, Hilliard is distanced from middle-class family life, evidenced again by his attitude toward the young son of the family, whom he terms "The Brat." Griffin's violence is presented as something he enjoys, suggested by the fact that he scarred the face of a detective when arrested for his initial crime, which included shooting a policeman. Griffin's anger over the class divisions that deny him Hilliard's lifestyle is put forward as a possible reason for his violent criminality. Enjoying the authority he now has over Hilliard, Griffin makes clear his frustration: "I got my guts full of you shiney-shoes, down-your-nose wise guys with white handkerchiefs in their pockets." Yet ultimately, this class struggle is refuted, as Griffin is labeled a "savage" and even his younger brother tries to escape Griffin's disturbed reality. The narrative conclusion assigns victory to the steady intelligence of the father and husband who orders the psychopath, "Get out! Get out of my house!" The changing representation of Bogart's "tough guy" persona from the positive individualism of the 1940s to the sexual

Figure 6: This publicity poster for *Suddenly* highlights the film's modeling of Baron as a psychologically disturbed murderer with a brutal lust for killing.

anxiety of *In a Lonely Place* (1950) and the psychopathic violence of *The Desperate Hours* is indicative of the shift in perceptions of machismo from World War II to postwar America.[56]

In *Suddenly,* there is a similar denial that the positive promotion of machismo in war makes society complicit in Baron's cold postwar violence. Baron has performed according to the "role" assigned him—just as Pidge is expected to do—but is now as much a threat to democracy as were the Allies' enemies. Baron represents a threat not only to the Benson home but to America. The narrative refutes the need to redefine masculinity, arguing instead that Baron's aggression makes him "an animal" or "goofy." Baron's challenge to traditional male identity is therefore contained by the end of film, when Ellen shoots and kills the assassin as he whimpers, "No, please, no." Ellen's momentary conversion to an honorary male proves for the narrative that violence, and war, are necessary when perpetrated for a socially justifiable cause. To reinforce the point, the toy gun that Tod had bought for Pidge causes enough confusion to enable this to occur. Traditional masculinity reasserts its authority through Ellen's acceptance of the rightness of Tod's preaching, proven by her willingness to kill Baron and her subsequent admission of her attraction to the sheriff when she offers to collect him the next morning for church.

This forceful narrative thrust is disturbed, then, only by Baron's contesting of Tod's self-assured masculinity and the impact that Sinatra's image has on the role. The role of John Baron was previously offered to Montgomery Clift,[57] whose generally vulnerable persona complicates films such as *The Heiress* (1949), leaving the audience with lingering doubts about the extent of his character's gold-digging motives, despite all the evidence against him.[58] The director Lewis Allen's consideration of Clift for the part in *Suddenly* suggests an intent to allow a greater level of sympathy for Baron than is sanctioned by the narrative. In the same way, Sinatra's image works against the narrative, as the star brings with him an image of male vulnerability constructed through his early feminized persona and his building 1950s masculine image. In his assessment of Marilyn Monroe's performance as Lorelei Lee in *Gentlemen Prefer Blondes* (1953), Richard Dyer demonstrates how Monroe's image of innocent sexuality offsets the director Howard Hawks's presentation of Lee as a manipulative female, who contrasts with the warm, straightforward Dorothy, played by Jane Russell.[59] The combined effect of narrative intent and ideological climate, confirmed by other home-invasion films, is to cast Baron's behavior as a simple case of individual psychological deviance.

However, Sinatra carries with him the cumulative impact of his portrayals of innocence as sailors on leave in *Anchors Aweigh* and *On the Town,* and as a returning soldier in *It Happened in Brooklyn,* making his serviceman a necessarily vulnerable figure. The absence of any demonstrations of violence by Sinatra's servicemen provokes a curiosity about what could have transformed Clarence Doolittle into a cold-blooded killer. The cold sneers and furtive glances delivered by Sinatra in close-up are peculiar to *Suddenly* and, added to the connections Baron makes between the experience of war and male bravado, disrupt the narrative's confident elevation of traditional masculinity. In addition, with Baron wearing Sinatra's trademark fedora all through the siege, significantly removing it only when preparing to attempt the assassination, the image of damaged masculinity is brought right up to date. Therefore, while the aim of the narrative is to contend that male violence is a positive force necessary to defend against threats from outside home and country, the film, despite itself, reveals the damage inflicted by the requirement to live up to an image of traditional American male identity.

"Let's Drink to the Return of the Conquering Hero": Machismo and Emotional Frailty in *Some Came Running*

Suddenly takes its place in a postwar trend of films that considered the traumatic effect of war on American masculinity and the difficulties of readjustment in the home environment. Kaja Silverman identifies a number of films of the immediate postwar period, such as *The Pride of the Marines, The Lost Weekend* (1945), *Gilda* (1946), and *The Best Years of Our Lives* (1946), that "are obliged to confer upon a female character the narrative agency which is the usual attribute of a male character" and in which "the hero no longer feels 'at home' in the house or town where he grew up, and resists cultural (re)assimilation."[60] In *The Best Years of Our Lives,* as in *The Pride of the Marines,* the issues of postwar adjustment and repositioned gender relations are relayed specifically through a narrative that deals with the experiences of war veterans. Air Force Captain Fred Derry (Dana Andrews), Army Sergeant Al Stevenson (Fredric March), and Homer Parish, a sailor who lost his hands in an aircraft fire (played by actual amputee Harold Russell) have difficulty adjusting to civilian life. Thrown together on their flight home, each of the men is wary of returning to his family, and when they come across each other in a bar on their first night back, it is testament to their lack of ease in their family homes, from which they have felt the need to escape. Al soon becomes aware that his family has run smoothly without him and is thrown into chaos only by his unannounced arrival. His attempt to impress his son with the souvenirs of battle he brings home is rebuffed by his son's objective account of the war as imparted to him in high school lectures. When Al returns to work at the local bank, his war experience is put to good capitalist use when he is put in charge of GI loans. When he is chastised for allocating loans on the basis of character rather than collateral, Al's disillusionment with the motives of big business signals his incompatibility with the civilian life to which he has returned. Al goes on to point out the cold professionalism of such business practices during his inebriated speech at a banquet hosted by the bank president to honor "our friend, our co-worker, our hero."

Fred, who spent the war dropping bombs on the enemy and was rewarded for his bravery with medals and officer status, returns to the local drugstore where he worked as a soda jerk and finds himself accepting orders in an impersonal chain store from the man who was previously his junior. Fred is soon fired from his job, after hitting a customer who suggests the United States chose the wrong allies and therefore Homer's physical sacrifice was in vain. When Fred's wife, Marie (Virginia Mayo), becomes so unimpressed by her husband's postwar desire to settle down that she leaves him, and his budding relationship with Al's daughter Peggy (Teresa Wright) is cut short by Al, Fred makes his way to an airfield in search of some direction. As he waits to fly east (only because east is the first destination available), the camera follows him through the lines of aircraft that are being dismantled to build prefabricated housing. Fred's pitch for a job with the scrap company suggests a realization that he needs to reinvent himself or become an anachronism like the fighter planes around him.

Homer's physical injury is the film's most obvious indicator of damaged masculinity and represents the character's struggle to come to terms with the adjustments that need to be made in his relationship with his fiancée, Wilma (Cathy O'Donnell). Homer's reluctance to reintroduce intimacy into their relationship culminates in a scene in which Homer relinquishes control to Wilma, allowing his fiancée to undress him for bed. By permitting himself a passive role, Homer becomes convinced of their ability to create a successful relationship, both physically and emotionally. In his analysis of *The Best Years of Our Lives,* Robert Warshow introduced in 1947 the issue of the American male's desire for sexual passivity, arguing that "the sailor's misfortune becomes a kind of wish fulfillment, as one might actually dream it: he *must* be passive;

therefore he can be passive without guilt."[61] Observing that each of the male characters is undressed and put to bed by the woman with whom he is, or will be, involved—Al by wife Millie (Myrna Loy) and Fred by Peggy—Warshow identifies a desire for sexual passivity in the men that illustrates their emotionally vulnerable status in their relationships. As Kaja Silverman notes, however, Warshow sees these characterizations as typical of Hollywood's representations of the American male, rather than viewing them as depictions of masculinity marked by their postwar context.[62]

Some Came Running provides further evidence of the direct connections made by Hollywood films between shifting definitions of male identity and the postwar experience. The intervening time period between the two films illuminates an increased focus on anxieties concerning the middle-class husband and the lifestyle he has created. In William Wyler's 1946 film, the middle-class home is ultimately reestablished as a positive environment in which the veteran is able to relocate his male identity, as indicated by the closing scenes in which Homer and Wilma are married and Fred and Peggy are reunited with talk of a future together. By 1958, *Some Came Running*'s year of production, the family home has become a symbol of the American male's self-indulgence and repression. Vincente Minnelli's melodrama represents middle-class home life in terms far different from the idyllic familial closeness of his 1944 film *Meet Me in St Louis,* drawing an image of masculine identity crisis that incorporates veterans and financial high achievers alike. Drawn from the novel by *From Here to Eternity*'s James Jones, *Some Came Running* takes a look at Middle America in 1948 through the eyes of returning war veteran Dave Hirsh (Sinatra). Dave's reluctant reacquaintance with his family and the new relationships he forms demonstrate the anxieties surrounding not only the veteran's adjustment to postwar society but also the newly defined masculine ideal.

Dave Hirsh's early morning arrival on a Greyhound bus in the Indiana town of Parkman ties the character immediately to a specific brand of masculinity based around his identity as a serviceman. Still dressed in his army uniform and carrying his belongings in a kit bag, Dave finds himself revisiting his past because of a night of overindulgence during which he mentioned to some army buddies that Parkman was his hometown, or "used to be," as he pointedly tells the bus driver. When Ginny Moorehead (Shirley MacLaine) follows him off the bus, she provides further clues as to Dave's lifestyle when she reminds him that he invited her to accompany him on a trip following his brawl in Chicago with her companion, local hoodlum Raymond. Dave's comment that "it's a little early for . . ." is followed by Ginny's suggestion that he take her to meet his family. However, Dave's unintentional return to Parkman bears little resemblance to a conventional homecoming, and his displays of machismo will prove to be unwelcome in a postwar America that sees itself as having moved beyond the violence of its recent past.

When Dave checks into the local hotel, the details of his male profile are fleshed out. His lack of sentimentality about his "home" town is evident when he asks for the best room in the house and remarks: "I once promised myself if I *had* to come back here I'd *have* the best room in the house." Dave carries his home around with him in his kit bag, from which he extracts his most prized possessions: a bottle of whiskey; the collected works of American writers Faulkner, Steinbeck, Wolfe, Hemingway, and Fitzgerald; and his own crumpled manuscript of a short story, which he tosses into a bin, retrieves, and throws away again. Dave's sense of displacement is confirmed on the arrival of his brother Frank (Arthur Kennedy). Their discussion reveals that Dave has been absent from Parkman for sixteen years—a place he refers to only as "where I was born"—and that, like John Baron, much of Dave's childhood was spent in a children's home, a fate to which his elder brother assigned him as their widowed father descended into alcoholism. That this act of abandonment still rankles is clear from Dave's insistence on reimbursing Frank for the expenses incurred at "Mrs. Dillman's home for little boys." Despite the obvious resentments still festering between them, Frank feigns delight at his brother's unannounced return, insisting that Dave accept his invitation to dine with the family. Frank's remark, "Not that it'd look funny if you didn't," betrays the motive of image maintenance behind his hospitality.

Keir Keightley has drawn attention to Dave's confused actions as the Greyhound bus pulls into town, when he frantically pats various areas of his body in an attempt to find his wallet. The image of Sinatra reaching into the crotch of his trousers, where he finally locates his money, introduces, Keightley correctly argues, the sense of lack incorporated in the film's discussion of masculinity in crisis.[63] The idea of incomplete masculinity is not limited to Sinatra's Dave Hirsh, however. Frank, or Mr. Hirsh, as many of the film's peripheral characters call him, has achieved a position of some standing in the community. As the owner of a jewelry store inherited from his father-in-law, a board member of a local bank, and a member of the committee set up to organize the town's centennial celebrations, Frank views himself as a man of influence. (Dave is fully aware that the most effective way of inflicting pain on his brother is to affect his carefully groomed image and therefore deposits a check in a rival bank.) Frank's professional success, coupled with the family life he has created with wife Agnes (Leora Dana) and daughter Dawn (Betty Lou Keim) in one of Parkman's large historic homes, means that he projects an ideal male image for public consumption.

Frank conforms to the postwar notion of mature male identity as bound up in marriage and fatherhood. Barbara Ehrenreich's analysis of the postwar period reveals the extent to which male maturity was said to be evidenced by marriage and a career, with the consequent labeling of single or professionally unsettled men as possible homosexuals or psychologically disturbed. Ehrenreich writes: "By the 1950s and '60s psychiatry had developed a massive weight of theory establishing that marriage—and, within that, the breadwinner role—was the only normal state for the adult male. Outside lay only a range of diagnoses, all unflattering."[64] This perspective is apparent in Frank's suggestion that they find a suitable companion for Dave and in his recommendation that his brother settle down and begin improving his financial status. (Dave's first two novels earned him a total of forty-eight dollars, and his bank deposit was accrued by gambling.) Yet the persona of mature masculinity Frank has constructed around a successful career and family unity is exposed as without basis. Despite his claim "I've worked hard for everything I've got; nobody's helped me," Frank has inherited his business through an opportune marriage and cultivates friendships that assist his social climbing. Professor Bob French (Larry Gates) and his daughter Gwen (Martha Hyer), the "intellectuals" whom Frank and Agnes invite to join them for an evening at the country club, are introduced to Dave as "really wonderful people," an assessment prefaced by Agnes's divulgence of how much land this "old" family owns. The relationship between Frank and his wife is similarly one that values appearance over substance. The public face of unity and flirtatiousness between "Mamma" and "Poppy" masks a cold, sexless marriage in which Agnes stays home at night sewing while Frank embarks on an indiscreet fling with his secretary, Edith (Nancy Gates), and hints at other affairs.

The welcome the married couple extends to Dave is just as transparently bogus. Though Agnes declares happily to Bob French, "We're hoping he'll stay," her unwilling participation in the family reunion is dictated by the necessity of maintaining appearances. Frank's warm reception likewise arises from the knowledge that the whole town has observed Dave's arrival. His hospitality is soon withdrawn when a latenight skirmish with Raymond lands Dave in jail. Frank's response is to advise the judge his brother will be leaving town, worry about the incident being reported in the local newspaper, and ask Dave, "How could you do this to *me*?" Frank views his brother's lifestyle as an embarrassment that might impinge on his own carefully constructed image of masculine maturity. He is concerned that the uncharacteristic behavior Dawn soon displays, coming home in the early hours of the morning following a night drinking with a middle-aged stranger, and then deciding to depart for New York, occurs as a result of Dave's bad influence, when, in fact, it is the sight of her father in the back of a car with his secretary that causes Dawn's restlessness.

Frank's attitude toward his brother's return reflects that of Parkman and postwar America. Ironically, the protection of the mythical image of the American home against the perceived threat to the values of Middle America was part of the reasoning for war. Dave's experiences as a young boy, however, make home and family an alien concept, and the substance of both seems to have deteriorated still further. Little gratitude is shown for Dave's wartime sacrifice, and while the town sets out to celebrate its centenary, the community's intent to disregard and move on from its more recent past is clear in its treatment of Dave. While family and friends drink a toast to "the return of the conquering hero," Dave's lifestyle is soon judged unacceptable in the altered society to which he returns.

Manhattan-drinking countryclub evenings are deemed the appropriate environment for the male persona to which Frank ascribes. When, bumping into the owner of the sweetshop he visited as a child, Dave refuses to allow her to call him "Mr. Hirsh," insisting instead, "It's still Dave," it becomes clear that the veteran's male identity is not based on vanity or status. Like Al in *The Best Years of Our Lives,* Dave's excessive drinking suggests his inability to assimilate in this postwar environment, while the community's shocked response to his behavior speaks of society's fears about veterans' abuse of alcohol. The "cocktail hour" was a feature of postwar middle-class life, drinks such as martinis suggesting something of the blandness and conformity of the gray flannel existence, as evidenced by the unimpressed look on Dave's face when Agnes asks whether he likes manhattans. Dave opts instead for triple measures of straight Scotch and spends his time in Smitty's bar either joining in illegal games of poker with local gambler Bama Dillert (Dean Martin) or getting reacquainted with Ginny. Alcohol is the means through which Dave connects to people, as is seen when he asks the bus driver and then the owner of the sweetshop to join him for a drink. When his displays of machismo spill out into the street in the form of violence, hourly news bulletins illustrate the town's displeasure. In recognition, Dave remarks wryly upon being arrested, "Welcome home, Dave."

Time's report of Sinatra's activities during filming suggests similar local disquiet about his expressions of machismo. Labeling him Frank "Lover Boy" Sinatra, *Time* recounted that, arriving in Madison with various "camp followers," the star proceeded to drink and gamble with redheads until the early hours, bully waiters, and poke fun at the locals, all of which failed to impress the Indiana residents excited about the descent of a film production on their town.[65] Dave's openly nonconformist behavior contrasts with the attitude of newfound friend Bama, who bears some resemblance to Dave's brother in his approach to his own lifestyle. Bama is mindful of the sensitivities of the smalltown "headquarters" he by chance inhabits and conducts his business in the back room of Smitty's and out of town rather than in the full glare of publicity. As a professional gambler, he likens himself to his late father, who gambled each year on whether his crop would come in, and exhibits none of the restlessness that has drawn Dave from freighters to oil rigs. Bama, rather, displays what Nick Tosches describes as Dean Martin's "emotional distance, that wall of *lontananza* between the self and the world,"[66] maintaining superficial relationships that allow him to operate undisturbed by either the law or female ties. In contrast, Dave's brawls in the streets of Parkman and beyond suggest an unbridled masculinity that was expected of him during the war and has been fully contained locally until his return.

Dave's relationships with women demonstrate further his postwar dislocation as he moves back and forth between them. His relationships with Gwen, a college lecturer in creative writing and criticism, and Ginny, who is excited to have secured a position at Parkman's brassiere factory, are complex and offer an outlet for the different elements that make up his masculine character. Ginny's garish makeup and tightfitting clothes mark her out as excluded from middle-class territory, and her job sewing female underwear in a factory emphasizes her working-class, sexualized identity. With Ginny, Dave is able to indulge in a lifestyle familiar to him as a serviceman (Figure 7). In Smitty's bar or on a gambling trip to the town of Terre Haute, Dave can give free expression to his passions for alcohol, violence, and, it is suggested, sex, as well as exercising male control, having Ginny patiently wait for him to allow her access to his world. At the same time, Ginny's maternal behavior toward Dave, seen in the delight she takes in tidying up the home he shares with Bama

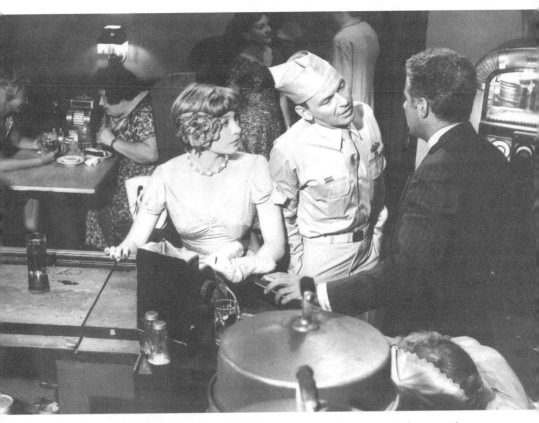

Figure 7: *Some Came Running* associates Dave's relationship with Ginny with masculine pursuits in male-dominated arenas, emphasized by this encounter with a receptive Ginny and hostile small-time gangster Raymond as Dave makes his way to an illegal poker game.

or helping him pack his suitcase, illustrates Dave's need for emotional protection.

His rejection of the one-dimensional machismo encouraged by the war is clear in his attitude toward the army uniform he wears for his arrival in Parkman. In *The Best Years of Our Lives,* to Fred's wife, Marie, her husband's masculinity is bound up in his air force uniform. Disappointed on seeing him for the first time in civilian clothes, she persuades him to don his uniform for a night out and only then is sexually attracted to him, declaring excitedly: "Oh, now you look wonderful. You look like yourself." Fred's reluctance to wear his uniform suggests an awareness that Marie is attracted to the false impression of his masculinity that it projects. In the same way, Dave's question to Agnes—"Do you suppose this costume will be all right at your club?"—reveals that the uniform's association with role playing, as John Baron suggests, indicates a brand of masculinity that no longer defines him. Agnes's positive reply—"Why not? It's the uniform of your country"—reflects the town's acceptance of the sense of heroism they believe the uniform represents, rather than its more earthy reality. Dave's first appearance in civilian clothes notably occurs when he drives out to Gwen's home to request her opinion on his unfinished manuscript, signifying his willingness to reveal the emotional frailty that exists beneath his displays of machismo.

Through Dave's stumbling relationship with Gwen, the narrative displays his attempts to both expose his emotional vulnerabilities and reconstitute his masculine identity for the changed society of postwar America. These two aims are seen to clash, ultimately because of the sense of repression that dominates Dave's unfamiliar environment. His demonstrations of machismo are a feature of his initial encounter with Gwen. Dave denies her the kind of objective distance she expects as a teacher when he asks her suggestively, "Would you like to teach *me?*" and invokes the kind of childlike imagery he will later resist. His crude sexual advances toward Gwen at the country club, when he pulls her closer to him on the dance floor and later invites her to his hotel room to look over his manuscript, are out of sync with the middle-class respectability of his companion and their environment. Gwen is a product of her educated, cultured upbringing, living on an estate with her father where books line the walls and a Canaletto hangs in the hallway. As the marriage of Frank and Agnes suggests, relationships in this world are marked by emotional and sexual repression. While Gwen expresses great interest in Dave's talent as a writer, she is reluctant to reveal her feelings for him as a man. Significantly, it is only after reading Dave's short story that she momentarily succumbs to his advances. This encounter takes place in the more natural setting of a wooden shack on the grounds of her father's home, with wild rabbits running past outside. Stripped of the accoutrements of her socially engineered repression, Gwen finally responds to Dave's unconstrained masculinity.

As Kaja Silverman notes, in *The Best Years of Our Lives* Peggy's attraction to Fred develops as a result of the emotional frailty with which he is associated, from his nightmares about the war, to the demeaning treatment he suffers in the drugstore, to his crumbling marriage. Her decision to pursue a relationship with Fred evidences her attraction to his weakness, "revealing in the process her investment not only in the former bombardier, but in the disintegration he increasingly comes to represent."[67] Similarly, in *The Manchurian Candidate,* Eugenie, or "Rosie," played by Janet Leigh, is attracted to Korean War veteran Bennett Marco (Sinatra), having observed the stranger's panic attack on a train journey. Gwen has already passed comment on Dave's first "more or less auto-biographical" novel as "a really powerful study of rejection." Unsure of his talent as a writer (he denies he even is a writer anymore at their first meeting), Dave exposes his vulnerabilities by requesting Gwen's assessment of his work. Her admission that his written words moved her to rare tears is a preface to her emotional and physical response.

However, the couple soon resumes their distant relationship as Gwen retreats from the displays of passion she labels "violence" and returns to intellectualizing her attraction to Dave. Dave takes a physically demonstrative approach, attempting to move Gwen closer to him as he pleads with her to reveal her feelings. In contrast, Gwen's controlled physical stance mirrors her desire to retain objectivity as she returns all conversation to Dave's work. The middle-class postwar society Gwen inhabits values Frank's lack of emotional and physical passion as evidence of adult masculinity, even if this belies an adulterous reality. Dave's open expressiveness is therefore viewed as immaturity, as several of Gwen's remarks suggest. When Dave appears upset at her insistence that she has no interest in "this sort of relationship," Gwen censures him, "Don't act like a little boy who's been slapped." When he repeats his desire to marry Gwen and proceeds to kiss her, the following exchange takes place:

> *Gwen:* "We'll have no more of that. I'm not one of your barroom tarts."
> *Dave:* "You're right, teacher. You're a hundred percent right. I've been a bad boy. I've been naughty. As a matter of fact, I don't even belong in your class."
> *Gwen:* "Quite possibly you don't."
> *Dave:* "Well, you won't get a chance to flunk me again."

Dave's use of the word "class" references Gwen's judgment of his emotional expressiveness as immature, as well as his alienation from the image of ideal male identity projected by her social class. Despite Gwen's assessment of Dave as lacking maturity, and Dave's own attempt to assimilate by abstaining from alcohol during their brief courtship, the film displays a postwar ambivalence toward male maturity. In addition to the negative portrayal of Frank, which suggests hegemonic masculinity to be severely flawed, Frank's own dissatisfaction with the compromises required for maturity comes in his confession to his secretary, Edith, that he feels old, "especially when I'm sitting next to an attractive young girl like you." Frank's mature male identity is socially desirable but ultimately unfulfilling.

Much of the discourse around the new male stars of the 1950s, epitomized by Clift, Brando, and Dean, circulated around notions of maturity. Sidney Skolsky's article for a 1957 edition of *Photoplay* set out to discuss "The New Look in Hollywood Men." Referring to the temperamental behavior of stars such as Anthony Perkins, Elvis Presley, and Brando, Skolsky writes: "The current movie heroes are boys trying to do a man's work. Most of them are adolescent, and this applies regardless of age. These heroes include boys who'd like to be men."[68] The stars' immature images are bound up in the kind of emotional intensity displayed by Montgomery Clift, whom Skolsky describes as "serious, moody, an individualist to the core."[69] In *The Young Lions* (1958), when Hope Plowman (Hope Lang) explains to her father her attraction to Noah Ackerman (Clift), telling him, "He's not just a man; he's a boy," the film draws on the sexual appeal of Clift's boyish sensitivity developed across roles such as George Eastman in *A Place in the Sun* (1951) and Robert E. Lee Prewitt in *From Here to Eternity.*

As is clear from Sinatra's musical characterizations of male vulnerability, Sinatra's star image disrupts direct connections made between emotionally expressive masculinity and immaturity, providing instead a new version of adult male identity. Similarly, Dave Hirsh resists definition in nonadult terms, taking on a paternal advisory role toward his niece, and by the end of the film acting as protector to Ginny. Even Bama is driven to remark on Dave's passive behavior as he waits for Gwen to telephone: "You ain't acting like no grown up man." Dave's response, "And how have you been?," questions Bama's own displays of machismo, which go on to land him in hospital with a broken arm caused by a fight and a bad case of diabetes exacerbated by excessive drinking.

Dave's mix of machismo and emotional frailty therefore appears as the film's most authentic representation of adult masculinity, an authenticity given added weight by the fact that Dave is the film's sole male participant in the war. Within this social framework, however, the veteran's machismo is still viewed as a sign of immaturity, and Dave's lifestyle is given as the reason for Gwen's ultimate dismissal of him: "I don't like your life. I don't like your thinking. I don't like the people you like. Now leave me alone. Stay away from me." Even though Dave's temporary abstinence from alcohol signals his willingness to conform to Gwen's notion of adult masculinity, she still rejects him. It seems significant that Gwen's father is able to see beyond the superficial in relation to Dave's lifestyle, the generational difference suggesting he is less affected by transient social attitudes. His recognition early on that "it isn't immediately apparent, but he's an extremely sensitive man," and his active encouragement of Dave's relationship with his daughter, however, have little impact.

By moving back and forth between Gwen and Ginny, Dave makes clear the dislocation that his complex brand of masculinity represents. As in *The Man with the Golden Arm*, Elmer Bernstein's dramatic score emphasizes the emotional instability of Sinatra's character in these pivotal scenes. Following each of Gwen's cold rejections, Dave finds succor in his relationship with Ginny. After their initial countryclub outing, Dave meets up with Ginny at Smitty's. And having been scolded by Gwen as a "little boy," Dave returns to Bama's home, where Ginny jumps straight into his arms. The contrasting ways in which the two women relate physically to Dave illustrate their varying abilities to connect with him emotionally. Gwen's severe expressions, assisted by having her hair tied tightly back, as she constantly moves away from Dave, hands by her side, are wholly dissimilar to Ginny's excited smiles when he returns home. Ginny's desire for his affection comes across in her need for physical closeness as she follows him from room to room and even into a wardrobe. While Gwen threatens to call the police if Dave puts his hands on her again, Ginny explains to her rival: "He just touches me and I fall apart."

Dave's ultimate decision to attempt a permanent relationship with Ginny is unsatisfying and reflects the narrative's lack of resolution with regard to postwar society's acceptance of Dave's complex male identity. Having been summarily dismissed by Gwen, Dave vents his anger on Ginny, berating her for her lack of intelligence and moral looseness. Bama's suggestion that Gwen has acted as a bad influence on Dave, his temperance adversely affecting his mood, sends Dave directly to a bottle of Scotch and to the woman who accepts his displays of machismo as part of his male persona. As he shakes his head and mutters, "Dames!"— in a very Sinatra-like manner—Dave reaches out again to Ginny, who makes two statements that differentiate her wholly from Gwen. Gwen's earlier request to Dave that he not be in love with her is in contrast with Ginny's plea to Dave to "be in love with *me*." Ginny's comment "I love you, but I don't understand you; now what's the matter with that?" provokes Dave's proposal of marriage and moves him to choose emotional sustenance above Gwen's intellectual approach to relationships. By deciding to marry Ginny, Dave reveals not only his need for the place of comfort she provides but also his desire to demonstrate a sense of male protectiveness, which Ginny's own frailties will allow him to do. When Bama expresses his consternation at Dave's decision, Dave explains, "I'm just tired of being lonely, that's all, and the way she feels about me, well, nobody ever felt that way about me before. And besides, maybe I can help her. I sure can't help myself."

Ironically, it is Ginny who ends up shielding Dave from Raymond's gunshots and being killed in the process. The chaos and garish style of the fairground scene depict the excess lurking beneath the surface of respectable postwar society, and it is in this arena, created by Frank, who has been organizing the centenary celebrations, that Dave's attempt to achieve emotional security with Ginny is ended. The final scene, in which the town reunites for Ginny's funeral, intimates a resolution of the social differences that have dominated the film. Yet there is still little to suggest that Dave's combination of machismo and emotional vulnerability will find acceptance in this community. Dave's attempt in his relationship with Ginny to dismiss his need for intellectual stimulation in favor of emotional expression also suggests a failure to fully reconcile the various elements of his masculine identity.

Sinatra's World War II veterans represent emotional vulnerability as an integral element of the postwar American male's identity. The characters' unfamiliar combination of machismo and emotional damage makes problematic their assimilation in postwar society, where they conflict with notions of ideal masculinity. In contrast to stars such as Brando and Clift, Sinatra resists associations of immaturity and sexual ambiguity that frequently circulate around emotionally expressive male images. Moving beyond the feminizing effect of his early music and film performances, Sinatra's 1950s recordings and album covers construct a persona that expresses emotional frailty in an urban masculine context. Building intertextually, Sinatra's emotionally vulnerable male persona reconstructs male identity in the postwar era as a complex mix of traits that breaks down traditional gender definitions and illustrates the broad nature of masculine identity.

5 Male Performance and Swingin' Bachelors

> Frank Sinatra is the most complete, the most fantastic symbol of American maleness yet discovered, for both good and bad reasons. . . . For example, if there is a *Marlboro Man,* who has a tattoo on his right wrist and rides herd or fishes trout, he is nothing compared to the *Chesterfield Man* . . . who looks at women as if he knew what they were all about, dresses, walks and talks as if he didn't care what they thought and lives as if the world and its women were pretty much built for him. He cuts, as we say, the *Marlboro Man,* that is, unless you dig fish and horses better than women, which is a sad state some times commented on by the more understanding writers of our generation.
>
> —Bill Coss

Bill Coss's hyperbolic summation of Sinatra's masculine image, published in *Metronome* in December 1957, was a response to the star's appearances on the early editions of *The Frank Sinatra Show.* The ABC series was sponsored by Chesterfield cigarettes, a brand that in-show vignettes suggested was prepared by the "Men of America" for the smoking pleasure of affluent urban consumers. Magazine advertisements for Chesterfield featuring Dean Martin and Jerry Lewis and Ronald Reagan stressed, respectively, the cigarette's mildness or the suitability of Chesterfield cartons as Christmas presents. In contrast, tie-ins with Sinatra's television series used "On the set with Sinatra" storyboards to relay the tuxedoed star's comments on the "man-size satisfaction" and "big, big pleasure" delivered by Chesterfield's product.[1]

Coss's description of Sinatra as a kind of midcentury "über-male" draws on the sense of potent urban sexuality that Chesterfield promotes, pitching Sinatra as a stylish, sophisticated contrast to the nature-loving loner of the Marlboro campaign. The television shows, which frequently opened with Sinatra appearing, raincoat over his shoulder, to the strains of "The Tender Trap," presented the star as the epitome of confident, hip virility. Yet the screen characterizations of swingin' bachelorhood evoked by this imagery relate as much to the complex ambiguities with which Sinatra's early image is branded as to the model of unmarried masculinity provided by *Playboy* magazine.

Sinatra's image of male heterosexuality is examined in this chapter as it develops from the vocal eroticism of the 1940s to the bachelor lifestyle of the 1950s. Despite the distinct differences that seem to exist in the sexual imaging of Sinatra through these two periods, the issues of performance and sexual objectification that lie at the core of Sinatra's swinger image are established as part of his early persona. The process of fetishization that occurs around Sinatra's voice combines with the singer's erotic performance style to initiate an image of the star as an object of desire, providing an unconventional male persona on which Sinatra's early screen roles draw. Much of the feminist debate around the cinematic representation of male and female performers contends that female stars alone are positioned as erotic objects, or, as in the case of Mary Ann Doane, concedes the possibility of male objectification while viewing such instances as mere "aberrations whose acknowledgement simply reinforces the dominant system of aligning sexual difference with a subject/object dichotomy."[2] Analyses of genres such as the epic and the musical, however, which clearly draw attention to the display of the male body, complicate this type of strictly defined positioning. Similarly, Sinatra's consistently objectified status has implications for the image of male sexuality his characters reveal.

Sinatra's sexual image becomes, in fact, a complex negotiation of male and female positionings that reconstructs male heterosexual masculinity in more rounded terms. Although Sinatra seems, in many ways, to epitomize the idea of the swingin' bachelor in the 1950s, lauded by *Playboy* magazine for his sexual exploits, and consistently playing hip, single urban men on film, *Playboy's* own ambivalence toward aspects of Sinatra's star image demonstrates the extent to which the star strays from this male model. Similarly, the roles that connect Sinatra most closely to this persona draw on the physical and class inadequacies surrounding the star to bring complexity to the figure of the swinger.

A variety of misreadings have occurred around the genres that play host to this type of male character and, more specifically, around Sinatra's films. For example, Bruce Babington and Peter William Evans describe the romantic comedies of the late 1950s and early 1960s as "the conformist comedies of a conformist era."[3] On the contrary, however, *The Tender Trap,* one of the first of this trend of films, represents a modern take on sexual relations, exposing the social construction of gender positions and, at the same time, drawing on Sinatra's building image as a swingin' star. Where the issue of performance arises around other male stars of this period and may suggest an undercurrent of homosexuality, Sinatra's role in *The Tender Trap* uses allusions to performance to challenge the notion of hypermale virility as a natural identity. *Pal Joey* provides the most famous visual image of Sinatra's swinger, hand touching his angled fedora, raincoat over his shoulder, and looking confidently toward his audience. A superficial reading of Joey Evans may view the character as epitomizing the playboy's predatory sexual arrogance. Richard Lippe, for example, sees Sinatra's performance largely as a celebration of masculine seduction: "*Pal Joey* endorses Sinatra's manipulation and exploitation of women but in contrast suggests that Hayworth, who attempts to counter his power position through tactics not dissimilar altogether from those he uses to satisfy his ego-centred needs, is 'unattractive.' Essentially, the film celebrates Sinatra's 'masculine' behaviour and holds Hayworth responsible for any unsavory connotations the narrative produces."[4] Lippe's analysis, however, skims the surface of a role that markedly moves away from conventional "masculine behaviour" and illuminates the relationship between sexual objectification and power through the context of a male character. As such, *Pal Joey* is highly representative of Sinatra's image of male sexuality, an image that constantly disrupts gender norms and challenges the simplicity of the playboy identity.

"Naked to the Larynx": The Voice and the Irrelevant Body

Sinatra's unconventional image of male sexuality initially builds around his voice, introducing the issues of performance and sexual objectification that will remain central to his masculine image. One psychologist's early theory on the reasons for Sinatra's popularity among young girls described the singer's style in terms of a dangerous asexuality that evidenced girls' fear of mature male sexuality. Poking gentle fun at Alice La Vere's conclusion that Sinatra's fans were "a bad marriage risk," *Down Beat* reported: "She says that girls who profess to find romance in the epicene (common to both sexes) voice of crooners are really running away from sexual truth. The kids, she added, are subconsciously driven by the desire to escape what seems gross and terrifying in males. They find a symbol of purity and sexlessness in crooners with choir boy voices."[5] La Vere's reading of Sinatra as a symbol of childlike sexual immaturity seems provoked by the airy "choir boy" tone of his voice and distinguishes him from the norms of adult male sexuality. Yet it conspicuously ignores Sinatra's sexually provocative singing style and his audiences' equally sexual response. Sinatra's use of *glissando,* curling notes at particular points during a song, which is apparent in recordings such as "You Go to My Head" and "Night and Day," injected an individualized sensuality into songs that on the surface were more about romance than sex.[6]

Recently released recordings confirm the reports of E. J. Kahn Jr. and Bruce Bliven that screams and "swooning," prompted by Sinatra's performance style, were a feature of the singer's live performances. Kahn wrote of Sinatra's young female fans: "They are reduced to helplessness by, for one thing, Sinatra's celebrated use of glissando; whenever he slides gently from one note to another, their admiration is exceedingly open-mouthed. They insist that they do not really scream but merely murmur 'Ooh' or 'Aah.'"[7] On the eve of Sinatra's televised concert at Madison Square Garden in October 1974, journalist Martha Weinman Lear recounted her experience of "swooning" during one of Sinatra's concerts at Boston's RKO Theatre in the mid-1940s. Refuting the theory propounded by sociologists that the physical and emotional vulnerability Sinatra conveyed provoked young girls' motherly instincts, the journalist analyzed her reaction to Sinatra:

> Look at him now, what do you see? A paunch, a jowl, a toupee. What could have driven me so crazy—the cuff links? But no, in the beginning he was no sartorial splendor. Suits hung oddly on him. Suits with impossible shoulders jutting like angle irons from that frail frame. . . . He had cabbage ears and the biggest damned Adam's apple you ever saw . . . So what drove me crazy? . . . The voice had that trick, you know, that funny little sliding, skimming slur that it would do coming off the end of a note. It drove us bonkers . . . whatever it's called, it was an invitation to hysteria. He'd give us that little slur—"All . . . or nothing at aallll . . ."—and we'd start swooning all over the place. . . . It was like pressing a button. It was pressing a button . . . the thing we had going with Frankie was sexy.[8]

Marking out the engagement between Sinatra and female audience members as fundamentally sexual, Weinman Lear highlights the knowing participation of both in the objectification of the star. The formation of Sinatra as an object of desire is key to the image that transfers to the screen and develops into the 1950s. Of central importance to this sexual image is the notion that Sinatra's objectified status is achieved through means other than his physicality.

While in the 1950s the issue of Sinatra's objectification is raised around the star's personalized style of dress, in the earlier decade Sinatra's sexuality is tied specifically to his voice. This emphasis on Sinatra's voice as the site of his sexuality results from both the singer's intentionally sensual vocal technique and the inadequacy of his physical make-up in terms of traditional heartthrob appeal. Commentators searching for reasons for the excesses of the audience response to Sinatra frequently focused on the question of Sinatra's lack of obvious physical attractiveness. In 1943 a *Newsweek* article, which expressed a lack of enthusiasm for Sinatra's voice, went on to query Sinatra's physical appeal, commenting: "As a visible male object of adulation Sinatra is even more baffling. He is undersized and looks underfed."[9] Dana Polan argues that as an unconventional object of desire, Sinatra destabilized notions of normative masculinity during World War II: "Significantly, part of the threat of Sinatra seems to reside in the sense that he doesn't correspond to traditional he-man norms. At the same time that the war effort claims to be turning men into heroes, Sinatra suggests that such a conversion may be the worst path to sexual attractiveness."[10] Polan rightly identifies the disruptive quality of Sinatra's male image during a period that valued the heroic use of masculine physical strength. Sinatra's appearance, however, goes further than to provide physical weakness as a new ideal of attractiveness. As Martha Weinman Lear's disdain for Sinatra's "frail frame" and "cabbage ears" reveals, female audiences were attracted to the singer despite, rather than because of, his physical inadequacies, making Sinatra's body largely irrelevant to his sexual appeal. The sobriquet "The Voice" only underlines the condensation of Sinatra into a bodyless version of male sexuality.

Parker Tyler's discussion of Sinatra in 1947 focused on the idea of the singer's powerful voice and frail body as two separate and seemingly incompatible entities. Comparing the relationship between Sinatra's voice and body to that of a ventriloquist and his dummy, Tyler accentuates the disconnection of the two in relation to the Sinatra aura.[11] Sinatra's origins as a voice to which a body was later added on the screen means that, for Tyler, Sinatra's sexuality remains located around his voice: "It makes little difference what songs he chooses or whether on the screen he is visible from the neck or the knees down. On his lips is the theme song of a boudoir Tarzan—not everything he might be in weight, it is true, but swinging, if the lady has a radio, from end to end of the Hit Parade and naked to the larynx."[12] Tyler's analysis articulates several factors that are central to Sinatra's image as a singer: that the image *is* highly sexual; that his sexuality circulates around his voice, almost to the exclusion of his body; and that Sinatra participates in his self-objectification, practicing male seduction (Tarzan) but ultimately positioning himself as an object of desire (naked to the larynx).[13]

As the site of his sexual appeal, Sinatra's voice therefore becomes fetishized, a process highlighted by the language of nudity used by Tyler and by the comments of a psychologist, whose reference to Sinatra performing "a sort of melodic strip tease in which he lays bare his soul"[14] supports the idea that the star's singing style, as well as being emotionally revealing, seeks a sexual response. Sinatra added to this fetishistic imaging with the bow ties that were a defining part of his early fashion style and which he regularly unraveled on stage, throwing them out to the audience. In this way, Sinatra can be compared to the "love goddesses" of World War II. Female stars such as Betty Grable and Rita Hayworth were defined as objects of desire through a fetishistic emphasis on, respectively, their legs or hair, acting as objects to which servicemen were able to direct masculine excess permissible in the war context. The use of Hayworth's image to adorn not only American fighter planes during World War II but additionally the H-bomb "Able Day," which was dropped on Bikini Atoll,[15] demonstrates the extent to which sexualized images of female stars reinforced the subject/object positions of masculinity and femininity. The sexual imagery surrounding Sinatra intervenes to disrupt the natural positioning implied by the frequent representation of female stars in this way. As a figure of masculinity on the home front, Sinatra provides a version of the "love goddess" for women, a kind of "love god," a term later used by *Playboy* magazine to describe Sinatra in terms of heightened sexual machismo but that here illustrates the star's deviance from the norms of gender positioning.[16] Reports of a request made by the crew of an American navy vessel for a photograph of Sinatra to pin on a bulkhead during the Bikini atom bomb tests only accentuate Sinatra's disruptive quality in relation to sexual imaging.[17]

Ziegfeld Boy: Role Reversal, Imaginary Relationships, and Glamour Shots

This distinctive sexual persona plays out in interesting ways in Sinatra's early film roles. The sexual naïveté most easily identifiable in the characters portrayed by Sinatra at RKO and MGM is introduced in his first film, *Higher and Higher,* in which Sinatra's relationship with Michèle Morgan's scullery maid extends only as far as waving to her each day across the courtyard. As one character remarks: "Well, guess you can't get into any trouble just waving." In *Step Lively,* the seductive power of a Sinatra vocal performance is drawn into the text by George Murphy as wheeler-dealer producer Gordon Miller, who, observing women reacting to an impromptu performance in a nightclub by Sinatra's playwright, comments, "If that guy was the Pied Piper of Hamlin, there wouldn't be a dame left in town." At MGM, however, Sinatra's roles display more of the complexities of Sinatra's image as it transfers to the cinema screen. Often playing the innocent pupil to Gene Kelly's navy "wolf," Sinatra's sexual immaturity contrasts directly with the worldliness of his costar's characters. Beyond this, however, issues of imaginary sexuality and objectification, prompted by the fetishization of Sinatra's voice and relegation of his body to inadequacy, are raised in a number of ways.

Sinatra and Kelly's second film together, *Take Me Out to the Ball Game,* best illustrates the cinematic development of Sinatra's sexual persona as it draws on factors stimulated by the star's prescreen image. Sinatra and Kelly play baseball players Dennis Ryan and Edward O'Brien, who spend the off-season playing the vaudeville circuit as song-and-dance men. Early scenes paint an already familiar picture of Sinatra's character as fearful of women. Therefore, when Ryan and O'Brien return for the start of the season and regale teammates with tales of their sexual conquests in the "The Boy Said No" number, the notion of imaginary sexuality is introduced around Sinatra. Recalling the "I Begged Her" routine in *Anchors Aweigh,* during which Sinatra and Kelly provide fellow servicemen with a similarly fictionalized account of their evening activities, the number creates a sense of unreality in relation to Sinatra's sexual persona.[18] The omission of names for Sinatra's love interests in both *Anchors Aweigh* (Pamela Britton) and *It Happened in Brooklyn* (Gloria Grahame) contributes further to the idea of sexual relationships that remain in the imaginary. One other highly symbolic scene in *Take Me Out to the Ball Game* references this illusory sexuality. Having serenaded the owner of the team, Katherine Higgins (Esther Williams), Ryan, whose idea of the perfect relationship is to marry a girl who plays baseball, engages in an imaginary game with his boss. As the two characters pass an invisible ball between them and feign touching base, the scene reiterates the imaginary nature of their relationship and of Ryan's, and Sinatra's, sexual persona.

The film additionally positions Sinatra as an objectified male, a space he occupies in most films of this period and, in more complex ways, through the 1950s. From his attempts to escape the amorous advances of a besotted bobby-soxer in *Higher and Higher*, to being chased by Betty Garrett around a taxicab on the streets of Manhattan in *On the Town*, Sinatra's characters are regularly on the receiving end of the attentions of predatory women. The implications this objectification has for traditional gender roles are spelled out in "I Begged Her," where Sinatra's part in the duet with Kelly reveals, "She begged me." As love interest Shirley in *Ball Game*, Betty Garrett again articulates both the sexual objectification of Sinatra and the reversal of roles that accompanies this displacement of sexual norms. Observing Ryan during a baseball game, Shirley is unimpressed by his appearance, asking, "Who's that skinny little runt?" When Ryan is injured by a single punch from a member of an opposing team (a recurring event in the film), Shirley picks him up and carries him over her shoulder to safety, signaling the reversal of roles by which their relationship will be defined. The film has some fun with psychologists' theory that the singing Sinatra provoked women's latent maternal feelings, as Shirley suggests about her tender treatment of the injured Ryan, "It's just the mother instinct." She is, however, soon seen in hot pursuit of Ryan around the bleachers, trying to convince him through song, "It's Fate, Baby, It's Fate."

Shirley openly claims the male role in her clearly sexual advances towards Ryan, sending him chocolates and flowers and inviting him to a clambake. Significantly, it is this relationship, with its disrupted sexual norms, that ultimately succeeds. Ryan's pursuit of Katherine, on the other hand, wherein he attempts to assume the traditional male role, is doomed to failure. The conspicuous objectification of Sinatra in the sequence during which Ryan attempts to strike up a relationship with Katherine signals his unnatural positioning in this traditional role. For example, when Katherine swims in the hotel pool, eagerly observed by Ryan, O'Brien, and Goldberg, who are watching from their hotel room, Williams assumes the conventional position of a female star set up to be viewed by both characters and audience. However, when Ryan is pushed out onto the balcony to attract her attention and prompted by his teammates to appear "nonchalant," Sinatra's pose, as he places his hand behind his head and juts out his chest, suggests an image comparable to a female star's glamour shot. Again, joining Katherine by the pool, Ryan/Sinatra serenades her with the song "The Right Girl for Me," taking up the role of active seducer. However, with Williams either out of shot or facing away from the camera, Sinatra becomes the objectified figure on screen. At one point leaning against a trellis, bathed in bright light and the sole focus of the camera, Sinatra is clearly glamorized in a style much more reminiscent of the treatment of female stars.

The scene recalls Sinatra's widely mocked appearance in the Jerome Kern biopic *Till the Clouds Roll By* (1946)—*Life* magazine described Sinatra's appearance as "a high point in bad taste"[19]—during which he performs "Ol' Man River." The scene is often derided today for its crass mismatching of a lyric concerned with the plight of blacks in the South with a cast dressed wholly in white. More interesting in relation to Sinatra's image, however, is the extent to which the scene resembles a Ziegfeld production number, complete with a stylized fantasy set, full orchestra, and numerous starlets. In the midst of such Hollywood glamour, however, Sinatra is given prime position, perched on top of a dais, his newly darkened hair accentuating the whiteness of his suit: the ultimate Ziegfeld Boy. Sinatra's screen playboys that hit the screen a decade later were not as distinct from this gender-crossing glamour-boy image as they might first appear. With an increasing focus on Sinatra's visual image, and with the physical and class inadequacies with which Sinatra is consistently branded, issues of performance and sexual objectification necessarily complicate the star's projection of male sexual bravado.

"What Manner of Love God Is This?": *Playboy* and the Definition of the Hip Bachelor

Toward the end of the 1960 musical *Can Can,* Judge Philippe Forestier, played by Louis Jordan, takes a final, alternative approach in his attempt to win the affections of Simone Pistache (Shirley MacLaine), the owner of the nightclub where the banned dance is performed. Ditching his subdued patrician style, Forestier transforms himself into an exaggerated version of his romantic rival, François Durnais, played by Sinatra. He explains to Simone: "You like flip, sophisticated fellows with a lot of fast answers. You like men who know how to make you laugh and then treat you badly. Well, that isn't so hard to learn." Having learned, the judge sports a suitably angled fedora, refers to Simone as his "little French pastry," and promises an evening during which they will "thrill the tourists at Maxim's." He concludes his courtship with a chorus of "It's All Right with Me," complete with *glissando,* hand gestures, and a final "Ring-a-ding ding ding." This deft caricature was, of course, of Sinatra, or, more accurately, Sinatra's swinger persona, rather than of *Can Can*'s French lawyer. There is, in fact, a multiplicity of performances on display here—Jordan plays Forestier impersonating Sinatra in his playboy persona as expressed through the character François Durnais— pointing to the extent to which ideas of performance underpin Sinatra's hip bachelor image. Equally, as Jordan's caricature suggests, the lessons to be learned in the playboy transformation have as much to do with an image of sophistication, projected through language, clothes, and lifestyle, as they do with a specific approach to sexual relations. While the advocate of the swingin' lifestyle, *Playboy* magazine, writes about Sinatra as the leading Hollywood version of its sophisticated, virile male, Sinatra's swinger is as much a performance as is the caricature provided by Jordan (or Forestier).

Through the 1960s, a further layer of performance would be added as Sinatra parodied (intentionally or otherwise) his playboy persona in roles such as *Come Blow Your Horn*'s (1963) middle-aged bachelor who tutors his younger brother in the ways of the world, and the cool private detective Tony Rome in *Tony Rome* (1967) and *Lady in Cement* (1968).[20] During the 1950s, however, Sinatra's image fails in a variety of ways to correspond with *Playboy*'s masculine model, or with other screen versions of this male type. Sinatra's inadequacy in meeting the conventions of an attractive male star, combined with the suggestions of imaginary sexuality that remain from his earlier roles, make performance a central component of his 1950s swinger. Sinatra is nevertheless perceived to be the ultimate hip bachelor, and his image therefore works to reveal the playboy itself as a constructed and performed figure.

Sinatra's first role as a romantically fickle bachelor was in the *Colgate Comedy Hour* television production of Cole Porter's "Anything Goes," which aired in November 1953. Appearing opposite unlikely costar Ethel Merman as nightclub singer Reno Sweeney, Sinatra plays Harry Dane, a showbiz agent who rebounds back and forth between pursuing Reno and rejecting her, while impersonating the infamous gangster "Angel Face" Nelson.[21] One month later, in December 1953, the first edition of *Playboy* hit the American newsstands, famously featuring Marilyn Monroe as its first centerfold. *Playboy,* through the guiding philosophy of founding editor Hugh Hefner, presented itself as a magazine for virile bachelors intent on escaping the trap of marriage. In 1954, *Playboy* advised single men how to avoid financially motivated, predatory women: "Woman has only one goal in life—marriage. . . . All woman wants is security. And she's perfectly willing to crush man's adventurous, freedom-loving spirit to get it. . . . The true playboy can enjoy the pleasures the female has to offer without becoming emotionally involved. Like the little bee, he flits from flower to flower, sipping the sweet nectars where he finds them, but never tarries too long at any one blossom."[22] However, the attempt to depict the single life as the male's "natural" state, as natural as the birds and the bees, masks the construction of a defined character for the playboy, a character that readers could learn to perform. Married readers could fantasize about a life far removed from suburban marriage, and single men could transform themselves into a model of hip virility, at the same time suggesting their newfound identity to be natural.

A determination to deny the extent to which alignment with *Playboy* masculinity might require an unnatural performance is evident in the magazine's claim that its readers were distinguished from the average American male in ways that went beyond a sexually liberal lifestyle. Responding in 1958 to a reader's complaint that the magazine failed to address "Mr. Average," one editorial claimed: "*Playboy* is edited for a special sort of guy—a bit above average in taste, education and income."[23] Another suggested that research revealed more than two-thirds of the magazine's readership to be college educated, while closer analysis showed less than 30 percent had been awarded a degree at the time of the survey.[24] Despite evidence to the contrary, *Playboy* credited its readership with an identity that was clearly defined as educated, white-collar professional, and superior in matters of taste. Hefner's subscription drive in the April 1956 issue of the magazine set out in clear terms the type of man to whom *Playboy* was directed:

> What is a playboy? Is he simply a wastrel, a ne'er-do-well, a fashionable bum? Far from it: he can be a sharp-minded young business executive, a worker in the arts, a university professor, an architect or engineer. He can be many things, providing he possesses a certain point of view. He must see life not as a vale of tears, but as a happy time; he must take joy in his work, without regarding it as the end and all of living; he must be an alert man, an aware man, a man of taste, a man sensitive to pleasure, a man who—without acquiring the stigma of voluptuary or dilettante—can live life to the hilt. This is the sort of man we mean when we use the word playboy.[25]

Hefner defined the playboy as strictly upper middle class, a work-hard, play-hard model of the modern urban bachelor, creating a male figure that bore a close resemblance to its married suburban counterpart in terms of class and professional aspirations.

As Barbara Ehrenreich's examination of *Playboy* reveals, the magazine's consumerist agenda connected in similar ways with the surrounding culture, differing only in the uses to which the playboy's money would be put. *Playboy*'s rebellion against marriage was expressed, in part, by encouraging its readers to enjoy their freedom from the financial demands of a wife by embarking on their own journey of conspicuous consumption from the base of their urban apartments. *Playboy* pointed them toward consumer items suited to their lifestyle, as Ehrenreich puts it: "not the power lawn mower, but the hi-fi set in mahogany console; not the sedate, four-door Buick, but the racy little Triumph; not the well-groomed wife, but the classy companion who could be rented (for the price of drinks and dinner) one night at a time."[26] As part of this consumerist agenda, *Playboy*'s approach to men's fashion is significant in reiterating its upper-middle-class identity. This strictly defined identity and its expression through style of dress becomes one of the ways in which Sinatra's swinger persona is distinguished from the *Playboy* model. In addition, the magazine's didacticism in relation to clothes exposes the need to school its readers in the performance of the hip urban bachelor.

As Becky Conekin's research illustrates, just as the magazine advised its readers on how to decorate their city apartments and which stereo to purchase, budding playboys were steered toward a fashion look that consisted of blazers and crew necks and eschewed European or Hollywood-style influences, or "the kind of gruesome garbage . . . touted as the hottest news from Majorca, the Italian Riviera, Cap d'Antibes and Southern California."[27] The magazine's first fashion editor, Jack Kessie (under the pseudonym Blake Rutherford), promoted a distinctly Ivy League style, implying that readers who were without the benefit of a top college education could create the circumstances for professional progress by adopting the style markers of this narrowly defined male identity. Writing in January 1955, Kessie made clear that a sense of understatement was key to the look: "Conservative in all departments we lean heavily towards those distinctive details of styling that point up the man as being *quietly* well dressed."[28] Readers were therefore instructed to aim to achieve a modern take on conventional styling, which would distinguish them from their elders and yet maintain a strong link with traditional, often English-inspired tailoring. The reader's transformation should all the while be presented as part of the natural maturing process. As Conekin remarks: "Nobody need know how recently the playboy had come by these marks of distinction."[29] This focus on class-based style and its naturalization set *Playboy* apart from the star the magazine nevertheless described as "surely the hippest of the hip."[30]

Sinatra was undoubtedly *Playboy*'s favorite male singer during the 1950s. He regularly topped the magazine's Annual Jazz Poll as the preferred male vocalist of both readers and musicians[31] and was frequently described as the Hollywood embodiment of the hip bachelor. In 1960, *Playboy* published an account of the filming of *Ocean's Eleven* and the Rat Pack's simultaneous nightly shows at The Sands in Las Vegas, terming the stars collectively "the innest in-group in the world."[32] Focusing on Sinatra in 1958, *Playboy* was moved to similar superlatives, contending that Sinatra "*is* a love god and no mistake—a bona fide sex idol, with the stamp of his epoch upon him. . . . It is doubtful that anyone, anywhere, makes out any better than Sinatra."[33] *Playboy* defines Sinatra as a thoroughly modern model of virility—its version of a "love god"— idealized for his sexually liberal lifestyle. The magazine connects Sinatra to its bachelor identity through reference to his sexuality and visual style, constructing him as both a figure of aspiration for men and an object of desire for women: "Hat set cockily on the back of his head, raincoat draped carelessly over a bony shoulder, this hip brand of love god, so different from the lush and limpid-eyed love gods of yore, casually ambles into the phantasies of females young and old, dances on the ceilings near their beds, bids them come fly with him down to Acapulco Bay. And if the real Sinatra were to make the offer, a goodly number would hop at the opportunity."[34] The combination of visual image, musical identity, and biography, *Playboy* suggests, authenticates Sinatra's swinger persona. At the same time, remaining consistent with commentary around Sinatra, the magazine feels the need to investigate the reasons for his appeal, a need prompted in part by *Playboy*'s WASP-inspired style conservatism: "He has none of the Latin mystery of a Valentino or the distingué hauteur of a Barrymore. He is, in fact, short and slight (140 pounds, including hair pieces). His face and neck still show the scars from the forceps used in a difficult birth. . . . He tends to overdress, with suits cut a bit too sharp and Windsor-wide knots in his ties. What manner of love god is this?"[35] As it settles on the dynamism of Sinatra's "personality" as the key to his success, *Playboy*'s confusion is, nevertheless, an indication of Sinatra's distinction from the bachelor figure that the magazine came to represent. Sinatra's personality becomes the means through which *Playboy* attempts to overcome some aspects of the star's image that are more troubling in terms of its definition of the urban single male. *Playboy*'s reference to Sinatra's tendency to "overdress" has all the undertones of class and ethnic prejudice that *Time* magazine expressed in its description of Sinatra's "George Raft kind of snazziness"[36] and immediately distances the star visually from *Playboy*'s bachelor model. Similarly, by detailing the inadequacy of Sinatra's appearance, going so far as to draw attention to his hairpieces, the article undermines Sinatra's male identity, even in the context of its use of superlatives around his sexuality. Even to *Playboy*, Sinatra's individualistic style betrays his working-class Italian American roots, and his unremarkable looks make his sexual appeal surprising. As *Playboy* usefully demonstrates, while the perception of Sinatra is often as the ultimate version of the 1950s' virile, hip urban male, a variety of issues work to complicate the simplicity of this image. In *The Tender Trap* and *Pal Joey*, issues of performance and objectification come to the fore, with the result that the decade's number-one swinger challenges the very notion that the urban playboy is anything more than a carefully constructed image.

"Plain Joker Like Me": Performance and Modern Sexual Relations in *The Tender Trap*

As *Playboy*'s consideration of Sinatra suggests, the star's swinger persona appears to be authenticated by its sheer consistency across the various media and by biographical insights into Sinatra's lifestyle. An article published by *Uncensored* in 1959, which detailed the course of one of his affairs, assured readers of Sinatra's insistent bachelor status, or, as the article put it: "When ladies pine for a vine-covered cottage with Frankie they wind up with the gate."[37] Capitol albums such as *Songs for Swingin' Lovers!, Come Fly with Me, A Swingin' Affair!* (1956), and *Sinatra's Swingin' Session!!* (1960) projected a sense of enthusiastic romance reiterated by the use of exclamation marks. The fun-loving optimism of the music was echoed on covers for albums such as *Come Fly with Me*, showing a smiling Sinatra surrounded by airplanes, framed by a bright blue sky, and holding the bejeweled hand of a woman who remains out of shot. Just as albums such as *In the Wee Small Hours* create a character through a marriage of lyrics and visual imagery, songs such as "Let's Get Away from It All" and "Come Fly with Me" create Sinatra's lifestyle image as a jet-setting romantic adventurer, which biographical commentary appears to confirm.

Similarly, Sinatra's adoption of this persona for his television shows has the effect of naturalizing the swinger image. His appearances on *The Frank Sinatra Show* occur outside the context of a film or album cover and therefore seem to present the "real" Frank Sinatra. Yet here, too, Sinatra is engaged in a performance, firstly as a television host, and additionally as a character who closely resembles his roles in *The Tender Trap* and *Pal Joey*. This persona is clearly marked out as a performance by the cinematic links Sinatra often makes. Opening shows in a Joey Evans–style pose, raincoat over his shoulder, to the musical accompaniment of "The Tender Trap," with cameras and crew exposed to the audience, Sinatra highlights connections with his screen characters that underline his swinger persona as a performance.[38]

The identification of Sinatra's swingin' bachelor as a performance has the effect of destabilizing the playboy masculinity of the characters with which this image is associated. While Charlie Reader and Joey Evans appear to be archetypes of the virile urban bachelor, the notion of the swinger as a natural identity for the American male is disrupted by the sense of performance that accompanies Sinatra's persona. Most discussions of performance in relation to the Hollywood playboy focus on the issue of disputed sexuality provoked by the best-known screen depiction of the 1950s bachelor lifestyle, the Rock Hudson/Doris Day romantic comedy *Pillow Talk* (1959). Cynthia Fuchs, for example, views the use of split screens as a demonstration of the film's disruption of gender but also sexual stereotypes. Brad Allen and Jan Morrow's taxi ride home following their first face-to-face encounter, during which their private thoughts are revealed to the audience as a stark contrast to their conversation, becomes a moment where the pair "collaborate in a flamboyant performance of heterosexual courtship, in effect 'passing' as a straight couple."[39] Steven Cohan argues that the bachelor's insistent heterosexuality as portrayed in *Pillow Talk* masks the threat of an underlying homosexuality. This "masculine masquerade," he contends, is revealed through a number of means, including Brad Allen's alter ego, Rex Stetson, and the suggestions of homosexuality that are set up around him, his more effete friend Jonathan Forbes (Tony Randall), and through the impact of Hudson's star image, which the actor's resolute bachelorhood had made troubling.

In addition, Cohan examines the significance of the urban bachelor's apartment, where divisions of public and private space allow for a performance of heterosexuality and a private expression of homosexuality. Cohan suggests that the separation of the playboy apartment into a public space or "active zone" (kitchen, dining room, and living room) and a private space or "quiet zone" (bedroom, bathroom, and study)—as defined by a two-part article published in *Playboy* in 1956—represents a division of the bachelor's sexuality and a masking of one element of the male identity. Cohan explains: "If the outer sphere of the apartment, with its orientation toward entertaining and exhibitionism, can be said to theatricalize bachelorhood as a public spectacle, then the inner sphere, with its connotation of shelter and security, can as easily be seen enclosing bachelorhood in a closet, that invisible edifice constructed to contain homosexuality entirely within the 'quiet zone' of culture, so to speak."[40] The extent to which dual identities and different versions of masculinity govern the narrative of *Pillow Talk* makes an analysis that focuses on a problematized heterosexuality almost unavoidable. In the case of *The Tender Trap,* however, performance revolves around quite different factors while drawing on Sinatra's star image. As Sinatra's objectification and modern images of female sexuality come into play, gender positions in relation to sexual relations are exposed as more socially constructed than natural, and masculine and feminine stereotypes are disturbed into less stable identities. Appearing just two years after the birth of *Playboy, The Tender Trap* references most closely the initial temper of the magazine while revealing the performativity of the confident virility of the hip urban bachelor.

The precredits opening sequence of *The Tender Trap* spells out the extent to which this will be an identifiably Sinatra styling of 1950s bachelorhood. Amid a desert background framed by blue skies and singing the title song, Sinatra saunters toward the front of the screen, swaying to the beat of the music, hands in the pockets of his light gray suit, wearing a fedora with the flourish of a white ribbon. This opening, which occurs outside the narrative, presents what had already become a recognizable visual image of Sinatra as well as draws on the idea of a swingin' lifestyle introduced by his performance of early Capitol songs such as "South of the Border" and "I'm Gonna Live till I Die," if not yet by a complete mood album. Sinatra's scat singing that accompanies the titles reinforces the sense of easygoing nonconformity that surrounds Sinatra's swinger persona. At the same time, the clear invocation of this persona implies that the film's characterization of the playboy will be affected by the complexities of Sinatra's star image, making Sinatra's return to MGM, after six years, closer in tone to his earlier performances with the studio than it at first appears. The title song, while performed in Sinatra's relaxed style of the period, reveals through its lyrics *The Tender Trap*'s narrative take on sexual relations, like *Playboy,* warning bachelors about a female obsession with marriage:

> Some starry night
> When her kisses make you tingle
> She'll hold you tight
> And you'll hate yourself for being single.

Marriage as a trap set by women into which unsuspecting bachelors fall roughly describes the narrative trajectory of the film. Its diverse depictions of male/female relationships, however, serve to complicate this polarized positioning of midcentury bachelorhood and marriage.

The lifestyle of Broadway theatrical agent Charlie Reader (Sinatra) is introduced in the first scene as the camera closes in on Charlie and his female companion Poppy (Lola Albright) "making out" on the sofa of his dimly lit apartment. The significance of Charlie's sexual performance as a marker of his masculinity is made clear when Poppy's sighs provoke his question "Is that the best you've got to say?" and the further comment "You can do better 'n that." Charlie's performance is brought to a halt by the unexpected arrival of old school friend Joe McCall (David Wayne), whose telegram has remained unopened amid the phone messages and unemptied ashtrays on Charlie's desk. Joe has been dispatched from Indianapolis to New York by his wife, Ethel, in the hope that a fortnight's break from each other will reinvigorate their eleven-year marriage. His stale relationship leads him to initially envy Charlie for his stylish apartment with a view of the Brooklyn Bridge, and for the stream of women who visit in steady succession, eager to cater to Charlie's domestic needs and sexual desires. Through the course of the film, Joe becomes embroiled in his own illicit relationship with one of Charlie's part-time lovers, Sylvia Crewes (Celeste Holm), but he is soon morally repulsed by Charlie's cavalier treatment of the women with whom he surrounds himself and, like Charlie, is ultimately saved from himself by marriage.

Postwar films such as *The Seven Year Itch* (1955), *Kiss Me, Stupid* (1964), and *Boys' Night Out* (1962) draw on the idea of the playboy lifestyle as the married man's fantasy, often making specific reference to a version of *Playboy* to give context to the male identity on show. In *The Seven Year Itch,* Tom Ewell plays a publisher who imagines himself living out the fantasies summoned up by an unpublished manuscript, "The Repressed Urge of the Middle-Aged Male." Left alone in the city while his wife and son spend the summer in the country, Ewell creates a fantasy figure out of Marilyn Monroe, the blonde who rents the apartment upstairs but is never given a name and whose "artistic" photograph appears in *US Camera* just as Monroe's did in *Playboy*. *Kiss Me, Stupid* plays with Dean Martin's swinger image, when the star is stranded in a small town where a couple of local songwriters attempt to plug their songs to him. Martin is the ultimate bachelor to Orville (Ray Walston), whose wife accuses him of reading *Playboy* and who likes to term himself a "swinger." In *Boys' Night Out,* three married men and one divorcé (James Garner), who make the daily train journey from the suburbs to their jobs in New York, hatch a plan to share the rent on a city apartment where they hope to install a fully paid-for female companion. Following the instructions given to them in an article in *Play-Mate* on "Ten Things Every Ideal Bachelor Pad Should Have," they place an advertisement for a "blonde, attractive companion" but mistakenly loan out their apartment to a sociology doctoral candidate played by Kim Novak, who surreptitiously observes them as part of her research for a book titled "The Adolescent Sexual Fantasies of the Adult Suburban Male." Novak succeeds in restricting the men to the less dangerous fancies of DIY and high-fat home-cooked meals because, as Novak tells her professor: "It's the modern pipe dream, doctor. Every book, every magazine, every ad, every movie they see. . . . The whole thing is a fantasy. Why, they don't really want this adventure. They've been sold that they're supposed to want it." *The Tender Trap* goes further, to suggest that even the single man secretly craves a more settled existence than the lifestyle he has been "sold."

In the early scenes of the film, Joe is transported into the married man's fantasyland. Poppy's premature departure is followed by the arrival of Jessica (Jarma Lewis), bearing a Wisconsin cheese and offering to spring-clean the apartment; neighbor Helen (Carolyn Jones), who collects Charlie's dog for his daily walk; and later Sylvia, who "hardly cleans up at all." Joe's incredulous reaction to this constant flow of attractive women points to Charlie's natural incompatibility with his identity as a playboy and additionally suggests that the single male's fantasy may be something other than bachelorhood. Joe asks his old friend, "Tell me one thing. How come you rate with girls like that?" Charlie's explanation— "Because I'm big and strong and fat"—is clearly flippant and is refuted by audience awareness of Sinatra's physique and the confirmation of his physical inadequacies when Charlie removes his shirt before taking a shower. When a further invitation comes via a phone call, Joe continues to probe: "Boy, what have you got?" Charlie's reply is revealing: "It's not what I've got, Joe. It's what I haven't got: a wife." His success with attractive women results from lack rather than hypermasculinity. Charlie explains that in New York, the games of sexual attraction are conducted in a fashion incomparable to the traditional rules of romance back in Indiana. He tells Joe: "They got a kind of an underground here. As soon as a bachelor sets foot in this town, the signals go out. And even before you get your bag unpacked, you're up to there in dames. Look, it's wonderful. Plain joker like me. I've got dames I haven't even called yet." Charlie's explanation introduces the idea of urban women as sexual predators. As one of New York's few eligible single men, Charlie insists his swingin' lifestyle has been forced upon him by the demands of the city's single women and that his physical mediocrity fails to equate with his level of success (Figure 8).

The conversation between the two school friends further confirms that Charlie is not a natural playboy. Joe's remarks about the women who flow in and out of Charlie's apartment provoke a response from Charlie that suggests his insecurity in his bachelor identity: "Don't think you're gonna beat my time with them the way you did with all the others." Their talk returns them to the junior prom, when Charlie, as he tells it, made the mistake of choosing a statuesque dancing partner rather than Ethel, a decision that led to a failed paternity suit. Charlie's remarks suggest his bachelor status is the result of poor judgment rather than a positive lifestyle choice and that he covets his friend's married identity. His assertion—"I would be happy to trade this rat race for your set-up in two seconds"—suggests that the juggling required by his lifestyle is work in itself, a view that will be confirmed later in the film by his two simultaneous engagements. Charlie's envy of Joe's relationship is based on an idealized image of married life and fatherhood. He reveres Ethel and pictures her greeting Joe in an apron on his return from work while the children rush at him yelling, "Daddy." Charlie refuses to discard his Americana vision of marriage, despite Joe's counterimage, which includes Ethel's obsession with wall-to-wall carpeting and his children's constant round of fencing and finger-painting lessons. While Charlie is distanced from the reality of married life, his envy of Joe's relationship suggests an alternative fantasy and further destabilizes any idea of him as a natural playboy.

In addition, Charlie's lack of the physical credentials that would support his identity as a man in sexual demand makes him an unusual version of the swinger. Brandon French suggests that this characterization of Charlie is in contrast with Sinatra's star image. French argues: "We are not meant to see Charlie as an extraordinary fellow with sensational sex appeal (i.e. Charlie is not Frank Sinatra, although Sinatra plays the part)

Figure 8: Sinatra exposes his inadequate body as Charlie discusses with childhood friend Joe his surprising good fortune with the predatory females of New York. (*The Tender Trap*)

but as an ordinary fellow from Indiana—in other words, like any man in the film audience."[41] French recognizes Charlie's mediocrity; however, he misses the point that while Sinatra undoubtedly has considerable sexual allure, the role clearly draws on aspects of Sinatra's image through which his extraordinariness is lessened, even as he retains his persona as a swingin' bachelor. Contrary to *Playboy*'s image of its readership as in various ways superior, Charlie's description of himself as a "plain joker" makes clear that he views himself as "Mr. Average."

This brings into play consistent imaging around Sinatra that points to his ability to attract a multitude of women despite his physical inadequacies. As well as in *Playboy*'s analysis, this type of commentary is evident in magazines addressed to a female market. *Woman's Home Companion,* for example, published a two-part series of articles on Sinatra in 1956 that suggested: "In appearance Frank Sinatra lacks almost everything you'd expect of a movie star. His ears stick out. He has a scar on his neck. He is far from handsome in the conventional sense. And he doesn't have the build of a Burt Lancaster or a Rock Hudson."[42] At the same time, the article reinforces the image of Sinatra as an emotionally vulnerable male whose attractiveness to glamorous women is in little doubt, revealing: "Frank's name has been linked with a list of stars and glamour girls that reads like Who's Who in New York and Hollywood. Sometimes on the same day, in the same paper, gossip columnists will have him staggering under a torch for half a dozen different women. . . . Wherever Frank goes, there is usually a woman in the background, waiting for him to finish his business. At his duplex bachelor apartment in Westwood, Hollywood girls are always popping in (blonds, brunettes and redheads)—just like in *The Tender Trap*—ready to do little chores for him."[43] The article's attempt to make direct connections between Sinatra's lifestyle and that of Charlie Reader suggests an authentication of the swinger persona but, at the same time, indicates the extent to which the persona of both star and character is governed by performance. Alongside Sinatra's physical inadequacy, the idea of performance builds through the ways in which *The Tender Trap* represents masculine and feminine social roles.

As Cohan, Fuchs, and Frank Krutnik have all noted, in *Pillow Talk,* Brad Dexter's use of the metaphor of a tree being chopped down, "stripped of its bark," and reconstructed as a breakfast nook and baby crib represents bachelorhood as the natural male state and marriage as castration.[44] In *The Tender Trap,* Joe alludes several times to the treehouse Charlie was prone to falling out of as a child. When he first arrives, Joe comments that Charlie's apartment bears favorable comparison with his childhood playhouse, and he later warns Charlie about his relationship with Julie Gillis (Debbie Reynolds), likening Charlie's inevitable move toward marriage to falling out of the treehouse. As an attempt to replicate the domestic arena in the grounds of the family home, the semi-independent treehouse symbolizes Charlie's ambivalence toward married life, envying Joe's existence and at the same time reveling in his own. Similarly, Charlie's bachelor apartment demonstrates the common features of single and married masculinity. Charlie's apartment resembles the family home in a number of ways, from the prominent television set in the living room to the dog housed in the kitchen. It contains none of the switches and gadgets that enable swift seduction in *Pillow Talk,* and even though the sofa folds out into a bed, the only one to sleep on it is Joe. The focus of the apartment is the bar, which could suggest an alcohol-filled bachelor lifestyle but is actually another marker of familiar 1950s domesticity, as evidenced by the way in which Joe takes over bartending duties on his arrival, since, as a true inhabitant of the suburbs, he mixes a better martini. Charlie's apartment has none of the private spaces where, as Steven Cohan suggests, the bachelor is able to express the natural masculinity he masks in public. As Poppy tidies her hair in the bedroom, Joe observes Charlie preparing himself for a date in the bathroom, and Helen strolls in and out of the kitchen to collect and return the dog, every area of Charlie's domestic life is exposed to scrutiny. Instead of enabling a performance of playboy masculinity that hides a desire for marriage, or, as Cohan argues, a performance of heterosexuality that masks a natural homosexuality, Charlie's apartment openly reveals the significance of both bachelor and husband personae as part of his male identity.

The lack of flamboyance in Charlie's apartment also serves to accentuate the character's personal style. The neutral colors in the apartment emphasize Charlie's orange shirt, his red sweater, the wide sashes on his fedoras, and his immaculate tuxedo. (Joe, in contrast, does not even own a tuxedo.) The focus on style during Sinatra's multiple costume changes references *Playboy*'s attention to men's fashion, and draws on the extra individualism of Sinatra's personal image. The objectification of Sinatra as a singer on stage and through his earlier screen roles comes into play as the audience is given a rare shot of Sinatra's bare torso. Charlie is admired by his dates, so that when he presents himself in a tuxedo to a waiting Sylvia and he twirls and declares, "And there you are," she responds, "My, but don't you look pretty." This objectification is representative of the deconstruction of male/female relations that occurs through Charlie's relationships. In some ways, the women's admiration for Charlie as an object of desire is aligned with *Playboy*'s definition of the hip bachelor as a man who attracts women without too much effort. Charlie's various companions therefore call to collect him at his apartment, and Jessica leaves him each time with a parting comment on his sexual performance: "Tiger!" Yet the way in which these women relate to Charlie is also a marker of the social construction of gender roles, their relationships with Charlie illuminating postwar changes in sexual relations. Frank Krutnik argues that 1950s and 1960s comedies "reduce their sexual drama to an at times surprisingly stark conflict between 'aggressive' male virility and a 'passively resistant' female virginity,"[45] with female characters becoming sexually active only as a means of ensnaring a husband. However, just as Charlie's virility is not expressed in aggressive terms, most of the female characters in *The Tender Trap* are far from sexually passive and instead represent elements of modern-day femininity.

Joe's initial confusion at Charlie's lifestyle leads him to ask: "Where am I? Where did all these tomatoes come from?" Charlie is horrified at Joe's underestimation of his companions: "Tomatoes? How dare you call these girls tomatoes?" Unlike the various women in *Pillow Talk,* who are pictured lounging in their apartments in negligees or who dance on stage at local nightspots, these are modern, urban career women, as Charlie explains: "For your information, Mr. McCall, Poppy is an important editor at Doubleday, and Jessica happens to be the buyer for the largest chain of women's stores in the South. Tomatoes, indeed. Tchh!" Each of the women—apart from Julie—defines herself in modern terms as professionally driven and sexually expressive. Rather than being duped by Charlie's attentions, they show every sign of being knowing participants in the game of sexual relations. They may tidy up his apartment, but all the while demonstrate an awareness that such behavior is part of the social constructedness of gender roles. For Poppy and Jessica, Charlie provides a way of experiencing a lifestyle of cosmopolitan nightclubs and sexual activity with an attractive single male until marriage becomes the preferred option. The women use Charlie until they tire of the single life, as Poppy reveals when she rejects Charlie's offer of guitar music and Spanish food in favor of a date with a "square" at Radio City Music Hall, explaining, "But he is going to call me tomorrow." When Charlie objects to her labeling him "a stinker," she answers matter-of-factly: "But sweetie, I never thought you were anything else."

These postwar women negotiate positions for themselves in ways that point forward to the modern female dilemma of achieving simultaneously successful career and personal lives, or "having it all." This is best expressed through Sylvia, the film's roundly admired model of femininity, whom Charlie describes as "probably the most wonderful woman on this earth or any other earth." As a violinist with the NBC orchestra, Sylvia aspires to professional success and enjoys an exciting urban lifestyle. When she reads in the trade papers that a particular male violinist has been appointed conductor of the summer symphony, she complains that they would never appoint a woman to the position, suggesting the ambition that she at various points denies. Having a personal life that remains unsatisfying, Sylvia articulates the problems posed for career women. At the same time, she has no illusions about Charlie as a male ideal. When Joe questions why she puts up with the careless treatment she receives from Charlie, she explains:

> We come to this town from Springfield and Des Moines and Fort Worth and Salt Lake City. We're young and we're pretty and we're talented. All we have to do to get married is stay home. But the boys back home don't have what we want. We've got our eyes on something else: a career, glamour, excitement, and this is the place to find it. So we come to New York, and we do pretty well. Not great, but pretty well. We make a career. We find the excitement and the glamour. We go to first nights. We buy little mink stoles. Head waiters call us by name, and it's fun, it's wonderful. Until one fine day we look around and we're thirty-three years old and we haven't got a man. . . . Joe, do you have any idea what's available to a woman of thirty-three? Married men, drunks, pretty boys looking for someone to support them, lunatics looking for their fifth divorce. It's quite a list, isn't it? So we set our cap for Charlie. He's eligible. He's attractive. He's employed, and reasonably sane.

Charlie provides the faint promise of a stable romantic future for Sylvia, even though he remains dedicated to the bachelor lifestyle. Her lack of emotional investment in the relationship is made clear when Joe challenges her, "But you don't love him, do you?," and Sylvia replies, "How did the word 'love' ever creep into this conversation?" Charlie again performs a role required of him until, after her short-lived engagement to Charlie, Sylvia is rewarded for her patience with a wedding to a well-dressed English neighbor of her former fiancé, who pursues *her* and demonstrates he is not a "square" when he asks to be invited to Charlie's next party, confessing, "I love brawls."

Alongside these relatively progressive models of femininity, Julie Gillis represents a positively backward version of the postwar woman. Julie comes across as the least likable character on screen; even the amiable Joe describes her as "the most terrifying child I ever met in my life" after listening to her plans for her future. Julie represents the kind of cynical female character depicted in a number of films of the postwar period, such as *Every Girl Should Be Married* (1948), *Three Coins in the Fountain* (1954), and *How to Marry a Millionaire* (1953). In each film, women view marriage obsessively as their prime objective and concoct elaborate schemes to bring their choice of husband to the point of proposing. Although Julie is less manipulative, she has a well-defined plan for her future. She explains her lack of enthusiasm when she wins the lead role in a Broadway show by telling Charlie, Sylvia, and Joe: "A career is just fine, but it's no substitute for marriage. . . . I mean, a woman isn't really a woman at all until she's been married and had children. And why? Because she's fulfilled." Julie is the product of the kind of cultural teaching described by Betty Friedan, which persuaded women that "truly feminine women do not want careers, higher education, political rights—the independence and the opportunities that the old-fashioned feminists fought for. . . . All they had to do was devote their lives from earliest girlhood to finding a husband and bearing children."[46] While Friedan would report in 1963 on women's dissatisfaction with the narrow identity prescribed for them, Julie is unshakable in her certainty that her goal is the route to happiness. She has all the specifications of the man she will marry, other than his blood type, despite never having met him, and has their plans for several years laid out, from their early married life in New York, to the Scarsdale public school their children will attend.

Because of her cold approach, Julie initially dismisses Charlie as a suitable date, feeling no "immediate chemistry" between them, even though she admits to him in a halfhearted compliment: "You're even attractive in an off-beat, beat-up kind of way." Julie remains convinced of their incompatibility until their encounter at the American Home Show, where Charlie and Joe have spotted Julie on television asking questions about "the kitchen of tomorrow," the symbol of suburban married life. When Charlie arrives to retrieve Julie and deliver her to rehearsals for her show, she persuades him to replace a bespectacled middle-aged salesman in a chair in a mock-up of a modern living room and is instantly attracted to him. The suggestion is that Charlie fits comfortably into this domestic setting. Tellingly, her attraction to him is confirmed when Charlie/Sinatra gives a rendition of the title song for her, signaling the path toward "the tender trap" that their relationship will take. The modern decor at the American Home Show is also significant as a marker that Charlie may incline naturally toward domesticity but would still provide a very modern version of a husband. When the couple later finish a date by retiring to Julie's parents' apartment, the chintz and flocked wallpaper are reminders of the traditions associated with Julie. Her response to Charlie's sexual advances is therefore quite different than Poppy's; she objects to Charlie's "nibbling" and moves activities away to watching television and flicking through books of classical art. When she discovers phone messages from Charlie's numerous female companions in the pocket of his suit, Julie demands he devote himself to her alone, explaining: "I'm going to try to make a man out of you. Because that's what I want to marry, a man." Julie represents the kind of woman *Playboy* warned its readers about. Her desire to mold Charlie into her idea of husband material—equating the husband role with male maturity—feeds into the notion of bachelorhood as a man's natural condition and marriage as the unfortunate result of feminine manipulation. As Joe describes her, Julie is "a trap with the trigger all set."

The final part of the narrative illustrates Charlie's ineptitude as a swingin' bachelor. Having dismissed Julie's talk of marriage with the question "Well, who asked ya?" Charlie promptly proposes to Sylvia. His feigned joviality as he hastily arranges their engagement party demonstrates the centrality of performance to his male image. During a break in the proceedings, Charlie embroils himself in a further mess by becoming simultaneously engaged to Julie and, the morning after the party, is summarily dumped by both fiancées, confirming his ineffectiveness as a playboy. After a working sojourn overseas, Charlie returns to attend Sylvia's wedding to her Englishman, where he is reunited with Julie. Talk of marriage provides a tidy narrative conclusion and suggests Charlie's fate as a married man was inevitable. However, Charlie has an uncertain masculine identity. He veers through the course of the film from basking in his swingin' lifestyle to envying what he considers to be his friend's domestic bliss, suggesting a less stable outcome is more likely. In *The Tender Trap,* Sinatra's representation of the hip urban bachelor as a performed identity combines with a deconstruction of sexual relations to depict playboy masculinity in terms that move away from gender stereotypes and toward more fluid identities. As narrow definitions of husband and bachelor are destabilized and career women demonstrate a knowing complicity in the relationship game, Sinatra's swinger strikes a distinctive tone, mixing a provocative modernity with the inadequacies fundamental to his image of male sexuality.

"Nobody Owns Joey but Joey": Sex and Power in *Pal Joey*

When John O'Hara was asked whether he had viewed Sinatra's performance in *Pal Joey,* the author replied: "No, I didn't have to see Sinatra: I invented him."[47] O'Hara's telling remark articulates what is central to Sinatra's performance as nightclub master of ceremonies Joey Evans—in effect, that Sinatra both embodies the role and, at the same time, makes use of the swingin' character in constructing his own playboy identity, which, as O'Hara indicates, is in itself an invention. In his comment O'Hara also assumes that the arrogant heel of the *Pal Joey* stories, or at least of the earlier Broadway musical, has been transferred wholesale onto the screen. Sinatra's characterization of Joey Evans, however, draws as much on the issues of class and objectification that surround the star's image as on the playboy persona constructed by both Sinatra and O'Hara. O'Hara's stories originally appeared in *The New Yorker* in the form of letters from "Your pal Joey" to a friend detailing Joey's various professional, sexual, and underworld adventures.[48] Following the book's publication in 1940, *Pal Joey* was adapted as a musical with songs by Rodgers and Hart and staged on Broadway in the same year. This original stage production was notable for giving Gene Kelly his first starring role on Broadway, which would lead to his first film role, alongside Judy Garland in *For Me and My Gal* (1942).[49] It also made its mark as a musical that unusually featured a largely unsympathetic main character and resolved its narrative in an unhappy ending, with Joey losing his nightclub and the two women in his life. Several adjustments were made for Columbia's film version, which included placing a more positive spin on the finale and toning down the unfamiliar sexual frankness of the stage production.

The significance of this less hardened narrative lies in the room it allows for the vulnerability inherent in Sinatra's image to be incorporated into the character of Joey Evans. Certainly, the original UK exhibitors' poster for *Pal Joey* represents Joey in anything but empowered terms. Seated between glamorous standing shots of Hayworth and Novak, with only Joey's pet dog Snuffy for company, Sinatra is pictured with his chin resting on his hand, looking morose. The poster's copy captures the mix of Joey's objectifying language and his ultimate powerlessness, asking audiences to: "Celebrate the story of Joey (*the heel!*) and his bosom pals! Both stacked: one rich (*the doll!*), one poor (*the mouse!*) . . . with y'r pal Joey caught in the ever-lovin' middle!" Like the part of Angelo Maggio in *From Here to Eternity,* Sinatra had long coveted the role of Joey Evans, and in his characterization of this confident swinger he reveals a sense of alienation similar to that exhibited by Maggio and various of his 1950s characters, making him just as much an underdog, despite initial appearances. In addition, as the conspicuous objectification of both Sinatra and Joey results in an image of powerless masculinity more akin to representations of sexualized women on screen, Sinatra's film swinger represents a significant departure from the kind of masculine masquerading exemplified by, for example, Rock Hudson's serial seducers.

The pre-titles opening sequence of *Pal Joey* establishes the essentials of Joey Evans's persona. Joey is being escorted to a train by two policemen, from whom we learn that he has been arrested for entertaining an underage girl in his hotel room who turned out to be the mayor's daughter. The policemen present the penniless Joey with a one-way ticket out of town and launch him onto the train so that he falls face-first onto the floor of the carriage. The credits sequence shows Joey en route to San Francisco. During the course of the journey he attempts a pickup on a ferry, makes a suggestive remark to an elderly lady behind a "Travelers Aid" desk, and quips to a taxi driver looking for business, "No, thanks. I've got my car and chauffeur meeting me." Joey is constructed as a sexually transgressive male, whose financial insecurity and unsettled way of life contribute to his position outside society's norms. While he clearly enjoys a sexually liberal lifestyle, it leaves him powerless to the extent that he can be physically humiliated by policemen who act to limit his transgressive behavior.

Joey's arrival at the Barbary Coast Club reveals more about what is central to his identity. These early scenes illustrate Joey's supreme confidence, as he disturbs bandleader and old friend Ned (Bobby Sherwood) in the middle of a performance and, learning that the club's master of ceremonies has failed to turn up—a regular occurrence—seizes the stage for an impromptu audition. Joey's sexual arrogance is evident as he watches the showgirls and rates each one, singling out Linda English (Kim Novak) for admiration, describing her as "pretty well arranged." These scenes also introduce the connection between Joey's sexuality and his career, which will continue through the narrative. Despite his attempt to convince Ned he is available for work because "You got to stay loose, you know," Ned's tired reply, "Oh, daddy, you're always available," confirms that Joey's career is consistently stalled by his unbridled sexual behavior. Having secured the emcee job, Joey continues to exude confidence, advising the club's manager, Mike (Hank Henry), that he has "a big following" and suggesting his picture is displayed out front. However, Mike has already evaluated Joey as a "bum" and is aware of gossip about the trouble Joey's flirtations with female customers have caused during previous club engagements. Showgirl Gladys (Barbara Nichols) confirms the rumors, informing Joey that her sister has told her tales about his predatory behavior in another club. Rather than being defined by his talent (which is taken as considerable, since Sinatra provides the performances), Joey's reputation is built on his sexuality. This heightened sexual emphasis continues as Joey's dressing room becomes the location for secret trysts with various showgirls, who also deliver his clean laundry and keep him supplied with coffee.

In the film's 1950s context, Joey's apparent ability to attract the opposite sex with ease and his sexually liberal lifestyle connect the character to the *Playboy* persona. His use of hip language works further to construct him in swinger terms, the original film trailer indicating the significance of Joey's particular "slanguage" to his male identity. Appearing off-set with a blackboard and pointer, Sinatra defines for prospective audiences words such as *mouse, gasser, loose,* and *poppin',* which form part of "Joey's Jargon." Discussing the film in *Photoplay,* Sinatra went through a similar list of definitions for terms such as *tomato* and *beetle.* Describing his costars, he continued: "Kim Novak is an out-and-out Gasser. . . . And Rita Hayworth is a real gone Barn Burner."[50] This hip brand of talking brings Sinatra's bachelor image into the text. Constructed in part through the various "swingin'" album titles and the 1960 *Ring-a-Ding Ding!* album, as well as through Sinatra's frequent use of words like "gasser," "crazy," and "broad" in stage and television performances, Sinatra's swinger persona resembles Joey's superficial identity as a highly sexual, hip urban male.[51] With Sinatra's image as background to the character, space is opened up for Joey's virile confidence to be read in more complex ways, as Philip K. Scheuer of the *Los Angeles Times* suggested in his review of the film: "His Joey is a rat, all right, among mice, but his environment has a lot to do with making him one and you can't quite submerge a sneaking sympathy for the Frankie part of him."[52] Both star and narrative combine, therefore, to problematize the characterization of Joey Evans as an uncomplicated playboy.

Much of the counterpoint to Joey's projection of heightened masculinity is set up through musical performance. Each of Sinatra's musical numbers (apart from the final "What Do I Care for a Dame?") has a narrative agenda but is equally significant in providing a stage, literal or otherwise, for Joey to display himself to an audience. Drawing on the seductive appeal of Sinatra's voice, from the outset Joey's singing provokes sexual interest, from the showgirl who squeals from offstage, "He's cute!," to society hostess Vera Prentiss Simpson (Rita Hayworth), who is intrigued by the voice she hears singing "There's a Small Hotel," even before she sees Joey on stage at her Nob Hill party. Joey's status as a willing sexual object is a central aspect of his identity and has implications for what, on the surface, is a highly masculine persona.

This is not to argue that Joey is the sole objectified character in the film, nor that Sinatra is the only star depicted as a desirable figure. The representation of both Novak and Hayworth conform at various points to Hollywood's traditional foregrounding of actresses as objects of desire. As Columbia's rising female star, and despite her character's "good girl" status, Novak is most openly put on display via the softly lit close-ups of the "My Funny Valentine" number, where Novak is framed by a heart-shaped prop, when seen stepping out of a bath, and through her attempt at a strip routine that allows for a level of audience voyeurism. Hayworth is given similar treatment during her rendition of "Bewitched," which culminates in her barely veiled naked form appearing behind a glass shower screen. In her seminal article "Visual Pleasure and Narrative Cinema," Laura Mulvey contends that cinematic sexual objectification is necessarily limited to female performers. Taking a psychoanalytical approach, Mulvey has argued: "In a world ordered by sexual imbalance, pleasure in looking has been split between active/male and passive/female. . . . In their traditional exhibitionist role women are simultaneously looked at and displayed, with their appearance coded for strong visual and erotic impact so that they can be said to connote *to-be-looked-at-ness.*"[53] Since Mulvey's strict categorization of "the gaze" into active male subjectivity and passive female objectivity, more recent discussions have recognized the positioning of male performers as erotic objects, both as characters in a film's narrative and as stars performing for the nondiegetic audience. For example, Miriam Hansen's analysis of Rudolph Valentino demonstrates the extent to which the Latin star's films drew attention to his physicality, most famously via his face, but additionally through fetishistic close-ups of parts of his body. Hansen notes, in particular, a close-up of Valentino's foot in the 1922 film *Blood and Sand.*[54]

During the 1950s, the objectification of male stars is particularly rife, assisted by genres that enabled men's bodies to be highlighted as part of the narrative or generic context. In epics such as *Ben Hur* (1959) and *Spartacus* (1960), for example, action scenes allowed for the legitimate display of the bodies of male stars such as Charlton Heston and Kirk Douglas, who represent the physical antithesis of Sinatra. Similarly, film musicals provided an arena for the appreciation of male physical performance. Steve Neale contends that, particularly in the western genre, the stylized presentation of male bodies in, for example, a shoot-out scene, is played down through the aggressive or fearful looks of other male characters, as well as through its use as a device of narrative resolution, specifically designed "to disavow any explicitly erotic look at the male body." Neale further suggests that the display of the male body in musicals results in a "feminization" of the stars involved.[55] However, a deeper exploration of masculine display and a move away from a concentration on the body may take these discussions further.

In the musical genre, for example, these desirable male objects are identifiable not only in energetic dance routines such as the barn-raising number in *Seven Brides for Seven Brothers* (1954), but also in the frequent use of groups of well-dressed male dancers to accompany female singers, such as in Judy Garland's "Get Happy" number in *Summer Stock* (1950) and Dolores Gray's "Thanks a Lot, but No Thanks" routine in *It's Always Fair Weather* in 1955. In the case of Fred Astaire's stylized wardrobe, Steven Cohan positions this concentration on his visual image firmly in the context of the film musical, arguing that, rather than objectifying Astaire, the star's style is part of the spectacle of the genre, drawing attention to "the theatricality of his musical persona."[56] In contrast, Sinatra's consistent association with an individual style that emphasizes specific elements, from the bow tie to the fedora, and that extends far beyond the film musical, means that his appearance is a continuous reference point for the ways in which he is viewed. For a male audience, Sinatra's visual image enhances a feeling of aspirational identification, as in the case of Boston's West Enders, who appreciate Sinatra's propensity for "individual display," or forms the basis of class criticism, as suggested by *Playboy*'s comments. For female audiences, the attention that Sinatra draws and that is drawn to his appearance allows the opportunity to approach this male star as an object of desire. Sinatra's objectified status works to reinforce Joey's presentation of himself in similar ways as a desirable male. Before he receives his first paycheck, Joey visits a tailor to have his suit altered, and later, as he is fitted for a tuxedo, Joey stands perched on a dais while the rest of the club's performers pause rehearsals to watch the event (Figure 9).

Joey and Vera are both aware of the extent to which sexual objectification is bound up in issues of power and control. As ex-stripper Vera Vanessa, or "Vanessa the Undresser" as Joey recalls, Vera has been subjected to the male gaze for economic reasons and now basks in her identity as a wealthy widow with the ability to reject this definition. Vera has reinvented herself as an opera-loving, philanthropic socialite with her past put firmly behind her. When Joey sings at her party and persuades her guests to bid for a performance by "Vera with the vanishing veils," therefore, he forces her to revisit her relinquished identity as an erotic object and puts in place the power plays that will define their relationship (Figure 10). The "Zip" routine, in which Vera is cast as an "artiste" who considers the works of Freud and Plato while stripping, draws on Hayworth's screen image as a female star with an excess of what Mulvey terms "to-be-looked-at-ness." In musicals such as *You Were Never Lovelier* (1942) and particularly *Cover Girl* in 1944, in which Hayworth represents

Figure 9: Joey and Vera trade power positions as she assumes control of his attire and he willingly becomes the object of male and female attention. (*Pal Joey*)

an object of desire for two generations of men, her body is displayed in musical numbers and celebrated as a thing of beauty. Hayworth's rendition of "Zip" recalls more directly her performance of "Put the Blame on Mame" in *Gilda,* as she moves her body in a strapless dress and peels off gloves, casting them in Sinatra's direction. Before he puts in a bid for Vera's performance, Joey's eyes move up and down her body, assessing her worth, and he continues to submit her to his close scrutiny as she runs through her routine. The look of pleasure on Joey's face comes not only from watching Vera's movements, but also from the knowledge that, in defining Vera as an erotic object, bought and paid for, he has assumed a level of control at the outset of their relationship.

While in moments such as the one just described Hayworth is clearly objectified in familiar terms, by tying up and taming the star's trademark long, flowing hair, the film suggests that Hayworth's days as a misunderstood femme fatale may be behind her. *Pal Joey* was Hayworth's final film under her Columbia contract, and while she had initially been intended for the part of Linda English when the film was originally discussed, by 1957 Harry Cohn considered her more suitable for the older role.[57] When it comes to replacing the original "love goddess," however, indications suggest it is less Novak than Sinatra who is positioned as the film's primary sexual object, whether perched on top of a step ladder to sing "I Could Write a Book" or giving a sexually charged performance of "The Lady Is a Tramp." Sinatra becomes the cinematic embodiment of the "love god" he represented during World War II and which *Playboy* later labeled him, but does so as a thoroughly objectified Joey whom Vera nicknames "beauty" and who plainly uses his sexuality for financial gain. Reversing the traditional Hollywood treatment of male and female stars, the film draws on the screen images of Sinatra and Hayworth to highlight the extent to which their characters stray from normalized definitions of male and female identity.

The relationship between Joey and Vera is played out through the direct connections made between sexual objectification and power. A shift in this power dynamic is signaled when Vera visits the Barbary Coast Club to exact her revenge on Joey for his behavior as a "boy auctioneer" when he returned Vera to her former identity as a performing object of desire. When Vera's actions result in Joey receiving a threat of dismissal, Joey turns up at Vera's hilltop home to assure her that, despite appearances, her only appeal for him lies in her "M.U.N.Y.—money." Having already planted the idea of a club of his own—"Chez Joey"—with Vera, Joey makes plain his awareness that his appeal for Vera lies in his sexuality and his readiness to make a fair exchange, confirming this with his exit line: "By the way, if you knew what you were throwin' away, you'd cut your throat." While he tells tales of engagements lined up at El Morocco and the Waldorf, believed by no one, he recognizes that Vera's money represents his sole chance of career progression.

Sinatra's performance of "The Lady Is a Tramp" (a song in itself about nonconformity) is used in the narrative to seal the relationship between Joey and Vera and their respective positions within it. Arriving at the club after hours (in another strapless dress), Vera demands a performance from Joey, reversing the power relations established by Joey at her society party by making him her personal erotic object. The club's sole customer, Vera positions herself at a table directly in front of the

Figure 10: Joey returns Vera to her sexualized identity as a stripper through the "Zip" routine, subjecting her to his and the audience's erotic gaze. (*Pal Joey*)

stage, all the better to focus her attention on Joey. Medium shots back and forth between the two characters mark out Vera's response to Joey as clearly sexual, as her eyes move up and down his body, echoing Joey's reaction to her "Zip" routine. As Joey walks slowly around Vera's table, in a style similar to a flirtatious striptease act, Vera's eyes follow him as she strains to keep him within her field of vision.

In contrast to Vera during her performance of "Zip," Joey revels in the chance to display himself in sexual terms, aware of the results it will achieve for him. The nods of appreciation that come from Ned additionally provide some male approval for the potency of the show. Sinatra's highly sexual performance only heightens the sense of erotic objectification around Joey. Beginning seated at a piano with a cigarette, Sinatra soon pushes both away, leaving nothing to obscure Vera's, and the audience's, view. The finger snapping and low slurs are trademarks of Sinatra's performance style and work as reminders that this is the star more than the character on stage, adding Sinatra's consistent willingness to objectify himself to Joey's self-definition. Sinatra's familiar shoulder shrugs and swift turns of the head, timed to correspond with trumpet blasts, increase the number's sexual charge, making it a vocally and physically erotic performance. When Sinatra ceases to sing or move, arms outstretched, on the line "It's oke," and the band also falls silent, Sinatra displays himself visually for the audience and, as Joey, for Vera. The final close-up of Hayworth's satisfied smile confirms that Sinatra's performance has turned Joey into a pure sexual object for Vera, who now takes the lead, instructing him, "Come now, beauty."

The scene that follows spells out the ground rules of the relationship between Joey and Vera. Having accompanied Vera to her yacht, Joey reminds her of his ambition to open a club of his own, "Chez Joey, a place with real class." Comparing their show-business experiences of "drafty dressing rooms" and "drunks tossing pennies," Joey fails to convince Vera that she should return to the stage. His own dream is for independence and respect: "No hokey waiters rattlin' plates when I'm on. No tough managers beltin' me around. Be my own boss. Nobody owns Joey but Joey." Seeing no other means of progression, however, the route he chooses to achieve this leaves him with neither. When Joey suggests that he and Vera could be "partners," the explicit agreement is that Joey will trade his sexuality for Vera's financial ability to provide him with his desired nightclub. Hayworth's rendition of "Bewitched" the next morning—the original lyrics of which include the line "Horizontally speaking, he's at his very best"—makes plain the arrangement. Joey is therefore characterized in terms far removed from the casual sexual autonomy of *Playboy*'s male figure. Rather than providing Joey with his longed-for independence, his willingness to sell himself for financial gain brings him under Vera's control. Having reduced Joey to a sexual object, Vera holds the reins of power, deciding on the cut of his suits and demanding he get rid of Linda so as to protect her relationship with Joey, her "investment." This ultimately leads to her closing down the club in order to prove "who owns Joey."

For Vera, Joey's heightened sexuality makes him, temporarily at least, a more attractive prospect than the high-toned escorts with whom she has previously been seen. However, Vera confines Joey to a compartment of her life, in part because of his gigolo identity, but also because of what is represented as Joey's lack of class. Joey's inability to remodel himself as an upper-middle-class *Playboy* ideal means that he is destined to remain excluded from social power. Rather than sharing her Nob Hill mansion, therefore, Joey is sidelined to Vera's yacht, a luxurious "hideout" that, nevertheless, represents the opposite of the personal wealth and sexual power of the *Playboy* apartment. Vera has transformed herself from a stripper to a society hostess, despite Joey's awareness that "underneath those furs, that is pure dame." However, she fails to invite Joey to her soirees because, as Joey guesses while spitting pips into a dish, he would be confused as to which fork to use. His attempt at broken French is in sharp contrast with Vera's fluent conversation with her French maid, and his picture of himself wearing white tie and tails and an opera hat as the host of his own nightclub remains in his imagination. The clothes that objectify Joey equally suggest his inability to reinvent himself, drawing on the overdressing of which Sinatra is accused and that positions the star in class terms. In one scene on Vera's yacht, the camera draws in on Joey's chosen outfit, which includes slippers embroidered with his name, burgundy pajamas and matching smoking jacket, and a cigarette holder. Later, he appears in a sailing sweater, cravat, and captain's hat, like a caricature of *Playboy*'s recommendations for a yachting weekend. Finally tiring of Vera's controlling ways, Joey rebuts her attempt to re-establish relations and open the club, and particularly her offer of marriage. Leaving behind the yacht and the yellow Thunderbird to which he has become accustomed, significantly Joey cannot quite relinquish his favorite indulgence.[58] With the camera panning across his monogrammed shirts and a closet full of suits, Joey sweeps them into his suitcase, justifying his actions, telling himself, "Why not? I earned them."

After Vera has magnanimously reunited Joey and Linda, *Pal Joey* closes with the couple heading, literally, into the sunset, toward San Francisco's Golden Gate Bridge, with talk of marriage and a family. Director George Sidney has since acknowledged the forced nature of this unlikely ending, commenting: "I don't believe there were too many in the audience who swallowed all that. . . . I think they thought as I did. That the minute the bum got across the bridge he'd be off."[59] Despite this contrived narrative resolution, however, *Pal Joey* remains an unusual casting of male/female relations. Sinatra's consistent willingness to objectify himself as a male star brings an added intensity to Joey Evans's self-characterization as an object of desire. Similarly, the powerlessness Joey experiences in his relationship with Vera, brought about by both his eroticized identity and his class inadequacies, references the essential vulnerabilities of

Sinatra's star image. Through the course of the film, the most famous of Sinatra's screen swingers comes to resemble less a figure of confident, predatory virility than a character possessing the same insecurities and sense of conflicted masculinity that typify Sinatra's star identity.

Sinatra's image consistently disturbs ideas of male heterosexual identity across the postwar period. As the "love god" of World War II, Sinatra is immediately positioned in ways unusual for a male star. Early screen roles draw on the casting of Sinatra as a physically unlikely erotic object, highlighting the issues of objectification and performance that continue to impact on the star's sexual persona. In the 1950s, biographical commentary and *Playboy*'s celebration of Sinatra seem to uphold the star's image as the quintessential Hollywood version of the magazine's carefully constructed bachelor identity. Yet Sinatra's physical and class inadequacies work to complicate his swinger persona. In *The Tender Trap* and *Pal Joey,* Sinatra's sexual image is drawn into the text as the films' characters display the heterosexual hipness of the bachelor identity, while exposing the performativity and class exclusivity of the modern playboy model. Sinatra's unconventional masculine image—virile, sexually objectified, and a challenge to traditional gender roles—represents an individualistic styling of postwar male sexual identity that fundamentally questions prevailing images of heterosexual masculinity.

Conclusion:
Chairman of the Board

The old Sinatra—the scrawny, temperamental crooner who punched parking-lot attendants and cursed at photographers—has given way to a new one—the jowly, horn-rimmed chairman of the board. The reason is simple: Sinatra *is* chairman of the board. From the Sunset Boulevard offices of Sinatra Enterprises, he rules a $25 million empire that reaches into real estate, banking, and almost every corner of entertainment. (Last week, when Sinatra sold his movie production company and his recording firm to Warner Brothers in exchange for a seat on the studio's executive board, there were some reports that he was broke. But one TV writer claims: "Frank is taking the first step to being the next Jack L. Warner.")

—*Newsweek*, "Chairman of the Board"

Newsweek's description of Sinatra's transition from "The Kid from Hoboken" to "The Chairman of the Board" emphasizes the shifts that occur around Sinatra's male identity in the 1960s. In 1965, the year of Sinatra's fiftieth birthday, Jack Warner was forced into issuing a public denial following reports that Sinatra was set to take charge of his family's Hollywood studio, insisting: "There is no evidence or reason for . . . speculation . . . that I am considering Mr. Sinatra as my successor as president of Warner Brothers Pictures—or that Mr. Sinatra desires to be my successor."[1] The notion of Sinatra as a Hollywood power player developed through the decade and indicated less a comprehensive change in the star's masculine persona than a variation in the ways in which the essentials of Sinatra's image of American male identity were represented. A variety of performances and events occurring in 1960 demonstrate how Sinatra's star image continues to revolve around issues of class, ethnicity, racial politics, emotional vulnerability, and sexuality. As his style of performance incorporates elements of excess, and commentary stresses a building image of power and control, Sinatra's male identity displays shifting areas of emphasis while remaining unaltered at its core.

Ocean's Eleven represents the apex of Sinatra's association with the group of male stars labeled by the press "the Rat Pack" or "the Clan." Sinatra, Dean Martin, Sammy Davis Jr., and, playing a less central role, Peter Lawford and Joey Bishop, presented on stage and screen a highly stylized, hypermasculine image, the tone of which was set by Sinatra. While there are distinctions to be drawn between Sinatra's persona as "Leader" of the Rat Pack and his image as a solo performer, the excesses of this striking group emphasize the shifts that occur around Sinatra's male identity through the 1960s. In *Ocean's Eleven,* Sinatra plays ex-commando Sergeant Danny Ocean, who reassembles his unit of the Eighty-second Airborne Division with a plan to relieve the top five Las Vegas casinos of their takings on New Year's Eve. Here, Sinatra's hip swinger continues its move toward parody that had begun in *Can Can* in the same year and would develop across films such as *Come Blow Your Horn* and Sinatra's two performances as private detective Tony Rome in the late 1960s. As Danny Ocean, Sinatra presents a figure of controlling sexuality to whom women are peripheral and always sexual objects. Dispensable young women provide massages, one-night stands are picked up in bars, and even Danny's wife, Bea (Angie Dickinson), from whom he is separated, is propositioned. To illustrate Sinatra's transition from swingin' ineptitude to cynical sexuality, "The Tender Trap" now serves as accompaniment to a strip routine performed in a burlesque joint.

Notably, Sinatra's virile excess is no longer tempered here by expressions of emotional vulnerability. The vulnerabilities associated with Danny are articulated by the character's male friends, who express concern about Danny's disintegrating marriage and, significantly, his response to the death of one of the members of the unit (Tony Bergdorf, played by Richard Conte). *Ocean's Eleven* is a film concerned with relationships between men and the male identities they construct. On its release, reviewers focused on the visual style and unrestricted morality of the stars and their characters. Archer Winsten of the *New York Post* suggested: "The picture is very plush, so chromium, so smooth, so much a display of performers who act as if a mere appearance would induce hysteria in the adoring public, that you wonder who's fooling whom."[2] The *Los Angeles Examiner* described *Ocean's Eleven* as "something you should keep your children away from."[3] Yet the film relates as much to the identity crisis of the veteran as does Sinatra's portrayal of Danny Miller in his first postwar film, *It Happened in Brooklyn*. Danny Ocean's planned casino raid is motivated largely by a desire to recapture the sense of masculine worth achieved during his World War II service as a commando. The incessant gambling and womanizing in which he has engaged since the war brings none of the gratification promised by *Playboy*, providing instead only instability through a faltering marriage and splintered friendships. The Las Vegas plot is driven by a need to revisit his formerly well-defined male identity in the heightened masculine environment Danny re-creates.

Danny's fellow servicemen are similarly unsettled. Sam Harmon (Martin) has been occupying himself as a lounge singer in Hawaii, war hero and ex–baseball player Josh Howard (Davis) now drives a dustcart, and Jimmy Foster (Lawford) is an unemployed patrician, reliant on the financial support of his mother. Like Danny, the men view their Vegas escapade as an opportunity to recover the strong and successful male identity afforded them by the war. Jimmy's description of the planned robbery as "a military operation, executed by trained men," and Danny's question, "Why waste all those cute little tricks that the army taught us, just because it's sort of peaceful now?," highlights their inability to disconnect from the past. Only Sam sounds a note of caution: "This ain't a combat team. It's an alumni meeting. Any of you liars want to claim that you're half the man you were in '45? Can you run as fast? Can you think as fast? Can you mix it up as good as you used to? Well, I sure can't. And Danny, if you want to try and catch lightning in a bottle, you go ahead, but don't try and catch yesterday." Sam recognizes the futility of the men's attempt to revert to a heightened male identity. He puts aside his objections, however, since reciprocal codes of loyalty dominate these male relationships. Danny saved Sam's life during World War II, and Sam's reluctant participation in the casino caper is a demonstration of his grateful allegiance.

Drawing on ethnic imaging around Sinatra, male friendships assume a high importance for Danny, by 1960 usurping his relationships with women. The men bask in the masculine arena they re-create, holding planning meetings around a pool table or in a bowling alley. Yet, as the ultimate failure of their "mission" demonstrates, their unwillingness to reformulate their male identities for the postwar environment accentuates their dislocation. Having watched the stolen money being cremated with their late friend, Danny departs Las Vegas, notably with his fellow ex-commandos rather than his wife. This closing scene, during which the characters pass in dark suits in front of a neon sign promoting the five stars' appearances at The Sands, reemphasizes the heavy stylization of Sinatra and the Rat Pack and the overriding impact of star identities on the film's characterizations. Moreover, their attempt to revisit their former identities has failed to resolve their sense of instability, demonstrating Sinatra's continued articulation of the problematic assimilation of the World War II veteran.

Like *Ocean's Eleven,* Sinatra's stage performances with Martin, Davis, and the remaining members of the Rat Pack illuminate the fundamentals of Sinatra's male identity in heightened form, demonstrating the shifts that reposition Sinatra in the 1960s context. The Rat Pack performances that took place at The Sands simultaneous to the filming of *Ocean's Eleven* were a particular focus of press commentary. Sinatra labeled the shows "The Summit," referencing the meeting between Eisenhower, de Gaulle, and Khrushchev in 1959. *Variety* continued this high-ranking theme with its review titled "Vegas' Zillion-$ Five; 'Summiteers' (Sinatra & 4) a Sizzler at the Sands." As the rest of this illustrious group is made anonymous, Sinatra is fêted as the main attraction, hugely successful in financial terms and drawing stars such as Bob Hope, Johnny Mathis, and Angie Dickinson into the audience. *Variety*'s description of the final show as "a gasser of a show that out-gassed the consistent procession of gassers which started opening night"[4] reiterates the hip imaging that circulates around the stars. *Playboy* presented a similar image, terming the Rat Pack "a very special gang of Hollywood rebels" and continuing: "'The Clan,' as they've been dubbed by others, possess talent, charm, romance and a devil-may-care nonconformity that gives them immense popular appeal—so much so that today they sit at the very top of the Hollywood star system, with Sinatra king of the hill. . . . This particular group, and this group alone, has cohesiveness in work, friendship, fun—and a wild iconoclasm that millions envy secretly or even unconsciously—which makes them, in the public eye, the innest in-group in the world."[5] For *Playboy,* the stars represent a unique collective of hip nonconformists who epitomize the magazine's philosophy. Beyond this general air of stylish individualism, however, the stars' performances illustrate Sinatra's shifting image in relation to racial politics.

The appearance on stage of a group of male stars consisting of two Italian Americans, one African American Jew, one son of an English aristocrat, and one American Jew was in itself a political act, presenting an image of racial, ethnic, and religious diversity that promoted the widest possible definition of American male identity. More specifically, the stars' references to their ethnic and racial origins and the context of civil-rights protests politicizes these performances. When Joey Bishop tells the audience, "Frank Sinatra and Dean Martin are gonna come out and tell you about some of the *good* work the Mafia is doing,"[6] or Martin refers to Sinatra as "the dago," the performances highlight Sinatra's continuous assertion of his Italian American identity and his reclamation of negative imagery.[7] Max Rudin suggests: "The vaudeville tradition that was the distant ancestor of their routines had relied on ethnic stereotypes: Irish and blacks, Germans and Jews, Italians and Poles—but as victims, as the lower-class butts of jokes. This was something altogether different, stars at the pinnacle of American entertainment who acted as if style and class and success were not at all incompatible with ethnic identification, whose act in fact proclaimed that they were truly American *because* they were Italian, or black, or Jewish."[8] Heading a stylish group of performers who have achieved unparalleled success while openly expressing their racial, ethnic, and religious identities, Sinatra claims a place for the immigrant at the center of American culture, implicitly proclaiming his victory over ethnic exclusion.

The ways in which the performers address Sammy Davis Jr.'s racial and religious identity are more complex in the context of America's increasingly volatile civil rights situation and illustrate Sinatra's altering political image. Racial references occur in the context of the shows' various excesses: Sinatra and Martin carrying placards proclaiming "We want free broads!" identifies the shameless sexual bravado of the performances and the stars' alienation from the modern protest culture. The racial jokes also belong to the shows' climate of irreverent mockery of the stars' identities and the prejudices to which they are subjected. Just as Davis plays with ethnic stereotypes, quipping about Sinatra and Martin "eating pizza every night" or coining the term "wopsicle," remarks that draw openly on America's discriminatory attitudes toward race and religion demonstrate the stars' contempt for bigotry. When Davis places his hand on Martin's shoulder, for instance, the following exchange takes place:

> *Martin:* "Zelda, I'll go out and I'll drink with you, I'll go pick cotton with you, I'll eat oranges with you, I'll go to shul with you, but don't touch me. Have you forgotten the South?"
> *Davis:* "I'm trying to, baby."
> *Sinatra (sings):* "I'm Alabamy bound."
> *Davis:* "You'll go there by yourself, I know that. Leader or no leader, I ain't going with you, baby."[9]

As Martin takes on a bigoted persona for his joke, it is clearly America's entrenched racism rather than Davis that becomes the butt of the stars' humor.

The almost postmodern approach to racial politics in these performances suggests a weariness at America's continued intolerance and is far removed from Sinatra's cinematic plea for tolerance in *The House I Live In* and the star's earnest lectures in high schools in 1945.[10] Clearly, there was an awareness among the stars that their style of racial politicking was open to misreadings. Following one racial jibe, Martin reassured the audience, relying on audience knowledge of Sinatra's political history to allay any confusion with regard to their perspective: "Believe me, I'm kidding. It's just a joke. With the champion here, do you think it ain't a joke?"[11] In his book detailing his experiences as Sinatra's valet from 1953 to 1968, George Jacobs refers to the *Amos 'n' Andy* impressions and racial jokes that are often misinterpreted, confirming Sinatra's unchanged attitude toward race: "He saw himself as a member of an oppressed minority and had total empathy for anyone who was similarly situated. Where race was concerned, the man was color blind, even if today he'd be viewed as criminally insensitive. Whatever he was doing came from the heart. A year or two later, when he'd sometimes call me 'Spook,' I took it as a brotherly nickname, not a racial epithet. Everybody in the Rat Pack had a 'ratty' nickname, and now so did I. I thought I had 'arrived.'"[12] Despite these assurances that the stars' humorous confrontation of racism evidences a change in style rather than substance, Sinatra's alternative means of addressing the race issue in an increasingly volatile civil-rights climate distances the star from the political mood. Sinatra's suggestion that Davis impersonate James Meredith (the University of Mississippi's first African American student, who was subjected to physical assaults), and, only weeks after the August 1963 March on Washington (attended by Davis), Martin's admission, "I wouldn't even march if the Italians were marching," suggests an insensitivity toward growing civil-rights tensions.[13] While this approach seems to position Sinatra as part of an obsolete tolerance agenda, the honorary doctorate he received in 1960 from the African American college Wilberforce University suggests his political past had not been entirely erased from his image. In addition, the star's less well-publicized activities indicate his early participation in the new wave of civil-rights protests inspired by Dr. Martin Luther King Jr. Sinatra's organization of a five-hour fund-raising tribute to King at Carnegie Hall on January 27, 1961, at which he, Martin, and Davis performed alongside Count Basie, Tony Bennett, and others, received less press attention than the Rat Pack's outrageous racial jokes. Yet the event demonstrates Sinatra's continued concern to contest America's attitudes toward racial identity.[14]

Just as Sinatra's early involvement with the issue of American intolerance was accompanied by his support for President Roosevelt, Sinatra's various insertions into the early 1960s civil-rights debate occurred alongside the star's public endorsement of Senator John F. Kennedy for the presidency in the 1960 race for the White House. Sinatra's association with Kennedy illuminates the extent to which the star's working-class Italian American identity remains problematic, despite his heightened stardom. Performing at fund-raising events, singing at the Democratic National Convention, and enlisting the support of other Hollywood stars, many of whom still bore an allegiance to Adlai Stevenson, Sinatra became the West Coast representative for the Kennedy campaign, surrounding the senator with an aura of Hollywood glamour subsequent presidential hopefuls would be at pains to achieve.[15] Kennedy's successful campaign concluded with the new president's Inaugural Gala in January 1961, organized and hosted by Sinatra. Commenting on the gala, columnist Murray Kempton wrote in the *New York Post* of the symbolic value of the event, at which a multitude of stars, including Mahalia Jackson, Gene Kelly, and Sidney Poitier performed: "All these people, the Sinatras, Nat Coles, Gene Kellys—the most inescapably valuable collection of flesh this side of the register of maharanis—were sons of immigrants or second-class citizens of not so long ago. They are in their wealth, their authority, their craft, the heirs of the Roosevelt revolution."[16] Leading this assortment of premier performers in an appearance before the president-elect, Sinatra more than anyone represented this working-class immigrant transition. Sinatra's personal closeness to Kennedy suggested the culmination of the star's defiance of exclusion, as the most infamous working-class Italian American befriended the Bostonian future president of the United States.

On the contrary, however, much of the response to Sinatra's close proximity to power indicated the extent to which Sinatra's working-class ethnic identity remained a cause for anxiety. During the campaign, Sinatra's alleged connections to organized crime were again raised by Hearst columnist Westbrook Pegler, who criticized Senator Kennedy's association with a man who "took part in the orgy in the Nacional Hotel in Havana at which Lucky Luciano was the guest of honor."[17] Following the election, the *New York World Telegram and Sun* expressed concern about the new president's lingering connection to the Rat Pack, commenting: "The spine-tingling worry persists in high places . . . that this unpredictable group of Hollywood characters may be presumptuous enough to assume they can have the run of the White House for the next four years."[18] The question raised by *Time* magazine in December 1960 about the possibility of Sinatra being appointed ambassador to Italy or "Secretary of Trouble"[19] was more lighthearted in tone but reflected still how Sinatra's image distanced him from notions of acceptable male identity. When, on the advice of an FBI report, the president reconsidered plans to vacation at Sinatra's home in 1962, opting instead to visit Republican Bing Crosby, Kennedy's public disassociation from Sinatra reiterated the star's ultimate alienation from social and political power, despite his level of success.[20]

Sinatra's plan in 1960 to produce and direct a film version of William Bradford Huie's *The Execution of Private Slovik* illustrates this same lack of power and shows the extent to which Hollywood was still governed by a restrictive political climate. Huie's book tells the story of the last American soldier to be executed by the United States Army for desertion following the Battle of the Bulge in 1944, the first such execution since the Civil War. The project reunited Sinatra with *The House I Live In* screenwriter Albert Maltz. As Maltz relates, Sinatra had a dual objective in bringing this book to the screen. His aim was to release a film whose narrative effectively articulated the inhumanity of war, but, in hiring Maltz as screenwriter, Sinatra was also intent on breaking the Hollywood blacklist. Maltz recalls: "I went up to see him, and we discussed the story, which we both agreed would say that the enemy in the war was not the United States Army, but the war itself. . . . Frank said that he had been thinking of hiring me for a long time and that it was very important to him to do so and to make this film. . . . He anticipated all the problems and the outcry from the American Legion-types, but he said he didn't care. He wanted to break the blacklist."[21] By revisiting the issue of anticommunist hysteria and its effects on the Hollywood film industry, Sinatra reasserted his liberal credentials at the beginning of the new decade, continuing to oppose the kind of red-baiting to which he and Maltz had been subjected during the late 1940s and early 1950s.

Much of the response to Sinatra's intended production indicated that the political climate in relation to Hollywood liberalism had altered little. On March 28, 1960, *Variety* published a full-page advertisement in which Sinatra announced the project and that he had hired Albert Maltz to write the script. The *New York Journal-American* responded in an editorial advising Sinatra to "dump Maltz and get yourself a true

American writer."[22] The *New York Mirror* continued the political assault on Sinatra and Maltz, asking: "What kind of thinking motivates Frank Sinatra in hiring an unrepentant enemy of his country—not a liberal, not an underdog, not a free thinker, but a hard revolutionist who has never done anything to remove himself from the Communist camp or to disassociate himself with the Communist record?"[23] A few months before this furor, Otto Preminger had openly challenged the blacklist, revealing the screenwriter for his 1960 film *Exodus* as another of the "Hollywood Ten," Dalton Trumbo. When *Spartacus* opened in October of the same year, Trumbo was again credited as author of the script.[24] By announcing his plans prior to production, however, Sinatra exposed the difficulties still involved in bringing to the screen liberal subjects written by those associated with the political left.

The *New York Post* was one of the few publications to criticize the press attacks on Sinatra. In an article titled "Sinatra's 'Sin,'" the paper countered: "The know-nothings have apparently declared total war on Frank Sinatra. A torrent of abuse from the Hearst press, from various veterans' groups and from smugly conformist film personalities of dubious talent is being heaped on the actor-producer's head. . . . Some of the lines being spoken by the flag-wrapped critics make us wonder how absurd this noisy production can get."[25] Fierce Republican supporter John Wayne was one of those in the Hollywood community who took exception to Sinatra's planned production, using the debate to question Senator Kennedy's political outlook, asking: "I wonder how Sinatra's crony, Senator John Kennedy, feels about him hiring such a man? I'd like to know his attitude because he's the one who is making plans to run the administrative government of our country."[26] This kind of attack on the presidential candidate Sinatra was so publicly supporting was, in part, responsible for the collapse of the project. Following a fortnight of pressure from sponsors, the Catholic Church, the right-wing press, and Joseph P. Kennedy, Sinatra paid Maltz his salary and abandoned his plans for the film.[27] Sinatra's initial retort to his critics had been: "I am prepared to stand on my principles and to await the verdict of the American people when they see *The Execution of Private Slovik*. . . . In my role as a picture maker, I have, in my opinion, hired the best man to do the job."[28] Sinatra's final statement demonstrated the continued existence of a powerful antiliberal lobby in Hollywood: "I had thought the major consideration was whether or not the resulting script would be in the best interests of the United States. . . . But the American public has indicated it feels the morality of hiring Albert Maltz is the more crucial matter, and I will accept this majority opinion."[29] Sinatra's admission of defeat illustrated the fragility of the star's image as a Hollywood power player, despite the heightened stardom and political connections that increasingly dominated his star identity.

Sinatra renewed his association with the story of Eddie Slovik in 1963, demonstrating shifts in Hollywood's political climate that allowed the explicit expression of an antiwar message on screen. Carl Foreman's *The Victors* (1963) follows Eli Wallach's U.S. army unit through Europe during World War II, casting a light on the detrimental effects of war on the spirit of both soldiers and civilians. One scene depicts the execution by firing squad of an unnamed private in December 1944, a clear reference to Slovik. While Wallach's men serve as unwilling witnesses to the event, the soundtrack accompaniment is a specially recorded Sinatra performance of "Have Yourself a Merry Little Christmas."[30]

The criticisms leveled at Sinatra in relation to his close association with Kennedy and the aborted *Private Slovik* film project have, of course, strong antiliberal political motivations. In addition, both episodes show how questions of power increasingly circulate around Sinatra while the star's class alienation is reaffirmed. Through the 1960s, commentary frequently identifies Sinatra as a controlling figure in the entertainment industry, an image that causes some discomfort. An article published in *Photoplay* in 1960 depicted Sinatra's Rat Pack as an exclusive club, Sinatra in particular abusing his industry power:

> The Clan has one thing the movie capital respects—power. And they use it. Led by Frank Sinatra, easily the most powerful—if benevolent—despot in Hollywood history, the clique manifests such a "one-for-all-and-all-for-one" zeal that, by comparison, the French Foreign Legion resembles an unfriendly society of anarchists. . . . The Clan has come in for much criticism lately—and most of it isn't just from those never asked to join. Professionally, Sinatra and his handful of cohorts control more power than is good for them—or the movie industry. Socially, The Clan is a law unto itself—condoning most of the behaviour common to any *nouveau riche* group. Their drinking bouts are already a commonly known fact of life in Hollywood.[31]

Despite begrudgingly allowing Sinatra a measure of benevolence, *Photoplay* is clearly disturbed by Sinatra's success, particularly in light of what the magazine views as the star's, and his friends', working-class behavior. The Rat Pack films and stage performances, as well as the group's lifestyle, all driven by Sinatra, circulate an image of the star as an industry insider, wielding considerable power with which many are uneasy. Such imaging is assisted by Sinatra's creation of Reprise Records in 1960. In the 1950s, Sinatra was one of a growing number of stars who became involved in film production, building companies such as Kent, Bristol, Essex, and Dorchester Productions, to which others, such as Artanis and Sinatra Enterprises, would be added in the following decade. In setting up Reprise, Sinatra indicated his desire for greater professional control in his main creative arena. As he drew artists such as Dean Martin, Sammy Davis Jr., and Rosemary Clooney onto the label, and in 1963 recorded a series of Reprise Musical Repertory Theatre albums of soundtracks to *Guys and Dolls, Finian's Rainbow, Kiss Me Kate,* and *South Pacific,* Sinatra appeared to be creating a select show-business grouping, of which he was clearly in control.[32]

In an article titled "Sinatra, Inc.," published in *Show Business Illustrated* in 1961, Sinatra admitted an increasing emphasis on business interests over creative activity. He explained to journalist Joe Hyams: "When I think of myself five years hence I see myself not so much an entertainer as a high-level executive, interested in business, perhaps in directing and producing films. . . . The things I'm involved in personally—such as acting and recording—steadily earn less money while the things I have going for me earn most. And that's the way I want it to be."[33] While Sinatra's plans suggest a shift away from a sense of exclusion toward an achievable establishment status, the disquiet expressed at Sinatra's progression indicates the star's continuous class alienation. In 1955, *Time* ridiculed the idea of Sinatra as a businessman, describing the star sitting "cockily in his ebony-furnished, 'agency modern' offices."[34] By the 1960s, Sinatra's success was being rebranded as a potentially disruptive force, just as Sinatra was returned to his New Jersey roots. In February 1960, an article titled "The Reign of King Frankie" in *American Weekly* suggested: "In Hollywood the whim of the tough and talented kid from Hoboken is almost law. Not since the late thirties when Louis B. Mayer ruled from his Metro throne, has anyone had such power."[35] In July of the same year, Richard Gehman wrote for *Good Housekeeping* about "The Disturbing Truth about Sinatra, His Changed Personality and Power." Describing Sinatra as "the most feared man in Hollywood," Gehman argued: "It would be disturbing indeed even if this enormous power were in the hands of a completely stable and predictable human being. When it is in the hands of a man torn by emotions that he apparently either cannot or does not care to control, it is something to view with alarm."[36]

The class-based discomfort evident in Gehman's remarks highlights the extent to which Sinatra remains tied to a working-class image. Whether represented in terms of unpredictable behavior or excessive levels of industry power, Sinatra remains a star alienated from cultural norms by his working-class identity.

Sinatra's most talked-about television appearance in 1960 produced a sharp contrast that illuminated the significance of the new decade in relation to his star image. The *Frank Sinatra Show* special "Welcome Home Elvis" aired on May 12, 1960, and concluded Sinatra's contract with ABC.[37] Designed to relaunch Presley's career following his return from army service and give Sinatra the kind of ratings his series had lacked, the show was a chaotic mix of performances, loosely pulled together by a seemingly disinterested Sinatra. Appearing in the midst of a pop-chart novelty song and a Japanese dance routine, Sinatra and his Rat Pack friends Davis, Lawford, and Bishop looked woefully out of place, despite being on the familiar turf of Miami's Fontainebleau Hotel. Wisecracks borrowed from their nightclub routines, and performed with indifference rather than spontaneity, neutralized the group's image of excess. With a structure aimed at returning to Presley the two years he had "lost" through army service, the show positioned Sinatra in a staid show-business past. As the audience screamed for the young singing idol, Sinatra was reduced to arguing for the quality of previous performances, displaying his Capitol album covers, and performing "Gone with the Wind" from *Only the Lonely,* an album two years old. A comic take on "You Make Me Feel So Young"—"You Make Me Feel So Old"—performed with daughter Nancy accentuated the shift in Sinatra's image from the swingin' hipster of a few years earlier to a disgruntled middle-aged father.

The duet performed by Sinatra and Presley brought into focus Sinatra's location in a passing era. He had expressed his distaste for rock 'n' roll in a 1957 article, remarking of Presley: "His kind of music is deplorable, a rancid-smelling aphrodisiac. . . . It fosters almost totally negative and destructive reactions in young people. . . . It is sung, played and written for the most part by cretinous goons."[38] Sinatra's unwillingness to give Presley more than a passing glance during their routine provided evidence of his lack of affinity with the singer, who symbolized the redefinition of Sinatra's style of popular music as entertainment for the older generation. As the two singers traded songs, Sinatra singing "Love Me Tender" and Presley "Witchcraft," and Presley imitated Sinatra's trademark shoulder shrugs, the host commented: "We work in the same way, only in different areas." While Sinatra's sharp movements evoked the potent sexuality of his male image, however, the more explicit dance moves Presley was known for pointed toward the less censored culture of the 1960s, which would make Sinatra's eroticized persona seem a tame contrast. To many, Presley's appearance on *The Frank Sinatra Show* marked a postarmy shift from his image as a youthful rebel to a show-business conformist. Karal Ann Marling, for example, views the performance as evidence that Presley had "lost his edge," explaining: "He made his first public appearance in a tux on Frank Sinatra's TV special, singing sedate duets with that middle-aged idol of the World War II generation."[39] However, the show was an even more patent illustration of the shifts occurring around Sinatra's star identity. As *The Hollywood Reporter* criticized "Frank's humble condescension to Elvis,"[40] and Sinatra's discomfort was manifest in his restrained performance, the star's ability to disrupt definitions of American male identity from his position at the hub of American culture was evidently diminishing.

Sinatra's screen career continued after 1960, until his final feature film role as an Irish police detective in *The First Deadly Sin* (1980). In contrast with the 1950s, his cinematic work during this period was of varying quality. Three inconsequential Rat Pack films—*Sergeants Three* (1961), *Four for Texas* (1963), and *Robin and the Seven Hoods*—followed *Ocean's Eleven,* and the inferior comedies *Marriage on the Rocks* (1965) and the infamous *Dirty Dingus Magee* (1970) added little to Sinatra's big-screen reputation. In a number of films, however, Sinatra gave the kind of powerful performance that was a feature of his earlier career and that illustrated the extent to which his male identity remained unchanged at its core. *The Manchurian Candidate* unquestionably provided Sinatra with his finest post-1960 role. Playing emotionally damaged Korean War veteran Bennett Marco, who attempts to thwart communist infiltration in the midst of American political corruption, Sinatra evoked the essential male vulnerability that underpins his screen image. Similarly, the New Jersey convict in *The Devil at 4 O'Clock* (1961), who rediscovers his conscience in the final reel; the independent and swingin' private eye of *Tony Rome* and *Lady in Cement;* and the liberal New York sergeant battling against corruption and authority in *The Detective* (1968) each drew on the fundamentals of Sinatra's alienated, sexual, and assertive screen persona.

From early screen roles that developed out of Sinatra's image as the singing idol of America's female youth, to performances that dramatized 1950s conflicts and debates, Sinatra's postwar Hollywood image evolved into a model of masculine diversity that consistently challenged the ways in which American male identity was defined. Depicting working-class exclusion, confronting ethnic stereotyping and racial bigotry, and creating a masculine image that expressed a potent sexuality and an emotional vulnerability in equal measure, Sinatra presented a fascinating star persona that illuminated the complexities of postwar culture and challenged dominant images of the American male. Postwar American male identity was redefined when Frankie went to Hollywood.

Notes

Introduction

1. O'Brian, "Jack O'Brian's TViews," 24.

2. DeLillo, *Underworld,* 24.

3. Pugliese, *Frank Sinatra;* Fuchs and Prigozy, *Frank Sinatra;* Hamill, *Why Sinatra Matters;* Gigliotti, *A Storied Singer;* Rojek, *Frank Sinatra;* Vare, *Legend;* Petkov and Mustazza, *The Frank Sinatra Reader;* Mustazza, *Frank Sinatra and Popular Culture.*

4. Friedwald, *Sinatra!;* Granata, *Sessions with Sinatra;* Horton, "One Good Take," 14–18.

5. McCann, *Rebel Males;* Braudy, "'No Body's Perfect,'" 275–99; Dyer, "Rock—The Last Guy You'd Have Figured?" 27–34; Cohan, *Masked Men,* 264–303.

6. Friedan, *The Feminine Mystique;* Wilson, *The Man in the Grey Flannel Suit.*

7. Whyte, *The Organization Man.*

8. Ellis, *Visible Fictions,* 91.

9. Ringgold and McCarty, *The Films of Frank Sinatra,* 74.

10. Ibid., 98.

11. Ibid., 162.

12. Alloway, "The Iconography of the Movies," 16.

13. Ibid., 17.

14. Klinger, *Melodrama and Meaning,* xvi.

15. Ibid., xx.

Chapter 1: The Postwar Success Story and Working-Class Alienation

1. Gans, *The Urban Villagers,* 195.

2. Quoted in Friedwald, *Sinatra! The Song Is You,* 125.

3. Bliven, "The Voice and the Kids," 33.

4. Kahn, *The Voice,* 86. Kahn's articles, published in October and November 1946, were consolidated, with additional material, in this book.

5. Brownstein, *The Power and the Glitter,* 93.

6. Giovacchini, *Hollywood Modernism,* 146–49.

7. Cripps, *Making Movies Black,* 95.

8. Diggins, *The Proud Decades,* 180 and 133.

9. Miller and Nowak, *The Fifties,* 133.

10. Packard, *The Status Seekers,* 12.

11. May, *Homeward Bound,* 164.

12. Ulanov, "Is Sinatra Finished?"

13. Two interviews given to the editor of *Metronome,* George Simon, were largely a blast at the newer songwriters' preference for novelty material rather than a more serious lyrical approach. Sinatra argued, "We must give people things that move them emotionally." Simon, "What's Wrong with Music!"; "Sincerity's a Thing Called Frank."

14. *Libby Zion Lecture,* Yale University, April 15, 1986.

15. Quoted in O'Brien, *The Frank Sinatra Film Guide,* 33.

16. *Person to Person,* CBS, September 14, 1956; *The Star Spangled Review,* NBC, May 27, 1950.

17. *Colgate Comedy Hour,* NBC, November 30, 1953; *Colgate Comedy Hour,* NBC, November 8, 1953.

18. *The Dinah Shore Show,* NBC, March 6, 1952.

19. Simon, "Sinatra Looks at Television . . . Television Looks at Sinatra," 15.

20. *The Frank Sinatra Show,* CBS, May 5, 1951.

21. In February 1951, Sinatra introduced his performance of "Take My Love" telling the audience it was becoming a hit "strangely enough." On the same show, Jackie Gleason remarked: "I'm worried about you. . . . I'd like to get some money out of you, and I'm worried you ain't got it," to which Sinatra replied: "Well, there's no sense in both of us worrying. Let me worry about it." *The Frank Sinatra Show,* CBS, February 3, 1951.

22. Will Friedwald refers to "Young at Heart" as "a hymn to recharged batteries," representing both in its positive lyrical message and in terms of its success the renewal of Sinatra's career. Friedwald, *Sinatra! The Song Is You,* 222.

23. Goodman, "The Kid from Hoboken," 42–47; "The Sinatra Story," 31–33, 52–54; Pryor, "The Rise, Fall and Rise of Sinatra," 17, 60–61.

24. Goodman, "The Kid from Hoboken," 42.

25. Quoted in Shaw, *Sinatra,* 192.

26. Ibid., 199.

27. Wiseman, *The Seven Deadly Sins of Hollywood,* 124.

28. Evans, "Why Does Frankie Hate So Hard?" 18, 19, and 53.

29. The second of Bill Davidson's three-part series for *Look* magazine in 1957 drew a similar picture of Sinatra's noncompliance with Hollywood codes of behavior, stressing his uncooperative attitude toward the press. The libel suit Sina-

tra filed against *Look* in relation to claims made in the series was later altered to question the magazine's very right to intrude on the star's personal life. Davidson, "Why Frank Sinatra Hates the Press," 123–24, 126, 128, 131–34, 136; "Frank Sinatra's Trial—The Case for Privacy," 8–9.

30. Larkin, "Sinatra: 'Why They Hate Me,'" 39.

31. Packard, *The Status Seekers*, 14.

32. Gans, *The Urban Villagers*, x, 8, and 229. Thomas Ferraro similarly highlights the significance of Gans's findings in relation to the West Enders' admiration for Sinatra but applies a solely ethnic reading to their response to the star. Ferraro, "'My Way' in 'Our America,'" 499–522; Ferraro, "Urbane Villager" in Pugliese, *Frank Sinatra*, 135–46.

33. Gans, *The Urban Villagers*, 192–93.

34. Ibid., 192. Richard Alba's research conducted during 1986–87 revealed that Sinatra was still being named by Italian Americans as a star with whom they identified. Alba, *Ethnic Identity*, 159.

35. Riesman, Glazer, and Denney, *The Lonely Crowd*, 28–48.

36. Whyte, *The Organization Man*, 7.

37. Ibid., 30.

38. Ibid., 3.

39. When Margo Channing (Bette Davis) lists the faults of her director boyfriend Bill Sampson (Gary Merrill) in *All about Eve*, his response is: "Well, everybody can't be Gregory Peck." In *The Seven Year Itch*, Tom Ewell's married man complains to neighbor Marilyn Monroe: "No pretty girl in her right mind wants me. She wants Gregory Peck."

40. William H. Whyte draws attention to *Woman's World* as an example of fictional texts that promote a philosophy of "acceptance." Whyte, *The Organization Man*, 242–44.

41. Quoted in Morella and Epstein, *Rebels*, 12.

42. Schatz, *Hollywood Genres*, 228–30.

43. Young's character in *Teacher's Pet* is drawn as particularly flawless. Psychology professor Dr. Hugo Pine is a noted expert in his field and, as he demonstrates in a nightclub on a date with Doris Day's journalism lecturer, is a proficient player of the bongo drums and can converse ably with members of the Watutsi tribe. As in most of these films, including *Young at Heart*, Young's character is contrasted with a less perfect male model, this time provided by Clark Gable's middle-aged, uneducated newspaper editor.

44. Mills, *White Collar*, 263.

45. Zinsser, *New York Herald Tribune*, quoted in Morella and Epstein, *Rebels*, 81.

46. Quoted in Ehrenreich, *The Hearts of Men*, 38.

47. Day revealed in a 1989 BBC documentary that the original *Young at Heart* script retained the *Four Daughters*–style ending, and it was at Sinatra's insistence that the script was altered so that Barney would survive. *I Don't Even Like Apple Pie*, BBC, 1989.

48. Screenwriter Budd Schulberg reports that the script was sent first to Brando,

who returned it without comment. Recalling Sinatra's Hoboken background, and knowing that the film was due to be shot in the same New Jersey location, Schulberg and Kazan approached Sinatra, who accepted the part. Spiegel, however, lacked confidence in his ability to attract finance on the basis of Sinatra's name and so set about persuading Brando to take on the role. Schulberg, "Secrets of Sinatra," reprinted in Vare, *Legend*, 209.

49. Preminger was so impressed with Sinatra's performance that he later expressed an interest in filming Mario Puzo's *The Godfather* with Sinatra in the role of Don Vito Corleone. When Sinatra declined, Preminger withdrew from the project, unwilling to accept another actor in the part. O'Brien, *The Frank Sinatra Film Guide*, 208.

50. Schulberg, "Secrets of Sinatra," 209.

51. Algren, *The Man with the Golden Arm*, 14.

52. Rosen, "Anatomy of a Junkie Movie," in Peary and Shatzkin, *The Modern American Novel and the Movies*, 194.

Chapter 2: Ethnic Stereotyping and Italian American Cultural Identity

1. Sinatra performed at the club for one week every summer through the 1950s and into the 1960s, in addition to Rat Pack performances. D'Amato also performed a managerial role at Sinatra's Cal-Neva Lodge on the California-Nevada border in the early 1960s. The two men formed a close friendship, celebrating their birthdays together every year until D'Amato's death in 1984. Sinatra served as one of the pallbearers at D'Amato's funeral.

2. Connolly and D'Acierno, "Italian-American Musical Culture and Its Contribution to American Music," 428.

3. Sinatra was also cast as an Irishman in a number of films, including *Take Me Out to the Ball Game* (1949), *Never So Few* (1959), and *None but the Brave* (1965).

4. *Sinatra: An American Original*, CBS, November 16, 1965.

5. Parsons, "Fabulous Frank Sinatra," 28, 78, and 80.

6. Wood, "Dining Alla Sinatra."

7. Vecoli, "The Making and Un-Making of the Italian American Working Class," 53–55. William F. Whyte confirms Italian Americans' regard for Mussolini in his study of an East Coast slum. Whyte, *Street Corner Society*, 274.

8. Polenberg, *One Nation Divisible*, 60.

9. Doherty, *Projections of War*, 131.

10. Quoted in Polenberg, *One Nation Divisible*, 50–51.

11. Ibid., 54. Polenberg notes that the organizers of such festivals were often unsure whether the events would unite their communities or highlight divisions.

12. Ibid., 59.

13. A short-lived television version of the show also aired on CBS in 1952, Vito Scott replacing Naish.

14. "A Day in New York with Frank Sinatra," *Life with Luigi*, CBS, October 10, 1950.

15. Hamill, *Why Sinatra Matters,* 48–49.

16. Ibid., 48.

17. Vecoli, "The Italian People of New Jersey," 291.

18. Quoted in Arnold Shaw, *Sinatra,* 110. A note in Sinatra's FBI file confirms that a photograph had been located (supplied by Lee Mortimer) picturing Sinatra disembarking from a plane in Havana with Joe and Rocco Fischetti. The date, noted as September 1947, however, fails to tally with Ruark's article published in February, and the discrepancy in the dates is not explained. Kuntz and Kuntz, *The Sinatra Files,* 26 and 99.

19. Mortimer, "Frank Sinatra Confidential," 29–36. *The Hollywood Reporter* labeled Mortimer's article "the most vicious attack ever printed on an entertainer . . . the filthiest piece of gutter journalism ever composed." Quoted in Shaw, *Sinatra,* 161. During his lecture at Yale, Sinatra confronted the rumor about Mafia intervention in his contract difficulties with Dorsey. He advised his audience that the matter was resolved through pressure from lawyer Sol Jaffe, who also acted on behalf of the American Federation of Radio Artists, and threatened to impede Dorsey's lucrative radio broadcasts. *Libby Zion Lecture,* Yale University, April 15, 1986.

20. Quoted in Gehman, *Sinatra and His Rat Pack,* 178.

21. Quoted in Shaw, *Sinatra,* 113. Mortimer was relentless in his attempts to associate Sinatra with organized crime, even referring to the star in a review of *It Happened in Brooklyn* as "Frank (Lucky) Sinatra." O'Brien, *The Frank Sinatra Film Guide,* 31. Some sections of the press were sympathetic to Sinatra's act of retaliation. Ed Sullivan called for the press to stop "kicking him around," and the editor of *Metronome* commented: "While disagreeing with the method of Frank's counterattack, I can't seriously question his choice of target." Quoted in Kahn, "What Will Sinatra Do Next?"

22. Quoted in Shaw, *Sinatra,* 110–11.

23. *Sinatra: An American Original,* CBS, November 16, 1965. The club in question was the Cal-Neva Lodge. When the chairman of the Nevada Gaming Control Board, Edward Olsen, filed a complaint in 1963 citing Giancana's illegal presence at the lodge, he received numerous letters expressing a distaste for Sinatra's male image. Olsen remarks: "The unfortunate thing that I found out . . . was that so many people had apparently an ingrained resentment of Sinatra because he had been successful, or he came from a poor background and made money, or something like that. And so many of these [letters] had racial overtones. People were just *bitter* about the man." Van Meter, *The Last Good Time,* 200.

24. *What's Inside Frank Sinatra's Coffin?* Channel 4, August 30, 2004.

25. D'Acierno, "Cinema Paradiso," 574.

26. Quoted in Goodman, "The Kid from Hoboken," 42; *The Rat Pack Captured* (June 20, 1965), Channel 4, 1998; *Sinatra: An American Original,* CBS, November 16, 1965. The benefit concert in St. Louis was raising money for Dismas House, a rehabilitation center for ex-offenders run by Father Dismas, nicknamed "the hoodlum priest."

27. Hamill, *Why Sinatra Matters,* 49.

28. *Dean Martin Roasts Frank Sinatra,* NBC, February 7, 1978. The *Dean Martin Celebrity Roasts* were a spinoff from *The Dean Martin Show* and ran on NBC between 1975 and 1984 as a series of "specials." Each of the shows, hosted by Martin, featured a performer who would be subjected to comedic disparagement by his fellow artists.

29. *Frank, Liza & Sammy: The Ultimate Event!,* Kodak Programs Inc., 1989. Mario Puzo confirmed that he drew on something he had read about Sinatra's contract with Dorsey in a gossip column—"It could have been Lee Mortimer"—as the basis for Johnny Fontane's career difficulties in *The Godfather.* "I tried to imagine how Frank would feel and think. I constructed a persona based on his legend." Nancy Sinatra, *Frank Sinatra* (1995), 50.

30. D'Acierno, "Introduction," xxx.

31. Guglielmo, "'No Color Barrier,'" 34 and 36.

32. Gennari describes male rap stars' cultural envy of Italian machismo, Sinatra being their main idol. He traces this crossover back to Marvin Gaye, who confessed: "My dream was to become Frank Sinatra. . . . I used to fantasize about having a lifestyle like his—carrying on in Hollywood and becoming a movie star. Every woman in America wanted to go to bed with Frank Sinatra. He was the king I longed to be." Gennari, "Passing for Italian," 36 and 38.

33. Hamill, *Why Sinatra Matters,* 46.

34. Moore, *The Kefauver Committee and the Politics of Crime, 1950–1952,* 237.

35. Kefauver initially lobbied for a committee on organized crime, with an eye on the 1952 Democratic vice presidential nomination. He eventually took his place on the Adlai Stevenson ticket in 1956. The late Benjamin "Bugsy" Siegel's mistress Virginia Hill added a touch of glamour to the New York proceedings, and the coverage was awarded an Emmy for Special Achievement for "bringing the workings of . . . government into the homes of the American people." Ibid., 201. Resisting a public appearance at the hearings, Sinatra was interviewed by a committee attorney, Joseph Nellis, in March 1951 in the office of Sinatra's lawyer at New York's Rockefeller Center. Sinatra admitted being acquainted with the Fischetti brothers but denied any business involvement or knowledge of their current whereabouts. Kuntz and Kuntz, *The Sinatra Files,* 111; Van Meter, *The Last Good Time,* 115.

36. Sinatra also indicated that his father's use of the name O'Brien as an amateur boxer, because of Irish control of boxing circles, served as a further incentive to retain his surname. Hamill, *Why Sinatra Matters,* 37–38.

37. *The Frank Sinatra Show,* ABC, November 29, 1957; *Frank, Dean and Sammy at The Sands,* Las Vegas, 1963.

38. Sinatra also recorded "(On the Island of) Stromboli" in 1949 and "Luna Rossa" in 1952.

39. Tosches, *Dino,* 52. Frank Krutnik observes that Martin toned down the overt Italian references that were a feature of his act with Jerry Lewis when critics of their

stage and television performances suggested they were becoming an annoyance. As Krutnik notes, however, the plastic surgery Martin chose to have performed on his nose had already indicated his readiness to present a more palatable ethnic image. Krutnik, *Inventing Jerry Lewis,* 58–59.

40. Goodman, "The Kid from Hoboken," 42–43.

41. Rogers St. Johns, "The Nine Lives of Frank Sinatra," 83.

42. In his entertaining analysis of Sinatra's masculine style, Zehme also quotes Sinatra's explanation for Joey Evans's specific look in *Pal Joey:* "I was so crazy about that suit from the movie, I didn't want to wear the coat over it—and that's why I put it over my shoulder." Zehme, *The Way You Wear Your Hat,* 131 and 115.

43. D'Acierno, *The Italian American Heritage,* 708.

44. Gans, *The Urban Villagers,* 82–83.

45. Pleasants, *The Great American Popular Singers,* 189.

46. Ibid., 190.

47. Talese, "Frank Sinatra Has a Cold," 104.

48. Goodman, "The Kid from Hoboken," 43.

49. Larkin, "Sinatra: 'Why They Hate Me,'" 92.

50. Talese, "Frank Sinatra Has a Cold," 102.

51. Ibid., 103. Arnold Shaw makes similar connections between Sinatra's attitudes and the *uomini rispettati.* Shaw, *Sinatra,* 17.

52. Talese, "Frank Sinatra Has a Cold," 124.

53. Gans, *The Urban Villagers,* 193n. Gans quotes Richard Gehman's reference to the Rat Pack motto: "Where's the action?"

54. Whyte explains the opposing attitudes through reference to two "Cornerville" inhabitants, college boy Chick and corner boy Doc: "Chick judged men according to their capacity for advancing themselves. Doc judged them according to their loyalty to their friends and their behavior in their personal relations." Whyte, *Street Corner Society,* 107 and 256–57.

55. Whyte gives the example of one college-educated man with political ambitions, who, taking fruit gratis from a fruit stall, explained that most of the stalls were rented from his uncle, and that if he ran for office, the stall-holders would have to vote for him or lose their stalls. Ibid., 89.

56. Yarwood, *Sinatra on Sinatra,* 89.

57. Quoted in Kelley, *His Way,* 186.

58. Quoted in O'Brien, *The Frank Sinatra Film Guide,* 66.

59. Biskind, *Seeing Is Believing,* 84.

60. Quoted in Kelley, *His Way,* 193. Joan Cohn concurred with this assessment after watching both Wallach's and Sinatra's tests, telling her husband: "He's [Wallach] a brilliant actor . . . but he looks too good. He's not skinny and he's not pathetic and he's not Italian. Frank is just Maggio to me."

61. Hamill, *Why Sinatra Matters,* 80.

62. Whyte, *Street Corner Society,* 126.

63. Quoted in Ringgold and McCarty, *The Films of Frank Sinatra,* 79.

Chapter 3: Anticommunist Witch Hunts and Civil Rights

Epigraph quoted in Greenwood and Stein, "Sinatra Given L.A. NAACP Award despite Rights Protest," 22.

1. Ibid., 22.
2. Sinatra, "Perspective on the Fourth of July," B5.
3. Meyer, "Frank Sinatra," 311–35.
4. Brownstein, *The Power and the Glitter,* 143–77.
5. Cripps, *Making Movies Black,* 200.
6. Kelley, *His Way,* 93–94.
7. Nelson, "Frank Sinatra and Presidential Politics," 49.
8. Whyte, *Street Corner Society,* 273–74.
9. Hamill, *Why Sinatra Matters,* 45.
10. Koppes and Black, *Hollywood Goes to War,* 66–69.
11. Gerstle, *American Crucible,* 204.
12. Ibid., 209.
13. Ceplair and Englund, *The Inquisition in Hollywood,* 98–100.
14. *60 Greatest Old-Time Radio Shows,* 42.
15. Sinatra, "What's This about Races?" 23–25; Sinatra, "Let's Not Forget We're *All* Foreigners," 7.
16. "The Voice Talks to the Boys," *Daily News,* October 24, 1945, 4, quoted in Meyer, "When Frank Sinatra Came to Italian Harlem," 175 and 161–76; Pozzetta, "My Children Are My Jewels," 72. The Benjamin Franklin High School was the subject of an OWI documentary that celebrated the school as an example of "democracy in action." Principal Leonard Covello pioneered the "community-centered school" during the 1930s and worked specifically with immigrant and racially defined communities. Gerald Meyer's research suggests the reporting of the incident and the use of terms such as "riots" grossly exaggerated what occurred at the school. The invitation issued to Sinatra was part of a campaign to both contest some of the press coverage of what had occurred and to reaffirm the school's commitment to integrated education.
17. "Frank Sinatra in Gary," 45–46; Wiener, "When Old Blue Eyes Was 'Red,'" 65; Kuntz and Kuntz, *The Sinatra Files,* 42–44; Kelley, *His Way,* 107–9. Both *Life* and Sinatra's FBI file suggest a connection between the students' actions and their parents' fears for their steel-mill jobs. The FBI file also reports communist suggestions that the mill owners had encouraged the dispute as a means of dividing white and black workers in the midst of pay negotiations.
18. Van Horne, *New York World-Telegram,* November 13, 1945 reprinted on CD sleeve notes to *Frank Sinatra, Volume Two.*
19. Kelley, *His Way,* 109.
20. As Thomas Cripps explains, the facts about this incident were distorted by the American forces. Although pilot Kelly and bombardier Levin worked together, the vessel they sank was a Japanese freighter that they mistook for the *Haruna,*

the largest cruiser in the Japanese navy. In order to divert attention from the mistake, the aspect of cooperation between religions was played up. The deceit was perpetuated, with the event being featured in *True Comics* and serving as the basis for Howard Hawks's *Air Force* (1943). Cripps, *Making Movies Black,* 31.

21. Cripps, "Racial Ambiguities in American Propaganda Movies," 136.

22. Doherty, *Projections of War,* 144–45.

23. The 1952 McCarran-Walter Act removed the ban on immigration from Asia and allowed Asian immigrants to become United States citizens.

24. Doherty, *Projections of War,* 137–45.

25. Ibid., 224–26.

26. Racist attitudes were, of course, not limited to the southern states. A report published in 1943 by the OWI revealed that the war had little effect on attitudes toward race. Ninety-nine percent of white southerners and seventy-six percent of white northerners were still in favor of segregated restaurants. Ibid., 205.

27. Cripps, "Racial Ambiguities in American Propaganda Movies," 137–41; Neve, *Film and Politics in America,* 80–81.

28. "Sinatra Flicker on Intolerance a Fine Attempt," 35.

29. Friedwald, *Sinatra! The Song Is You,* 323.

30. Cripps, *Making Movies Black,* 199–200.

31. Dick, *Radical Innocence,* 97.

32. Doherty, *Projections of War,* 205–6.

33. Kuntz and Kuntz, *The Sinatra Files,* 58; Wiener, "When Old Blue Eyes Was 'Red,'" 64.

34. *The Frank Sinatra Show,* CBS, November 13, 1951.

35. *America, I Hear You Singing,* Reprise, 1964.

36. *The Main Event: Frank Sinatra in Concert Madison Square Garden,* Braveworld, 1990.

37. CD accompanying Nancy Sinatra, *Frank Sinatra: An American Legend.*

38. In his statement before HUAC, Maltz referred to *The House I Live In* as one of the screenplays for which the committee was urging he be blacklisted. Fellow screenwriter Samuel Ornitz, in a statement he was prevented from reading, also listed *House* among the work of the "unfriendly" that "attacked anti-Semitism or treated Jews and Negroes sympathetically." Kahn, *Hollywood on Trial,* 89 and 99.

39. Kuntz and Kuntz, *The Sinatra Files,* 58.

40. Brownstein, *The Power and the Glitter,* 86–87.

43. Kelley, *His Way,* 106.

44. Sinatra, "As Sinatra Sees It," 3. The title of this "Letter of the Week" reads as a response to Westbrook Pegler's *Journal-American* column "As Pegler Sees It."

43. Ibid., 46.

44. The letter, received in August 1943, came from a concerned Californian who had heard Sinatra on the radio the evening before: "How easy it would be for certain-minded manufacturers to create another Hitler here in America through the influence of mass-hysteria! I believe that those who are using this shrill whis-

tling sound are aware that it is similar to that which produced Hitler. That they intend to get a Hitler in by first planting in the minds of the people that men like Frank Sinatra are O.K. therefore this future Hitler will be O.K." Kuntz and Kuntz, *The Sinatra Files,* 4.

45. Sinatra's FBI file lists a variety of organizations with which he was alleged to have been associated, from Action for Palestine to the Committee for a Democratic Far Eastern Policy. Kuntz and Kuntz, *The Sinatra Files,* 69–76 and 40–67.

46. Kahn, *The Voice,* 31.

47. Nelson, "Frank Sinatra and Presidential Politics," 50. One of Sinatra's responses to press attacks was to alter the lyrics of one of his hit songs, "Everything Happens to Me," during a concert at New York's Paramount Theater: "They asked me down to Washington/ To have a cup of tea/ The Republicans started squawking/ They're as mad as they can be/And all I did was say 'hello' to a/man named Franklin D./Everything happens to me." Brownstein, *The Power and the Glitter,* 94. In November 1944, before FDR was reelected later that month, Pegler wrote: "There are among the Roosevelt political following some thorough Americans who support him though they know that thereby they put themselves in alliance with the Communists." Tuck, *McCarthyism and New York's Hearst Press,* 16.

48. Wiener, "When Old Blue Eyes Was 'Red,'" 65. In *Gentleman's Agreement,* Smith is named several times as an example of anti-Semitic Americanism.

49. The 1947 HUAC hearings subpoenaed Hollywood employees who had a strong left-wing history, while the hearings that took place between 1951 and 1954 and resulted in a blacklist and graylist were much more wide-ranging.

50. Following the second broadcast by the committee on November 2, 1947, Sinatra asked: "If this . . . Committee gets a green light from the American people, will it be possible to make a broadcast like this a year from today?" In addition to their two radio broadcasts, members of the committee flew to Washington and presented a petition to the clerk of the House of Representatives seeking redress against the various "abuses of civil rights" perpetrated by the hearings. The 1948 report of the California Committee on Un-American Activities labeled the Committee for the First Amendment a "recently created Communist front in the defense of Communists and Communist fellow-travelers." Kahn, *Hollywood on Trial,* 141–44 and 219–220; Kuntz and Kuntz, *The Sinatra Files,* 57.

51. Goff, "Sinatra, Commie Playboy." Sinatra answered criticism of his appearance at Madison Square Garden from Gerval T. Murphy, a director of the Supreme Council of the Knights of Columbus, as follows: "That was no Red Rally. It was a rally sponsored by the Veterans Committee of the Independent Citizens Committee of the Arts, Sciences, and Professions. While Murphy was hunting witches, the committee was urging passage of legislation to provide housing for veterans. I was trying to help veterans get homes to live in. If that was subversive activity, I'm all for it. . . . The minute anyone tries to help the little guy, he's called a Communist. . . . The guy's a jerk." Kelley, *His Way,* 110.

52. Tuck, *McCarthyism and New York's Hearst Press,* 45.

53. Ibid., 46.

54. Hamill, *Why Sinatra Matters,* 144.

55. Shaw, *Sinatra,* 114.

56. Ibid., 114.

57. Mortimer, "Frank Sinatra Confidential," 31.

58. Bogart, *Bogart,* 131.

59. Meyer, "Frank Sinatra," 325.

60. Kuntz and Kuntz, *The Sinatra Files,* 67–69.

61. Meyer, "Frank Sinatra," 326.

62. Brownstein, *The Power and the Glitter,* 119.

63. Whitfield, *The Culture of the Cold War,* 19.

64. Cripps, *Making Movies Black,* 153; Polenberg, *One Nation Divisible,* 108.

65. Graham, *Framing the South,* 18–19.

66. Whitfield, *The Culture of the Cold War,* 21.

67. Ibid., 21.

68. The Civil Rights Act of 1964 and the Voting Rights Act of 1965 were more substantial pieces of legislation.

69. Sinatra, "The Way I Look at Race," 35.

70. Ibid., 35–44. NBC's *The Nat King Cole Show* premiered in November 1956 and broke new ground for African Americans on television but was canceled after just over a year following a continuous struggle to attract sponsors and Cole's refusal to be moved to an unfavorable time slot. Cole's succinct comment on the reason for the show's failure was, 'Madison Avenue's afraid of the dark.' "The Unforgettable Nat King Cole," *Arena,* BBC, 1988; MacDonald, "Black Perimeters," 255–64.

71. Quoted in Mustazza, "Introduction," 11.

72. *Home of the Brave* (1949) changes the Jewish soldier in Arthur Laurents's play to an African American suffering posttraumatic stress and the effects of racism in World War II. *Intruder in the Dust* (1949) tackles the unfair justice system some years prior to *To Kill a Mockingbird* (1962) in the trial of a proud black landowner accused of shooting a white man in the back.

73. Graham, *Framing the South,* 36.

74. Brown, *Kings Go Forth,* 110.

75. Curtis and Paris, *Tony Curtis,* 148.

76. Gardner, *Ava,* 142.

77. Dyer, *Films and Filming,* quoted in Ringgold and McCarty, *The Films of Frank Sinatra,* 143.

78. *The Los Angeles Mirror-News,* quoted in ibid., 143.

Chapter 4: Vulnerable Masculinity and Damaged Veterans

1. Mellen, *Big Bad Wolves,* 193.

2. Cohan, *Masked Men,* 220.

3. Ibid., 259–63.

4. Unnamed psychologist quoted in Kahn, *The Voice,* 48.

5. Erenberg, "Swing Goes to War," 157.

6. Smith, *God Bless America,* 50–121. As Smith's study shows, there were a variety of reasons why songs written to inspire the nation's patriotism were largely unpopular. As well as increased cynicism regarding the motives for war following the disillusionment created by World War I, the fast turnover of hits in the radio age and the emergence of the teenage market in the mid-1940s gave the war song an environment in which to fail. Frank Loesser's "Praise the Lord and Pass the Ammunition" achieved a level of success in 1942 but fell far short of the popularity of "Over There."

7. As Stowe points out, although white swing bands were undoubtedly more commercially successful as a result of record-industry bias, and African American musicians were subject to the prejudices of individuals in the music world, the early 1940s saw several white bandleaders making steps toward the creation of racially integrated bands, for example, Benny Goodman's hiring of Teddy Wilson and Lionel Hampton and Billie Holiday's tenure with Artie Shaw. Stowe, *Swing Changes,* 142–43 and 127–30.

8. "Miller over There," *Metronome,* September 1944, 26, and "Miller a Killer!," *Metronome,* November 1944, 15, quoted in ibid., 154–55.

9. Smith, *God Bless America,* 123–24.

10. Erenberg, "Swing Goes to War," 156.

11. Sinatra was, of course, not the only male singer performing in the field of popular music at this point. Dick Haymes, for example, followed Sinatra into the James and Dorsey bands, and Bing Crosby was still topping polls for favorite male singer. However, Sinatra's rise to prominence as a solo singer from 1942 onward associates him particularly with America's war years and with the ballads that formed its soundtrack.

12. Feather, "Frankly Speaking."

13. "I'll Walk Alone" made the top of the Hit Parade eight times in 1944 and was nominated for an Academy Award the same year, losing out to "Swingin' on a Star." Smith, *God Bless America,* 31.

14. Benjamin, "Sad Sack."

15. As Eberwein notes, the term "Mama Boys" appears here before "Mama's boy" is taken up by Philip Wylie in *Generation of Vipers* (1942). Eberwein, "As a Mother Cuddles a Child," 151.

16. Ibid., 155.

17. Sinatra commented in *Ebony* in 1958: "It is Billie Holiday whom I first heard in 52nd Street clubs in the early 1930s, who was and still remains the greatest single musical influence on me." Sinatra, "The Way I Look at Race," 42. Ava Gardner is said to have remarked regarding Holiday: "I used to hear her every night when I was first married to Frank. He said that, more than anyone, she taught him to handle a lyric." Pleasants, *The Great American Popular Singers,* 185.

18. Furia, "Sinatra on Broadway," 164.

19. Ibid, 167 and 173. As Furia notes, songs that appeared in Broadway musicals,

before the Rodgers and Hammerstein integrated musical approach took hold, had what he terms "particularity." Having their own situation, character, and narrative unrelated to the show's plot meant they could be extracted from their surroundings by a singer such as Sinatra and go on to become a "standard," rather than being resigned to the status of "show tune," a fate assigned to most songs from later musicals. Though Sinatra appeared in the film version of *Higher and Higher,* of course, he was unable to take advantage of the original score, since all but one of the Rodgers and Hart songs were discarded by RKO and replaced by tunes supplied by Jimmy McHugh and Harold Adamson.

20. Ibid., 164–65.

21. "One for My Baby" was introduced by Fred Astaire in *The Sky's the Limit* (1943). Astaire begins his rendition with a feeling of self-pity but finishes angrily smashing glasses and a bar stool into the mirrored walls of a barroom. This contrasts with Sinatra's subdued rendition in *Young at Heart,* when Sloan performs the song in a bar after a heated argument with Doris Day's Laurie. Sammy Davis Jr. paid tribute to Astaire's performance in *Robin and the Seven Hoods* (1964), dancing across a bar and shooting guns in the "Bang Bang" number.

22. *Sinatra Concert,* Royal Festival Hall, London, BBC, June 1, 1962.

23. Friedwald, *Sinatra! The Song Is You,* 247.

24. Connolly and D'Acierno, "Italian-American Musical Culture and Its Contribution to American Music," 423–24.

25. Friedwald, *Sinatra! The Song Is You,* 204.

26. *The Dean Martin Show,* NBC, February 1, 1958.

27. Granata, *Sessions with Sinatra,* 92.

28. Shaw, *Sinatra,* 102.

29. Lahr, "Sinatra's Song," 86.

30. Israel, *Kilgallen,* 220. Dorothy Kilgallen, in particular, pitched an image of Sinatra as rather pathetic. As Lee Israel describes it, "She hounded Frank Sinatra in the fifties, when he was not yet in a position to hit back, delineating him as the despairing victim of his unsuccessful marriage to Ava Gardner." In 1956 she followed her column pieces with a series titled "The Real Frank Sinatra Story," in which she suggested an agent from William Morris had been assigned to Sinatra to "try to keep him from slashing his wrists." Kilgallen, "The Real Frank Sinatra Story," 36.

31. Quoted in Shaw, *Sinatra,* 165.

32. Dyer, "Resistance through Charisma," 115.

33. Horton, "One Good Take," 15.

34. Place and Peterson, "Some Visual Motifs of *Film Noir,*" 68.

35. Christopher, *Somewhere in the Night,* 15–16.

36. Naremore, *More Than Night,* 187; Christopher, *Somewhere in the Night,* 223–24.

37. Although the voice is not Crosby's, the intention to represent it as such is clear from the similar voice and the song "June in January," one of Crosby's signature tunes.

38. Nancy Sinatra suggests that her father's adoption of the fedora was not meant to project a specific image, but his reasoning does indicate something of the vulnerability with which it can be associated: "The funny thing is, he wore them as a response to his receding hairline; it was just an easier way of dealing with it in public. He didn't realize what a tumult it would start." Zehme, *The Way You Wear Your Hat,* 116 and 17.

39. Shaw, *Sinatra,* 211.

40. *Sinatra Concert,* Royal Festival Hall, BBC, June 1, 1962; *The Frank Sinatra Show,* October 19, 1959; *The Voice of Our Time,* PBS, 1991. Some episodes of Sinatra's ABC series concluded with an image of Sinatra, raincoat over his shoulder, departing the studio lot alone.

41. Starr, "The Marlboro Man," 49.

42. As Bruce Lohof explains, the Marlboro Man underwent a series of transformations as the campaign used a variety of tattooed figures and eventually settled on a cowboy minus tattoos in 1963. Lohof quotes an agency executive: "We asked ourselves what was the most generally accepted symbol of masculinity in America, and this led quite naturally to a cowboy." Lohof, "The Higher Meaning of Marlboro Cigarettes," 235.

43. The difficulties with this image in advertising terms are suggested by the failure of the UK campaign for Strand cigarettes in 1959. Drawing heavily on Sinatra imaging, the black and white television advertisements featured a young man in an overcoat and hat, walking alone in the city streets after dark. A British television program in 2003 noted that the popularity of the advertisements and the theme tune "The Lonely Man," which topped the UK charts, nevertheless failed to translate into increased sales. The promotional line, "You're never alone with a Strand," failed to override the visual imagery, which suggested instead, "You're always alone with a Strand." Although an argument based around cultural differences between the U.S. and UK markets could be made, it seems clear that the image was simply not one to which men aspired, even if they were able to identify with the figure. *100 Greatest TV Adverts,* Channel 4, May 3, 2003.

44. Even behind the machismo of the Marlboro Man, there are issues of the feminine that impact on the strength of this image, since the campaign was constructed as a means of counteracting the feminizing effect of the company's new filtered cigarettes. Lohof, "The Higher Meaning of Marlboro Cigarettes," 235.

45. Naremore, *Acting in the Cinema,* 85. Pudovkin refers to the battleship in *Battleship Potemkin* (1925) as an example of an "active object" that has narrative agency rivaling that of the characters themselves. In appropriating Pudovkin's term, Naremore uses it less broadly to discuss objects used by characters and actors to signal emotions or character traits.

46. Ibid., 86–87. The scene in question is when Sheldrake (Fred MacMurray) confronts Baxter about his loaning out his apartment in return for professional advancement.

47. Starr, "The Marlboro Man," 52–53.

48. Horton, "One Good Take," 15.

49. The opening exchange between Barney and Laurie illustrates his cynical rudeness and her positive persistence; Barney continues working while Laurie works her way through lighters and matches in an effort to light his cigarette.

50. Quoted in Ringgold and McCarty, *The Films of Frank Sinatra,* 87; Morella and Epstein, *Rebels,* 81.

51. In *Libra,* Don DeLillo reiterates this myth by having Oswald watch *Suddenly* prior to JFK's assassination: "He felt connected to the events on the screen. It was like secret instructions entering the network of signals and broadcast bands. . . . They were running a message through the night into his skin." DeLillo, *Libra,* 369–70.

52. O'Brien, *The Frank Sinatra Film Guide,* 67.

53. Brod, "Masculinity as Masquerade," 14.

54. Wexman, "Kinesics and Film Acting," 208.

55. Kimmel, *Manhood in America,* 225.

56. Cohan makes similar assertions in Cohan, *Masked Men,* 120–21.

57. O'Brien, *The Frank Sinatra Film Guide,* 67.

58. *The Heiress* omits direct reference to Maurice's guilt or otherwise, whereas in Henry James's *Washington Square,* readers are told that the character is a gold-digger. Dyer, *Stars,* 134.

59. Ibid., 155–56.

60. Silverman, *Male Subjectivity at the Margins,* 52–53.

61. Warshow, *The Immediate Experience,* 161.

62. Silverman, *Male Subjectivity at the Margins,* 89–90.

63. Keightley, "The Man in the Gray Sharkskin Suit."

64. Ehrenreich, *The Hearts of Men,* 15.

65. "Frankie in Madison," 40.

66. Tosches, *Dino,* 51.

67. Silverman, *Male Subjectivity at the Margins,* 78.

68. Skolsky, "The New Look in Hollywood Men," 41. This article is also discussed in Cohan, *Masked Men,* 201–3 and 239–41.

69. Skolsky, "The New Look in Hollywood Men," 42.

Chapter 5: Male Performance and Swingin' Bachelors

Epigraph in Coss, "Frank Sinatra," 15. Sinatra's only screen connection to the western is in the 1956 film *Johnny Concho,* in which, rather than reinforcing the cowboy's image of independence and heroism, Sinatra plays this male archetype as a coward.

1. *Celebrity Sell,* n.p.

2. Doane, *Femme Fatales,* 21.

3. Babington and Evans, *Affairs to Remember,* 197.

4. Lippe, "Kim Novak," 10.

5. "Frankie Fans Make Poor Wives," 33.

6. "Night and Day" became one of Sinatra's early theme songs after he performed the song in *Reveille with Beverly* in 1943 and used it to open radio shows of *Old Gold Presents Songs by Sinatra* from 1945 to 1947.

7. *The Unheard Frank Sinatra*, vols. 1–4; Kahn, *The Voice*, 52 and 67–68; Bliven, "The Voice and the Kids," 31–33. Jack Egan, press agent for the Tommy Dorsey Orchestra, confirmed that Sinatra's performance style and the audience response to it stretched back to his early days with the band: "You know, right then and there, when he went into the slurring bit, the kids started screaming, just the way they did later at the Paramount. And there was nothing rigged about it either. . . . No, those screams were real!" Simon, *The Big Bands*, 166.

8. Lear, "The Bobby Sox Have Wilted, but the Memory Remains Fresh," 47–48.

9. Kahn, "The Voice," 19.

10. Polan, *Power and Paranoia*, 124–25.

11. Tyler, *The Magic and Myth of the Movies*, 36.

12. Ibid., 36–37.

13. Sinatra's comments regarding the way to use a microphone, and the particular analogy he uses, reinforce the notion that he intentionally takes this traditionally female position of an object of desire: "You don't crowd it, you must never jar an audience with it. . . . You must know when to move away from the mike and when to move back into it. It's like a geisha girl uses her fan." Lahr, "Sinatra's Song," 80.

14. Kahn, *The Voice*, 48.

15. Martin, "Gilda Didn't Do Any of Those Things You've Been Losing Sleep Over!," 202.

16. Reisner, "The Word on Frank Sinatra," 63.

17. Kahn, *The Voice*, 49–50. Adela Rogers St. Johns also reported that a navy PT boat in World War II had been named *Oh, Frankie*. Rogers St. Johns, "The Nine Lives of Frank Sinatra," 85.

18. Kelly's image of potent sexuality is also significantly undermined by suggestions of fantasy coming from this musical number, as well as the fact that his girlfriend Lola never materializes. Joe Brady has been set up as "the best wolf in the whole navy." However, Lola remains part of the imaginary, and not even her voice is heard at the end of the telephone.

19. O'Brien, *The Frank Sinatra Film Guide*, 204.

20. *Come Blow Your Horn* works as a parody of *Pal Joey* and *The Tender Trap*. The opening titles feature a succession of images of Sinatra in Joey Evans–like poses, and Sinatra's character, Alan Baker, inhabits a heightened version of Charlie Reader's New York apartment, in which he is visited by several women. In this case, as Alan grooms his younger brother Buddy (Tony Bill) as his successor by styling him in sophisticated clothes and introducing him to one of his companions, Sinatra's character begins to view himself as a dangerously out-of-date, middle-aged anachronism. The 1950s playboy itself seems under attack as a dated figure, when Buddy hosts a party in Alan's apartment that is attended by artistic types

and pseudointellectuals wearing black polo necks, a sharp contrast with the more sophisticated image of the playboy. In *Lady in Cement,* Sinatra seems to have toughened up enough to be able to reference his public breakup with Ava Gardner. Rome tells Raquel Welch's character: "Maybe you're the kind of dame collects hoods. I used to know a broad collected bullfighters."

21. "Anything Goes," *Colgate Comedy Hour,* NBC, November 8, 1953. Performance is introduced in this initial playboy role as Harry takes on a number of disguises on board a ship bound for England, including dressing as a sailor, wearing women's clothes, and putting on a false moustache, while a borrowed passport incorrectly identifies him as "Angel Face" Nelson.

22. Zollo, "Open Season on Bachelors," 38.

23. Cohan, *Masked Men,* 271.

24. *Playboy* 2, no. 9 (September 1955): 36–37, quoted in Conekin, "Fashioning the Playboy," 449.

25. Emphasis in original. "What Is a Playboy?" Subscription Page.

26. Ehrenreich, *The Hearts of Men,* 50.

27. Kessie, "Ivy Action," 20, quoted in Conekin, "Fashioning the Playboy," 460.

28. Emphasis in original. Kessie, "The Well Dressed Playboy," 39, quoted in Conekin, "Fashioning the Playboy," 458–59. Conekin ends her discussion by noting a shift at the end of the 1950s toward a more fantasy-inspired look to correspond with a more glamorous lifestyle suggested by new fashion director Robert L. Green's articles. For example, readers are told how easy it is to "plan a swinging weekend on the Continent . . . and still be back in the office, refreshed and glowing, Monday morn" while wearing the proper attire—a Prince of Wales plaid suit and poplin raincoat by London Fog. Though she does not take this point much further, Conekin suggests that by focusing more on a fantasy approach, the magazine assumed its didacticism had worked and that the readership no longer needed to be told to dress in Ivy League style: it simply did. Conekin, "Fashioning the Playboy," 461; "Wardrobe for a Jet Weekend," 38–39.

29. Conekin, "Fashioning the Playboy," 460.

30. Reisner, "The Word on Frank Sinatra," 64.

31. By 1963, Sinatra had won *Playboy*'s All-Star Jazz Poll seven times. "*Playboy* Interview: Frank Sinatra," 35.

32. Legare, "Meeting at the Summit," 34. Not all readers were quite so enamored; some of them attacked the article's "reverential and admiring tone." Reader's letter quoted in Shaw, *Sinatra,* 268.

33. Emphasis in original. Reisner, "The Word on Frank Sinatra," 63.

34. Ibid., 63.

35. Ibid., 63.

36. Goodman, "The Kid from Hoboken," 42.

37. Masters, "The Nite Sinatra Had One Peer Too Many," 33.

38. *The Frank Sinatra Show,* ABC, November 29, 1957; *The Frank Sinatra Show,* ABC, January 31, 1958.

39. Fuchs, "Split Screens," 237.

40. Cohan, *Masked Men,* 271–75.

41. French, *On the Verge of Revolt,* 74–75.

42. Taves, "The Personal Story of the Tender Tough Guy Who Won't Behave," 39. This unfavorable comparison to Rock Hudson highlights the very different ways in which these stars need to be viewed in terms of their depictions of playboy masculinity.

43. Ibid., 39–40.

44. Cohan, *Masked Men,* 276–77; Fuchs, "Split Screens," 241; Krutnik, "The Faint Aroma of Performing Seals," 60.

45. Krutnik, "The Faint Aroma of Performing Seals," 59.

46. Friedan, *The Feminine Mystique,* 13–14.

47. Shaw, *Sinatra,* 225.

48. O'Hara explained to Broadway columnist Earl Wilson in a 1946 interview that motivation for the stories came following a heavy drinking session: "Remorse set in. I asked, 'What kind of god damn heel am I? I must be worse 'n anybody in the world.' Then I figured, 'No, there must be somebody worse than me—but who? Al Capone, maybe.' Then I got it—maybe some night club masters of ceremonies I know. . . . That was my idea. I went to work and wrote a piece about a night club heel in the form of a letter." Quoted in Matthew J. Bruccoli's Introduction to O'Hara, *Pal Joey,* x.

49. Columbia originally intended to have Gene Kelly reprise his performance in the film version of *Pal Joey,* which had been mooted for some years. MGM's refusal to loan out their star for a follow-up to his successful 1944 collaboration with Rita Hayworth in *Cover Girl,* however, left the project on the shelf, with periodic attempts to resurrect the story in the 1950s using such contrasting actors as Brando and Jack Lemmon. O'Brien, *The Frank Sinatra Film Guide,* 102.

50. "Speaker: Frank Sinatra." 84.

51. Sinatra used terms such as these constantly through the 1950s. During his April 1959 concert in Melbourne, Australia, he used words such as *broad, crazy,* and *mothery* in his performance of various songs. In November 1957 he opened an edition of his television show telling the audience: "We think this one's gonna be a gasser. Gasser defined means, well, it's a grabber." *Sinatra: A Tour de Force,* Bravura, 1990; *The Frank Sinatra Show,* ABC, November 29, 1957.

52. Quoted in Ringgold and McCarty, *The Films of Frank Sinatra,* 138.

53. Mulvey, "Visual Pleasure and Narrative Cinema," 837.

54. Hansen, "Pleasure, Ambivalence, Identification: Valentino and Female Spectatorship," 289.

55. Neale, "Masculinity as Spectacle," 18.

56. Cohan, "'Feminizing' the Song-and-Dance Man," 63.

57. Prior to the film's release, the casting of Hayworth and Novak generated most of the press interest. Rumors that Harry Cohn was grooming Novak as a replacement for his now middle-aged "love goddess" Hayworth led to suggestions that the

billing of the three stars was causing problems. Sinatra's public response was to argue that Hayworth's successful history with the studio meant that she deserved top billing. As he put it: "Rita Hayworth *is* Columbia." Accepting second billing, Sinatra played up to his and Joey's swinger image as he joked: "I don't mind being in the middle of that sandwich." Roberts-Frenzel, *Rita Hayworth,* 191.

58. In 2002, Ford used this clip of Sinatra, as Joey, saying good-bye to his Thunderbird as part of an advertising campaign promoting a new retro version of the Thunderbird Roadster.

59. Pickard, *Frank Sinatra at the Movies,* 111.

Conclusion

1. Bryson, "Sinatra at Fifty," 71. Bryson's article includes photographs of Sinatra and Warner chatting in expansive offices at Warner Bros. and Sinatra boarding his private jet helicopter.

2. Quoted in Shaw, *Sinatra,* 268–69.

3. Quoted in Tosches, *Dino,* 329–30.

4. Duke, "Vegas' Zillion-$ Five," 1 and 111.

5. Legare, "Meeting at the Summit," 43.

6. Ibid., 18.

7. Except where noted, examples come variously from *Frank, Dean and Sammy at The Sands, Las Vegas, 1963; Frank Sinatra, Dean Martin and Sammy Davis Jr. at Villa Venice, Chicago, Live 1962;* and *Rat Pack: From Vegas to St. Louis.*

8. Rudin, "Fly Me to the Moon," 57.

9. Davis counters these remarks later in the show, telling Martin, "I'll go to church with you, but don't touch me," and asking, "How do you like standing in the back of the bus, Dean?" *Frank, Dean and Sammy at The Sands, Las Vegas, 1963.*

10. Sinatra also predicts a future era of political correctness when, introducing Martin's rendition of "I Can't Give You Anything but Love," he informs the audience that the song was originally written for the Broadway show *Blackbirds of 1926.* Following Davis's askance look, Sinatra apologizes but argues that no one would name the song "Purple Birds of 1926." *Frank, Dean and Sammy at The Sands, Las Vegas, 1963.*

11. *Frank Sinatra, Dean Martin and Sammy Davis Jr. at Villa Venice, Chicago, Live 1962.*

12. Jacobs and Stadiem, *Mr. S,* 56.

13. Just as Davis's involvement with white actresses such as Kim Novak and his marriage to May Britt created difficulties for the star, Davis was fully aware that his closeness to Sinatra—whom he happily called "The Leader" in stage performances— problematized his image as an African American performer. While attending a rally in Birmingham, Alabama, in support of Martin Luther King Jr., his need to assert his racial identity and demonstrate his allegiance to the movement was illustrated by his remarks: "This should prove, once and for all, that my

leader is your leader: Martin Luther King." *Kings of Black Comedy: A Funny Thing Happened . . . to Sammy Davis Jr.,* Channel 4, February 23, 2002.

14. This event took place one week after John F. Kennedy's inauguration. As Taylor Branch notes: "Although the event attracted no national attention, it raised $50,000 for the SCLC and established King as the possessor of a celebrity-drawing power that ambitious politicians could not ignore." A further benefit concert for the SCLC, starring Sinatra with the Count Basie Orchestra, was planned for November 26, 1963, but was canceled following Kennedy's assassination. Branch, *Parting the Waters,* 385; Sinatra, *Frank Sinatra: An American Legend,* 178.

15. Roz Wyman, the Los Angeles city councilwoman who had the task of providing celebrities for events in the campaign, confirmed that Sinatra's influence in Hollywood made him an invaluable recruiting sergeant for the cause, eclipsing any assistance Kennedy's brother-in-law Peter Lawford could provide: "Sinatra was the one most able to pick up the phone and get us anybody. . . . Peter couldn't. Peter didn't have the clout. But Sinatra certainly had an incredible reach. I was always impressed with what Frank could do." Brownstein views the Sinatra-Kennedy relationship as the solidification of the association between show business and politics that would come to represent an unbreakable connection between fame and power. Brownstein writes: "In the popular imagination, the friendship between Sinatra and Kennedy symbolized the union of politics and show business, as if the two men were ambassadors for distinct branches in the American aristocracy of fame. . . . The apparently easy and casual association between the glamorous president and the powerful star provided a tangible symbol for the attraction between Hollywood and Washington unequalled before or since. It suggested new rewards at the pinnacle of American life, adding forever to fame's appeal a proximity to power, and to power's allure a proximity to fame." Brownstein, *The Power and the Glitter,* 151 and 155–56.

16. Quoted in Shaw, *Sinatra,* 275–76.

17. Quoted in Brownstein, *The Power and the Glitter,* 161.

18. Ibid., 160–61. In an article titled "'Rat Pack' in the White House?" Hearst journalist Ruth Montgomery seemed similarly perturbed, suggesting that "some Washington residents" were concerned that "the Rat Pack may be making a nest for itself in the White House after next January 20." Quoted in Shaw, *Sinatra,* 272.

19. Ibid., 271–72. The article also suggested Martin might be named "Secretary of Liquor" and Davis ambassador to Israel.

20. The lunch attended by Herbert Hoover and President Kennedy on March 22, 1962, in which Hoover detailed to Kennedy the information he had uncovered about the circle of Mob connections the president had created around himself through his association with Sinatra and various female companions, was not recorded in documentary form. Kuntz and Kuntz, *The Sinatra Files,* 164. Earl Wilson notes that when Bobby Kennedy's files were opened to the public in 1974, they revealed that the family's cynical, politically expedient attitude toward Sinatra was evident

back in 1960. The Kennedys' civil-rights advisor recommended to an aide that JFK should not meet Sinatra "in public" at a Constitutional Rights Conference in 1960 at which both were to appear. The aide expressed the hope, however, that Sinatra would assist with a voter registration drive in Harlem, "where he is recognized as a hero of the cause of the Negro." Wilson, *Sinatra,* 177.

21. Quoted in Kelley, *His Way,* 272.

22. Quoted in Gehman, *Sinatra and His Rat Pack,* 186.

23. Quoted in Kelley, *His Way,* 273.

24. The release of *Spartacus* provoked similar vitriolic outbursts from both the American Legion and columnists such as Hedda Hopper, who advised her readers: "That story was sold to Universal from a book written by a Commie and the screen script was written by a Commie, so don't go to see it." Douglas, *The Ragman's Son,* 332.

25. Quoted in Gehman, *Sinatra and His Rat Pack,* 187.

26. Sinatra responded to Wayne's attack with an advertisement in the Hollywood trade papers stating: "This type of partisan politics is hitting below the belt. I make movies. I do not ask the advice of Senator Kennedy on whom I should hire. Senator Kennedy does not ask me how he should vote in the Senate." Quoted in Kelley, *His Way,* 273.

27. Sinatra is said to have been unconcerned about the threat from General Motors to cancel their sponsorship of three upcoming television specials, telling business partner Nick Sevano: "Fuck 'em. There will be other specials." However, when priests began denouncing Sinatra's involvement with Maltz, and Governor Wesley Powell of New Hampshire accused Senator Kennedy of "softness toward communism," the pressure brought to bear by the Kennedy patriarch finally ended the project. A memo dated March 29, 1960, in Sinatra's FBI file reports that, according to Dalton Trumbo, John Kennedy requested that Sinatra delay his announcement to the press with regard to his hiring of Maltz until after the New Hampshire primaries. Once the announcement was made, Peter Lawford recalls, Joe Kennedy's ultimatum to Sinatra was: "It's either Maltz or us. Make up your mind." Kelley, *His Way,* 274; Kuntz and Kuntz, *The Sinatra Files,* 125.

28. Quoted in Gehman, *Sinatra and His Rat Pack,* 187.

29. Quoted in Kelley, *His Way,* 274–75. *The Execution of Private Slovik* was eventually made as a television movie in 1973 starring Martin Sheen. The film depicts Slovik as a benign ex–petty criminal, who had settled down with a wife and career before being drafted and was emotionally ill prepared for frontline duty.

30. Although Slovik was executed on January 31, 1945, and the character remains unnamed in the scene, as the only United States soldier executed in World War II for desertion, it is clearly Slovik's story to which the film refers. Foreman is reported to have revealed that Sinatra recorded this version of the song especially for the film and requested no payment, because of the subject matter. *Perfectly Frank* (April/ May 2001): 27 and 29.

31. "Sinatra's Mob," 8 and 53. The magazine's caption accompanying *Ocean's Eleven*'s closing image of the group's exit from Las Vegas sees the men less as stylish than threatening: "Any resemblance to a bunch of hoodlums is coincidental."

32. The Reprise Musical Repertory Theatre consisted of various artists signed to the label. In addition to Sinatra's frequent collaborators, these included performers such as Bing Crosby, Jo Stafford, and Debbie Reynolds.

33. Quoted in Shaw, *Sinatra,* 281.

34. Goodman, "The Kid from Hoboken," 42.

35. John C. Bowes, "The Reign of King Frankie," *American Weekly* (February 1960), quoted in Shaw, *Sinatra,* 260.

36. Gehman, "The Enigma of Frank Sinatra," 184.

37. "Welcome Home, Elvis," *The Frank Sinatra Show,* ABC, May 12, 1960.

38. Quoted in Miller, *Flowers in the Dustbin,* 169–70.

39. Marling, *As Seen on TV,* 166.

40. Quoted in Shaw, *Sinatra,* 267.

Bibliography

Adamowski, T. H. "Frank Sinatra: The Subject and His Music." *Journal of Popular Culture* 33, no. 4 (Spring 2000): 1–11.

Alba, Richard D. *Ethnic Identity: The Transformation of White America.* New Haven, Conn.: Yale University Press, 1990.

Algren, Nelson. *The Man with the Golden Arm.* 1949. New York: Pocket Books, 1956.

Alloway, Lawrence. "The Iconography of the Movies." In Ian Cameron, ed., *Movie Reader,* 16–18. London: November Books, 1962.

Anderson, Christopher. *Hollywood TV: The Studio System in the Fifties.* Austin: University of Texas Press, 1994.

Auster, Albert. "Frank Sinatra: The Television Years—1950–1960." *Journal of Popular Film and Television* (Winter 1999): 166–75.

Babington, Bruce, and Peter William Evans. *Affairs to Remember: The Hollywood Comedy of the Sexes.* Manchester, U.K.: Manchester University Press, 1989.

Baker, Aaron, and Juliann Vitullo. "Screening the Italian-American Male." In Peter Lehman, ed., *Masculinity: Bodies, Movies, Culture,* 213–26. New York: Routledge, 2001.

Benjamin, George. "Sad Sack." *Modern Screen* (January 1946). Accessed at http://www.songsbysinatra.com/reprints

Biskind, Peter. *Seeing Is Believing: How Hollywood Taught Us to Stop Worrying and Love the Fifties.* London: Pluto Press, 1983.

Bliven, Bruce. "The Voice and the Kids." *New Republic* 6 (November 1944). In Steven Petkov and Leonard Mustazza, eds., *The Frank Sinatra Reader,* 30–33. New York: Oxford University Press, 1995.

Boddy, William. *Fifties Television: The Industry and Its Critics.* Urbana and Chicago: University of Illinois Press, 1990.

Bogart, Leo. *The Age of Television: A Study of Viewing Habits and the Impact of Television on American Life.* New York: Frederick Ungar, 1958.

Bogart, Stephen, with Gary Provost. *Bogart: In Search of My Father.* London: Sidgwick and Jackson, 1995.

Branch, Taylor. *Parting the Waters: America in the King Years, 1954–1963.* New York: Simon and Schuster, 1988.

Braudy, Leo. "'No Body's Perfect': Method Acting and 50s Culture." In Laurence Goldstein and Ira Konigsberg, eds., *The Movies: Texts, Receptions, Exposures,* 275–99. Ann Arbor: University of Michigan Press, 1996.

Braudy, Leo, and Marshall Cohen, eds. *Film Theory and Criticism.* 1974. New York: Oxford University Press, 1999.

Bremner, Robert H., and Gary W. Reichard, eds. *Reshaping America: Society and Institutions, 1945–1960.* Columbus: Ohio State University Press, 1982.

Brinkley, Alan. "The New Political Paradigm: World War II and American Liberalism." In Lewis A. Erenberg and Susan E. Hirsch, eds., *The War in American Culture: Society and Consciousness during World War II,* 313–31. Chicago: University of Chicago Press, 1996.

Brod, Harry. "Masculinity as Masquerade." In Andrew Perchuk and Helaine Posner, eds., *Masculine Masquerade: Masculinity and Representation,* 13–19. Cambridge, Mass.: MIT Press, 1995.

Brode, Douglas. *The Films of the Fifties.* New York: Citadel, 1976.

Brown, Joe David. *Kings Go Forth.* 1957. London: Pan Books, 1958.

Brownstein, Ronald. *The Power and the Glitter: The Hollywood–Washington Connection.* New York: Pantheon, 1990.

Bryson, John. "Sinatra at Fifty." *Look* 14 (December 1965): 61–66, 68, 71–22, 74.

Butler, Jeremy G., ed. *Star Texts: Image and Performance in Film.* Detroit, Mich.: Wayne State University Press, 1991.

Cameron, Ian, ed. *Movie Reader.* London: November Books, 1962.

Cannistraro, Philip V., and Gerald Meyer, eds. *The Lost World of Italian American Radicalism: Politics, Labor, and Culture.* Westport, Conn.: Praeger, 2003.

Celebrity Sell: Star Endorsements in the Classic Age of Advertising. London: Prion, 2001.

Ceplair, Larry, and Steven Englund. *The Inquisition in Hollywood: Politics in the Film Community, 1930–1960.* Garden City, N.Y.: Anchor Press, 1980.

"Chairman of the Board." *Newsweek* (October 28, 1963): 59–60.

Christopher, Nicholas. *Somewhere in the Night: Film Noir and the American City.* New York: Holt, 1997.

Cohan, Steven. "'Feminizing' the Song-and-Dance Man: Fred Astaire and the Spectacle of Masculinity in the Hollywood Musical." In Steven Cohan and Ina Rae Hark, eds., *Screening the Male: Exploring Masculinities in Hollywood Cinema,* 46–69. London: Routledge, 1993.

——. *Masked Men: Masculinity and the Movies in the Fifties.* Bloomington: Indiana University Press, 1997.

Cohan, Steven, and Ina Rae Hark, eds. *Screening the Male: Exploring Masculinities in Hollywood Cinema.* London: Routledge, 1993.

Conekin, Becky. "Fashioning the Playboy: Messages of Style and Masculinity in the Pages of *Playboy* Magazine, 1953–1963." *Fashion Theory* 4, no. 4 (2000): 447–66.

Connolly, Robert, and Pellegrino D'Acierno. "Italian-American Musical Culture and Its Contribution to American Music." In Pellegrino D'Acierno, ed., *The Italian American Heritage: A Companion to Literature and Arts,* 387–490. New York: Garland, 1999.

Coss, Bill. "Frank Sinatra: Mr. Personality." *Metronome* (December 1957): 14–15.

Cripps, Thomas. "Racial Ambiguities in American Propaganda Movies." In K. R. M. Short, ed., *Film and Radio Propaganda in World War II,* 125–46. London: Croom Helm, 1983.

Cripps, Thomas. *Making Movies Black: The Hollywood Message Movie from World War II to the Civil Rights Era.* New York: Oxford University Press, 1993.

Cunningham, Barbara, ed. *The New Jersey Ethnic Experience.* Union City: Wm. H. Wise, 1977.

Curtis, Tony, and Barry Paris. *Tony Curtis: The Autobiography.* London: Mandarin, 1994.

D'Acierno, Pellegrino. "Cinema Paradiso: The Italian American Presence in American Cinema." In Pellegrino D'Acierno, ed., *The Italian American Heritage: A Companion to Literature and Arts,* 563–690. New York: Garland, 1999.

——. "Introduction: The Making of the Italian American Cultural Identity—From La Cultura Negata to Strong Ethnicity." In Pellegrino D'Acierno, ed., *The Italian American Heritage: A Companion to Literature and Arts,* xxiii–liii. New York: Garland, 1999.

——, ed. *The Italian American Heritage: A Companion to Literature and Arts.* New York: Garland, 1999.

Davidson, Bill. "Why Frank Sinatra Hates the Press." *Look* (May 28, 1957): 123–24, 126, 128, 131–34, 136.

Davis, Sammy, Jr. "The Frank Sinatra I Know." *Down Beat* (August 22, 1956). Reprinted in *Down Beat* (August 1998): 26–27.

——. *Yes I Can.* London: Cassell, 1965.

Davis, Sammy, Jr., with Jane Boyar and Burt Boyar. *Why Me?* London: Michael Joseph, 1989.

DeLillo, Don. *Libra.* London: Penguin, 1989.

——. *Underworld.* London: Picador, 1998.

Dick, Bernard F. *Radical Innocence: A Critical Study of the Hollywood Ten.* Lexington: University Press of Kentucky, 1989.

Diggins, John Patrick. *The Proud Decades: America in War and Peace, 1945–1960.* New York: Norton, 1988.

Doane, Mary Ann. *Femmes Fatales: Feminism, Film Theory, Psychoanalysis.* London: Routledge, 1991.

Doherty, Thomas. *Projections of War: Hollywood, American Culture, and World War II.* New York: Columbia University Press, 1993.

Douglas, Kirk. *The Ragman's Son.* London: Pan Books, 1988.

Douglas-Home, Robin. *Sinatra.* London: Michael Joseph, 1962.

Duke, Forrest. "'Vegas' Zillion-$ Five; 'Summiteers' (Sinatra & 4) A Sizzler at the Sands." *Variety* (February, 24, 1960): 1 and 111.

Dyer, Richard. *Heavenly Bodies.* New York: St. Martin's Press, 1986.

————. *The Matter of Images: Essays on Representation.* New York: Routledge, 1993.

————. "Resistance through Charisma: Rita Hayworth and *Gilda.*" In E. Ann Kaplan, ed., *Women in Film Noir,* 115–22. 1978. London: British Film Institute, 1998.

————. "Rock—The Last Guy You'd Have Figured?" In Pat Kirkham and Janet Thumim, eds., *You Tarzan: Masculinity, Movies and Men,* 27–34. New York: St. Martin's Press, 1993.

Dyer, Richard. *Stars.* 1979. London: British Film Institute, 1998.

Eberwein, Robert. "'As a Mother Cuddles a Child': Sexuality and Masculinity in World War II Combat Films." In Peter Lehman, *Masculinity: Bodies, Movies, Culture,* 149–66. New York: Routledge, 2001.

Ehrenreich, Barbara. *Fear of Falling.* New York: Pantheon Books, 1989.

————. *The Hearts of Men: American Dreams and the Flight from Commitment.* New York: Anchor Books, 1983.

Ellis, John. "Stars as a Cinematic Phenomenon." In Jeremy G. Butler, ed., *Star Texts: Image and Performance in Film and Television,* 300–15. Detroit, Mich.: Wayne State University Press, 1991.

————. *Visible Fictions: Cinema, Television, Video.* London: Routledge, 1982.

Erenberg, Lewis A. "Swing Goes to War: Glenn Miller and the Popular Music of World War II." In Lewis A. Erenberg and Susan E. Hirsch, eds., *The War in American Culture: Society and Consciousness during World War II,* 144–69. Chicago: University of Chicago Press, 1996.

Erenberg, Lewis A. *Swingin' the Dream.* Chicago: University of Chicago Press, 1998.

Erenberg, Lewis A., and Susan E. Hirsch, eds. *The War in American Culture: Society and Consciousness during World War II.* Chicago: University of Chicago Press, 1996.

Evans, Pip. "Why Does Frankie Hate So Hard?" *Photoplay* (May 1959): 18–19, 53.

Fagiani, Gill. "The Italian Identity of Frank Sinatra." *Voices in Italian Americana* 10, no. 2 (1999): 19–32.

Feather, Leonard G. "Frankly Speaking." *Metronome* (May 1943). Accessed at http://www.songsbysinatra.com/reprints

Ferraro, Thomas J. "'My Way' in 'Our America': Art, Ethnicity, Profession." *American Literary History* 12, no. 3 (Fall 2000): 499–522.

———. "Urbane Villager." In Stanislao G. Pugliese, ed., *Frank Sinatra: History, Identity, and Italian American Culture,* 135–46. New York: Palgrave Macmillan, 2004.

Fine, Gary Alan. "The Psychology of Cigarette Advertising: Professional Puffery." In Jack Nachbar and John L. Wright, eds., *The Popular Culture Reader,* 63–74. Bowling Green, Ky.: Bowling Green University Popular Press, 1977.

Foreman, Joel, ed. *The Other Fifties: Interrogating Midcentury American Icons.* Urbana: University of Illinois Press, 1997.

Frank, Alan. *Sinatra.* 1978. London: Hamlyn, 1984.

"Frankie Fans Make Poor Wives." *Down Beat* (March 26, 1947). Reprinted in *Down Beat* (August 1998): 33.

"Frankie in Madison." *Time* (August 25, 1958): 40.

"Frank Sinatra in Gary." *Life* (November 12, 1945): 45–46.

"Frank Sinatra's Trial—The Case for Privacy." *Metronome* (March 1958): 8–9.

French, Brandon. *On the Verge of Revolt: Women in American Films of the Fifties.* New York: Frederick Ungar, 1978.

Friedan, Betty. *The Feminine Mystique.* 1963. London: Penguin, 1965.

Friedman, Lester D., ed. *Unspeakable Images: Ethnicity and the American Cinema.* Urbana: University of Illinois Press, 1991.

Friedwald, Will. *Sinatra! The Song Is You: A Singer's Art.* New York: Da Capo Press, 1997.

Frye Jacobson, Matthew. *Whiteness of a Different Color: European Immigrants and the Alchemy of Race.* Cambridge, Mass.: Harvard University Press, 1999.

Fuchs, Cynthia J. "Split Screens: Framing and Passing in *Pillow Talk.*" In Joel Foreman, ed., *The Other Fifties: Interrogating Midcentury American Icons,* 224–51. Urbana and Chicago: University of Illinois Press, 1997.

Fuchs, Jeanne, and Ruth Prigozy. *Frank Sinatra: The Man, the Music, the Legend.* Rochester, N.Y.: University of Rochester Press, 2007.

Fulford, Robert. "Sinatra with Sweetening." *New Republic* (November 18, 1957): 22.

Furia, Philip. "Sinatra on Broadway." In Leonard Mustazza, ed., *Frank Sinatra and Popular Culture: Essays on an American Icon.* Westport, Conn.: Praeger, 1998. 162–73.

Gabler, Neal. *Winchell: Gossip, Power and the Culture of Celebrity.* New York: Knopf, 1994.

Gans, Herbert J. *The Urban Villagers: Group and Class in the Life of Italian-Americans.* New York: The Free Press, 1962.

Gardner, Ava. *Ava: My Story.* London, U.K.: Bantam Press, 1990.

Garrow, David J. *Bearing the Cross: Martin Luther King Jr. and the Southern Christian Leadership Conference.* London: Jonathan Cape, 1988.

Gehman, Richard. "The Enigma of Frank Sinatra." *Good Housekeeping* (July 1960): 58–60, 179–84.

———. *Sinatra and His Rat Pack.* New York: Belmont Books, 1961.

Gennari, John. "Passing for Italian: Crooners and Gangsters in Crossover Culture." *Transition* 72 (1996): 36–48.

Gerstle, Gary. *American Crucible: Race and Nation in the Twentieth Century.* Princeton, N.J.: Princeton University Press, 2001.

———. "Interpreting the 'American Way': The Working Class Goes to War." In Lewis A. Erenberg and Susan E. Hirsch, eds., *The War in American Culture: Society and Consciousness during World War II,* 105–28. Chicago: University of Chicago Press, 1996.

Gigliotti, Gilbert L. *A Storied Singer: Frank Sinatra as Literary Conceit.* Westport, Conn.: Greenwood Press, 2002.

Gilbert, Roger. "The Swinger and the Loser: Sinatra, Masculinity and Fifties Culture." In Leonard Mustazza, ed., *Frank Sinatra and Popular Culture: Essays on an American Icon,* 38–49. Westport, Conn.: Praeger, 1998.

Giovacchini, Saverio. *Hollywood Modernism: Film and Politics in the Age of the New Deal.* Philadelphia: Temple University Press, 2001.

Gledhill, Christine, ed. *Home Is Where the Heart Is: Studies in Melodrama and the Woman's Film.* London: British Film Institute, 1987.

Goff, Kenneth. "Sinatra, Commie Playboy." *Red Betrayal of Youth.* 1948. Accessed online at http://www.songsbysinatra.com/reprints

Goldstein, Laurence, and Ira Konigsberg, eds. *The Movies: Texts, Receptions, Exposures.* Ann Arbor: University of Michigan Press, 1996.

Goldstein, Patrick. "The Birth of Cool Politics: When glamorous JFK hit L.A. for the Democratic Convention, Hollywood Was Enamored, and Campaigns Would Never Be the Same." *The Los Angeles Times* (August, 13, 2000). Accessed online at http://www.latimes.com

Goodman, Ezra. "The Kid from Hoboken." *Time* (August 29, 1955): 42–47.

Gordon, Milton M. *Assimilation in American Life: The Role of Race, Religion and National Origins.* New York: Oxford University Press, 1964.

Gould, Jack. "TV: Frank Sinatra Show." *New York Times* (October 19, 1957): 30.

Graham, Allison. *Framing the South: Hollywood, Television, and Race during the Civil Rights Struggle.* Baltimore, Md.: John Hopkins University Press, 2001.

Granata, Charles L. *Sessions with Sinatra: Frank Sinatra and the Art of Recording.* Chicago: A Cappella, 1999.

Green, Robert L. "Wardrobe for a Jet Weekend." *Playboy* 6, no. 4 (April 1959): 38–39.

Greenwood, Leonard, and Jeannine Stein. "Sinatra Given L.A. NAACP Award despite Rights Protest." *The Los Angeles Times* (May 15, 1987): 22.

Guglielmo, Jennifer, and Salvatore Salerno, eds. *Are Italians White?: How Race Is Made in America.* New York: Routledge, 2003.

Guglielmo, Thomas A. "'No Color Barrier': Italians, Race, and Power in the United States." In Jennifer Guglielmo and Salvatore Salerno, eds., *Are Italians White?: How Race Is Made in America,* 29–43. New York: Routledge, 2003.

Halberstam, David. *The Fifties.* New York: Villard Books, 1993.

———. "Sinatra at Sunset." *Playboy* (April 1998): 76, 154–57.

Hamill, Pete. "Sinatra: The Legend Lives." *New York Magazine* (April 1980). In Ethlie

Ann Vare, ed, *Frank Sinatra and the American Dream,* 133–46. New York: Boulevard Books, 1995.

———. *Why Sinatra Matters.* Boston: Little, Brown, 1998.

Hansen, Miriam. "Pleasure, Ambivalence, Identification: Valentino and Female Spectatorship." *Cinema Journal* 25, no. 4 (Summer 1986): 6–32. In Jeremy G. Butler, ed., *Star Texts: Image and Performance in Film and Television,* 266–97. Detroit, Mich.: Wayne State University Press, 1991.

Harris, Jay S., ed. *TV Guide: The First 25 Years.* New York: New American Library, 1978.

Haygood, Wil. *In Black and White: The Life of Sammy Davis, Jr.* New York: Knopf, 2003.

Hodgson, Godfrey. *America in Our Time: From World War II to Nixon, What Happened and Why.* New York: Random House, 1978.

"Hokey Tunes 'Bug' Frank." *Down Beat* (March 25, 1953). Reprinted in *Down Beat* (August 1998): 33.

Horton, Robert. "One Good Take: Sinatra, 1915–1998." *Film Comment* (July–August 1998): 14–18.

Howlett, John. *Frank Sinatra.* London: Plexus, 1980.

Iaconelli, Richard. "Frank Sinatra and the Great American Style." In Leonard Mustazza, ed., *Frank Sinatra and Popular Culture: Essays on an American Icon,* 183–97. Westport, Conn.: Praeger, 1998.

Israel, Lee. *Kilgallen.* New York: Dell, 1979.

Jacklosky, Rob. "Someone to Watch Over Him: Images of Gender and Class Vulnerability in Early Sinatra." Paper presented at *The Conference: Frank Sinatra—The Man, the Music, the Legend.* Hofstra University, New York. November, 12–14, 1998.

Jackson, Martin A. "The Uncertain Peace: *The Best Years of Our Lives* (1946)." In John E. O'Connor and Martin A. Jackson, *American History/American Film: Interpreting the Hollywood Image,* 147–65. New York: Frederick Ungar, 1979.

Jacobs, George, and William Stadiem. *Mr. S: The Last Word on Frank Sinatra.* London: Sidgwick and Jackson, 2003.

Jancovich, Mark. "Placing Sex: Sexuality, Taste and Middlebrow Culture in the Reception of *Playboy* Magazine." *Intensities: The Journal of Cult Media* 2 (Autumn/Winter 2001). Available online at http://www.cult-media.com

Kahn, E. J., Jr. "Phenomenon: The Fave, the Fans, and the Fiends." *New Yorker* (November 2, 1946). In Steven Petkov and Leonard Mustazza, eds., *The Frank Sinatra Reader,* 34–47. New York: Oxford University Press, 1995.

———. "Phenomenon: The Voice with the Gold Accessories." *New Yorker* (October 26, 1946). In Ethlie Ann Vare, ed., *Legend: Frank Sinatra and the American Dream,* 27–29. New York: Boulevard Books, 1995.

———. "The Slaves of Sinatra." In Richard Peters, *The Frank Sinatra Scrapbook,* 63–67. London: Souvenir Press, 1982.

———. *The Voice: The Story of an American Phenomenon, Frank Sinatra.* London: Musicians Press, 1947.

————. "What Will Sinatra Do Next?" *Look* (August 5, 1947). Available online at http://www.songsbysinatra.com/reprints

Kahn, Gordon. *Hollywood on Trial: The Story of the 10 Who Were Indicted.* New York: Boni and Gaer, 1948.

Kaplan, E. Ann, ed. *Women in Film Noir.* 1978. London: British Film Institute, 1998.

Kaufman, Michael, ed. *Beyond Patriarchy: Essays by Men on Pleasure, Power, and Change.* New York: Oxford University Press, 1987.

Keightley, Keir. "The Man in the Gray Sharkskin Suit: Masculinity, Individualism and the Popular Reception of Frank Sinatra, 1953–1962." Paper presented at *The Conference: Frank Sinatra—The Man, the Music, the Legend.* Hofstra University, New York. November 12–14, 1998.

Kelley, Kitty. *His Way: The Unauthorized Biography.* London: Bantam Press, 1986.

Kessie, Jack. "Ivy Action: The Right Look for the Beach, Boating, Tennis and the Links." *Playboy* 4, no. 7 (July 1957): 20.

————. "The Well Dressed Playboy: *Playboy*'s Position on the Proper Male Attire." *Playboy* 2, no. 2 (January 1955): 38–39.

Kilgallen, Dorothy. "The Real Frank Sinatra Story." *New York Journal-American* (February 26, 1956): 1, 36.

Kimmel, Michael S. "The Cult of Patriarchy: American Social Character and the Legacy of the Cowboy." In Michael Kaufman, ed., *Beyond Patriarchy: Essays by Men on Pleasure, Power, and Change,* 235–49. New York: Oxford University Press, 1987.

————. *Manhood in America: A Cultural History.* New York: The Free Press, 1996.

Kirkham, Pat, and Janet Thumim, eds. *You Tarzan: Masculinity, Movies, and Men.* New York: St. Martin's Press, 1993.

Klinger, Barbara. *Melodrama and Meaning: History, Culture, and the Films of Douglas Sirk.* Bloomington: Indiana University Press, 1994.

Koppes, Clayton R. "Hollywood and the Politics of Representation: Women, Workers, and African Americans in World War II Movies." In Kenneth Paul O'Brien and Lynn Hudson Parsons, eds., *The Home-Front War: World War II and American Society,* 25–40. Westport, Conn.: Greenwood Press, 1995.

Koppes, Clayton R., and Gregory D. Black. *Hollywood Goes to War: How Politics, Profits, and Propaganda Shaped World War II Movies.* London: I. B. Tauris, 1987.

Krutnik, Frank. "The Faint Aroma of Performing Seals: The 'Nervous' Romance and the Comedy of the Sexes." *The Velvet Light Trap* 26 (Fall 1990): 57–72.

————. *In a Lonely Street: Film Noir, Genre, Masculinity.* London: Routledge, 1991.

————. *Inventing Jerry Lewis.* Washington, D.C.: Smithsonian Institution Press, 2000.

Kuntz, Tom, and Phil Kuntz, eds. *The Sinatra Files: The Secret FBI Dossier.* New York: Three Rivers Press, 2000.

Lahr, John. "Sinatra's Song." *New Yorker* (November 3, 1997): 76–95.

Lane, Laura. "From Brando to Presley." *Photoplay* November 1956: 56–61, 121–22.

Lardner, John. "Synthetic Fun." *New Yorker* (November 2, 1957): 106–9.

Larkin, Louis. "Sinatra: 'Why They Hate Me.'" *Redbook* (August 1959): 39, 92–94.

Lear, Martha Weinman. "The Bobby Sox Have Wilted, but the Memory Remains Fresh." *New York Times* (October 13, 1974). In Steven Petkov and Leonard Mustazza, eds., *The Frank Sinatra Reader,* 47–50. New York: Oxford University Press, 1995.

Lears, Jackson. "A Matter of Taste: Corporate Cultural Hegemony in a Mass-Consumption Society." In Lary May, ed., *Recasting America: Culture and Politics in the Age of Cold War,* 38–56. Chicago: University of Chicago Press, 1989.

Legare, Robert. "Meeting at the Summit: Sinatra and His Buddies Bust 'Em Up in Vegas." *Playboy* (June 1960): 34–37, 48, 97–100.

Lehman, Peter, ed. *Masculinity: Bodies, Movies, Culture.* New York: Routledge, 2001.

Leonard, George J. "Preface: Making a Point of It." In Pellegrino D'Acierno, ed., *The Italian American Heritage: A Companion to Literature and Arts,* xv–xxii. New York: Garland, 1999.

Levy, Shawn. *Rat Pack Confidential.* New York: Doubleday, 1998.

Lhamon, W. T., Jr. *Deliberate Speed: The Origins of a Cultural Style in the American 1950s.* Washington, D.C.: Smithsonian Institution Press, 1990.

Lippe, Richard. "Kim Novak: A Resistance to Definition." *CineAction!* 7 (December 1986): 5–20.

Lohof, Bruce A. "The Higher Meaning of Marlboro Cigarettes." In Jack Nachbar and John L. Wright, eds., *The Popular Culture Reader,* 233–42. Bowling Green, Ky.: Bowling Green University Popular Press, 1977.

MacDonald, J. Fred. "Black Perimeters—Paul Robeson, Nat King Cole and the Role of Blacks in American TV." *Journal of Popular Film and Television* 7, no. 3 (1979): 246–64.

Malone, Michael. *Heroes of Eros.* New York: E. P. Dutton, 1979.

Manchester, William. *The Glory and the Dream: A Narrative History of America, 1932–1972.* London: Michael Joseph, 1975.

Mann, Denise. "The Spectacularization of Everyday Life: Recycling Hollywood Stars and Fans in Early Television Variety Shows." In Jeremy G. Butler, ed., *Star Texts: Image and Performance in Film,* 333–60. Detroit, Mich.: Wayne State University Press, 1991.

Marchand, Roland. "Visions of Classlessness, Quests for Dominion: American Popular Culture, 1945–1960." In Robert H. Bremner and Gary W. Reichard, eds., *Reshaping America, Society and Institutions, 1945–1960,* 163–182. Columbus: Ohio State University Press, 1982.

Marling, Karal Ann. *As Seen on TV: The Visual Culture of Everyday Life in the 1950s.* Cambridge, Mass.: Harvard University Press, 1994.

Martin, Angela. "'Gilda Didn't Do Any of Those Things You've Been Losing Sleep Over!': The Central Women of 40s Films Noirs." In Ann Kaplan, ed., *Women in Film Noir,* 202–28. 1978. London: British Film Institute, 1998.

Masters, Eric. "The Nite Frank Sinatra Had One Peer Too Many!" *Uncensored* 9, no. 3 (September 1959): 33–35, 72.

May, Elaine Tyler. *Homeward Bound: American Families in the Cold War Era.* New York: Basic Books, 1988.

May, Lary, ed. *Recasting America: Culture and Politics in the Age of Cold War.* Chicago: University of Chicago Press, 1989.

McCann, Graham. *Rebel Males: Clift, Brando and Dean.* London: Hamish Hamilton, 1991.

McGilligan, Patrick. *Cagney: The Actor as Auteur.* London: A. S. Barnes, 1975.

McNally, Karen. "Films for Swingin' Lovers: Frank Sinatra, Performance and Sexual Objectification in *The Tender Trap* and *Pal Joey.*" *Scope: An Online Journal of Film Studies* (May 2002). Available online at http://www.nottingham.ac.uk/film/journal

———. "'Sinatra, Commie Playboy': Frank Sinatra, Post-War Liberalism and Press Paranoia." *Film Studies* (Winter 2005): 43–53.

———. "'Where's the Spinning Wheel?': Frank Sinatra and Working-Class Alienation in *Young at Heart.*" *Journal of American Studies* 41 (2007): 115–33.

———. "'Your Blood's the Same as Mine': *The House I Live In* and the Post-War Push for Tolerance." *Film and History* CD-Rom Annual 2003.

Mellen, Joan. *Big Bad Wolves: Masculinity in the American Film.* London: Elm Tree Books, 1978.

Meyer, Gerald. "Frank Sinatra: The Popular Front and an American Icon." *Science and Society* 66, no. 3 (Fall 2002): 311–35.

———. "When Frank Sinatra Came to Italian Harlem: The 1945 'Race Riot' at Benjamin Franklin High School." In Jennifer Guglielmo and Salvatore Salerno,eds., *Are Italians White?: How Race Is Made in America,* 161–76. New York: Routledge, 2003.

Miller, Douglas T., and Marion Nowak. *The Fifties: The Way We Really Were.* New York: Doubleday, 1975.

Miller, James. *Flowers in the Dustbin: The Rise of Rock and Roll, 1947–1977.* New York: Simon and Schuster, 1999.

Mills, C. Wright.*White Collar: The American Middle Classes.* New York: Oxford University Press, 1951.

Moore, William Howard. *The Kefauver Committee and the Politics of Crime, 1950–1952.* Columbia: University of Missouri Press, 1974.

Morella, Joe, and Edward Z. Epstein. *Rebels: The Rebel Hero in Films.* New York: The Citadel Press, 1971.

Mortimer, Lee. "Frank Sinatra Confidential: Gangsters in the Night Clubs." *American Mercury* (August 1951): 29–36.

Mulvey, Laura. "Visual Pleasure and Narrative Cinema." *Screen* 16, no. 3 (1975). In Leo Braudy and Marshall Cohen, eds., *Film Theory and Criticism,* 833–44. 1974. New York: Oxford University Press, 1999.

Mustazza, Leonard, ed. *Frank Sinatra and Popular Culture: Essays on an American Icon.* Westport, Conn.: Praeger, 1998.

———. "Introduction." In Leonard Mustazza, ed., *Frank Sinatra and Popular Culture: Essays on an American Icon,* 1–19. Westport, Conn.: Praeger, 1998.

———. *Sinatra: An Annotated Bibliography, 1939–1998.* Westport, Conn.: Greenwood, 1999.

———. "Sinatra's Enduring Appeal: Art and Heart." In Steven Petkov and Leonard Mustazza, eds., *The Frank Sinatra Reader,* 3–9. New York: Oxford University Press, 1995.

Nachbar, Jack, and John L. Wright, eds. *The Popular Culture Reader.* Bowling Green, Ky.: Bowling Green University Popular Press, 1977.

Nadel, Alan. *Containment Culture: American Narratives, Postmodernism, and the Atomic Age.* Durham, N.C.: Duke University Press, 1995.

Naremore, James. *Acting in the Cinema.* Berkeley: University of California Press, 1988.

———. *More Than Night: Film Noir in Its Contexts.* Berkeley: University of California Press, 1998.

Neale, Steve. "Masculinity as Spectacle: Reflections on Men and Mainstream Cinema." *Screen* 24, no. 6 (November/December 1983): 2–16. In Steven Cohan and Ina Rae Hark, eds., *Screening the Male: Exploring Masculinities in Hollywood Cinema,* 9–20. London: Routledge, 1993:

Nelson, Michael. "Frank Sinatra and Presidential Politics." In Stanislao G. Pugliese, ed., *Frank Sinatra: History, Identity, and Italian American Culture,* 47–70. New York: Palgrave Macmillan, 2004.

Neve, Brian. *Film and Politics in America: A Social Tradition.* London: Routledge, 1992.

O'Brian, Jack. "Jack O'Brian's TViews: To Be Frank—A Long Show." *New York Journal-American* (October 19, 1957): 24.

O'Brien, Daniel. *The Frank Sinatra Film Guide.* London: B. T. Batsford, 1998.

O'Brien, Kenneth Paul, and Lynn Hudson Parsons, eds. *The Home-Front War: World War II and American Society.* Westport, Conn.: Greenwood Press, 1995.

O'Connor, John E., ed. *American History/American Television.* New York: Frederick Ungar, 1983.

O'Connor, John E., and Martin A. Jackson, eds. *American History/American Film: Interpreting the Hollywood Image.* New York: Frederick Ungar, 1979.

O'Hara, John. *Pal Joey.* 1940. London: Prion, 1999.

Packard, Vance. *The Status Seekers: An Exploration of Class Behaviour in America.* 1959. Harmondsworth, U.K.: Penguin, 1961.

Parsons, Louella. "Daddy-O!" *Tell It to Louella.* In Ethlie Ann Vare, ed., *Frank Sinatra and the American Dream,* 76–82. New York: Boulevard Books, 1995.

———. "Fabulous Frank Sinatra." *Photoplay* (November 1943): 28, 78, and 80.

Peary, Gerald, and Roger Shatzkin, eds. *The Modern American Novel and the Movies.* New York: Frederick Ungar, 1978.

Pendergast, Tom. *Creating the Modern Man: American Magazines and Consumer Culture 1900–1950.* Columbia: University of Missouri Press, 2000.

Perchuk, Andrew, and Helaine Posner, eds. *Masculine Masquerade: Masculinity and Representation.* Cambridge, Mass.: MIT Press, 1995.

Perfectly Frank (April/May 2001): 27 and 29.

Peters, Richard. *The Frank Sinatra Scrapbook.* London: Souvenir Press, 1982.

Petkov, Steven, and Leonard Mustazza, eds. *The Frank Sinatra Reader.* New York: Oxford University Press, 1995.

Pettigrew, Terence. *Raising Hell: The Rebel in the Movies.* Bromley: Columbus Books, 1986.

Pickard, Roy. *Frank Sinatra at the Movies.* London: Robert Hale, 1994.

Place, Janey, and Lowell Peterson. "Some Visual Motifs of *Film Noir.*" In Alain Silver and James Ursini, eds., *Film Noir Reader.* 64–77. New York: Limelight, 2000.

"Playboy Interview: Frank Sinatra." *Playboy* (February 1963): 35–40.

"Playboy's Penthouse Apartment." Part I, *Playboy* (September 1956); Part II, *Playboy* (October 1956). In Joel Sanders, ed., *Stud: Architectures of Masculinity,* 55–67. New York: Princeton Architectural Press, 1996.

Pleasants, Henry. *The Great American Popular Singers.* New York: Simon and Schuster, 1974.

Polan, Dana. *Power and Paranoia.* New York: Columbia University Press, 1986.

Polenberg, Richard, ed. *America at War: The Home Front, 1941–1945.* Englewood Cliffs, N.J.: Prentice-Hall, 1968.

———. *One Nation Divisible: Class, Race and Ethnicity in the United States since 1938.* New York: Penguin, 1980.

———. "World War II and the Bill of Rights." In Kenneth Paul O'Brien and Lynn Hudson Parsons, eds., *The Home-Front War: World War II and American Society,* 11–24. Westport, Conn.: Greenwood Press, 1995.

Pozzetta, George E. "'My Children Are My Jewels': Italian-American Generations during World War II." In Kenneth Paul O'Brien and Lynn Hudson Parsons, eds., *The Home-Front War: World War II and American Society,* 63–82. Westport, Conn.: Greenwood Press, 1995.

Pratley, Gerald. *The Cinema of Otto Preminger.* New York: Zwemmer, 1971.

Pryor, Thomas. "The Rise, Fall and Rise of Sinatra." *The New York Times Magazine* (February 10, 1957): 17, 60–61.

Pugliese, Stanislao G., ed. *Frank Sinatra: History, Identity, and Italian American Culture.* New York: Palgrave Macmillan, 2004.

Reisner, Robert George. "The Word on Frank Sinatra." *Playboy* (November 1958): 62–66, 84–88.

Riesman, David, Nathan Glazer, and Reuel Denney. *The Lonely Crowd: A Study of the Changing American Character.* 1950. Garden City, N.Y,.: Doubleday, 1953.

Ringgold, Gene, and Clifford McCarty. *The Films of Frank Sinatra.* New York: Citadel Press, 1989.

Roberts-Frenzel, Caren. *Rita Hayworth: A Photographic Retrospective.* New York: Harry N. Abrams, 2001.

Rockwell, John. *Sinatra: An American Classic.* London: Elm Tree Books, 1984.

Rogers St. Johns, Adela. "The Nine Lives of Frank Sinatra." *Cosmopolitan* (May 1956): 82–89.

Rojek, Chris. *Frank Sinatra.* Cambridge, U.K.: Polity Press, 2004.

Rosen, Robert C. "Anatomy of a Junkie Movie." In Gerald Peary and Roger Shatzkin, eds., *The Modern American Novel and the Movies,* 189–98. New York: Frederick Ungar, 1978.

Rudin, Max. "Fly Me to the Moon: Reflections on the Rat Pack." *American Heritage* (December 1998): 52–65.

Sanders, Joel, ed. *Stud: Architectures of Masculinity.* New York: Princeton Architectural Press, 1996.

Schatz, Thomas. *Hollywood Genres.* Philadelphia: Temple University Press, 1981.

Schulberg, Budd. "Secrets of Sinatra: Inside Tales of His Life and Career." *New Choices for Retirement Living* (December 1993/January 1994). In Ethlie Ann Vare, *Frank Sinatra and the American Dream.* 205–11. New York: Boulevard Books, 1995.

Scott, Ian. *American Politics in Hollywood Film.* Edinburgh: Edinburgh University Press, 2000.

Shaw, Arnold. *Sinatra: Retreat of the Romantic.* 1968. London: Hodder Paperbacks, 1970.

Shindler, Colin. *Hollywood Goes to War: Films and American Society, 1939–1952.* London: Routledge, 1979.

———. *Hollywood in Crisis.* London: Routledge, 1996.

Short, K. R. M., ed. *Film and Radio Propaganda in World War II.* London and Canberra: Croom Helm, 1983.

Shumway, David R. "Watching Elvis: The Male Rock Star as Object of the Gaze." In Joel Foreman, ed., *The Other Fifties: Interrogating Midcentury American Icons,* 124–43. Urbana: University of Illinois Press, 1997.

Silver, Alain, and James Ursini, eds. *Film Noir Reader.* New York: Limelight, 2000.

Silverman, Kaja. *Male Subjectivity at the Margins.* London: Routledge, 1992.

Simon, George T. *The Big Bands.* New York: Collier Macmillan, 1974.

———. "Sinatra Looks at Television,Television Looks at Sinatra." *Metronome* (November 1950): 14.

———. "Sincerity's a Thing Called Frank." *Metronome* (December 1953). Available online at http://www.songsbysinatra.com/reprints

———. "What's Wrong with Music!" *Metronome* (February 1948). Available online at http://www.songsbysinatra.com

Simon, Ronald C. "Frank Sinatra and '50s Television: Creating a Persona." Paper presented at *The Conference: Frank Sinatra—The Man, the Music, the Legend.* Hofstra University, New York. November 12–14, 1998.

"Sinatra Flicker on Intolerance a Fine Attempt." *Down Beat* (November 1, 1945). Reprinted in *Down Beat* (August 1998): 35.

Sinatra, Frank. "As Sinatra Sees It." *New Republic* (January 6, 1947): 3, 46.

———. "Let's Not Forget We're *All* Foreigners." *Digest Magazine* (July 1945). reprinted in *Perfectly Frank* (December 1992): 7.

———. "Perspective on the Fourth of July: The Haters and Bigots Will Be Judged; Some Words from a 'Saloon Singer' to Those Who Still Haven't Figured Out the Whole Point of America." *Los Angeles Times* (July 4, 1991): B5.

———. "The Way I Look at Race." *Ebony* (July 1958): 34–38, 40, 42–44.

———. "What's This about Races?" *Scholastic* (September 17, 1945). In Ed. Leonard Mustazza, *Frank Sinatra and Popular Culture: Essays on an American Icon,* 23–25. Westport, Conn.: Praeger, 1998.

Sinatra, Nancy. *Frank Sinatra: An American Legend.* London: Virgin Books, 1995.

———. *Frank Sinatra: My Father.* London: Hodder and Stoughton, 1985.

Sinatra, Tina, with Jeff Coplon. *My Father's Daughter: A Memoir.* New York: Simon and Schuster, 2000.

"Sinatra's Mob: The Real Low Down on the Rat Pack." *Photoplay* (November 1960): 8–9, 53.

"The Sinatra Story." *Photoplay* (January 1955): 31–33, 52–54.

Sklar, Robert. *City Boys: Cagney, Bogart, Garfield.* Princeton, N.J.: Princeton University Press, 1992.

Skolsky, Sidney. "The New Look in Hollywood Men." *Photoplay* (July 1957): 41–43, 111–12.

Smith, James F. "Bobby Sox and Blue Suede Shoes: Frank Sinatra and Elvis Presley as Teen Idols." In Leonard Mustazza, ed., *Frank Sinatra and Popular Culture: Essays on an American Icon,* 50–68. Westport, Conn.: Praeger, 1998.

Smith, Kathleen E. R. *God Bless America: Tin Pan Alley Goes to War.* Lexington: University Press of Kentucky, 2003.

"Solid-Gold Sinatra." *Newsweek* (October 21, 1957): 70.

"Speaker: Frank Sinatra. Subject: What Is a Woman?" *Photoplay* (January 1958): 28, 84.

Spigel, Lynn. *Make Room for TV: Television and the Family Ideal in Postwar America.* Chicago: University of Chicago Press, 1992.

Starr, Michael E. "The Marlboro Man: Cigarette Smoking and Masculinity in America." *Journal of Popular Culture* 17, no. 4 (Spring 1984): 45–57.

Stowe, David W. *Swing Changes: Big Band Jazz in New Deal America.* Cambridge, Mass.: Harvard University Press, 1994.

Studlar, Gaylyn. "Valentino, 'Optic Intoxication', and Dance Madness." In Steven Cohan and Ina Rae Hark, eds., *Screening the Male: Exploring Masculinities in Hollywood Cinema,* 23–45. London: Routledge, 1993.

Talese, Gay. "Frank Sinatra Has a Cold." *Esquire* (April 1966). In Steven Petkov and Leonard Mustazza, eds., *The Frank Sinatra Reader.* 99–129. New York: Oxford University Press, 1995.

Taves, Isabella. "The Personal Story of the Tender Tough Guy Who Won't Behave— Frank Sinatra." *Woman's Home Companion* (May 1956): 38–41.

Tosches, Nick. *Dino: Living High in the Dirty Business of Dreams.* London: Minerva, 1993.

Tuck, Jim. *McCarthyism and New York's Hearst Press: A Study of Roles in the Witch Hunt.* Lanham, Md.: University Press of America, 1995.

Tuska, Jon. *Dark Cinema: American Film Noir in Cultural Perspective.* Westport, Conn.: Greenwood Press, 1984.

Tyler, Parker. *The Magic and Myth of the Movies.* 1947. London: Martin Secker and Warburg, 1971.

Tynan, John. "Sinatra: He's Frank." *Down Beat* (November 28, 1957): 15–16.

Ulanov, Barry. "Is Sinatra Finished?" *Modern Television & Radio* (December 1948). Available online at http://members.aol.com/artanis103

Van Meter, Jonathan. *The Last Good Time: Skinny D'Amato, the Notorious 500 Club, the Rat Pack and the Rise and Fall of Atlantic City*. London: Bloomsbury, 2003.

Vare, Ethlie Ann, ed. *Legend: Frank Sinatra and the American Dream*. New York: Boulevard Books, 1995.

Vecoli, Rudolph J. "The Italian People of New Jersey." In Barbara Cunningham, ed., *The New Jersey Ethnic Experience*. Union City: Wm. H. Wise, 1977. 275–93.

———. "The Making and Un-Making of the Italian American Working Class." In Philip V. Cannistraro and Gerald Meyer, eds., *The Lost World of Italian American Radicalism: Politics, Labor, and Culture*, 51–75. Westport, Conn.: Praeger, 2003.

"The Voice." *Newsweek* (December 20, 1943). In Ethlie Ann Vare, ed., *Frank Sinatra and the American Dream*, 18–19. New York: Boulevard Books, 1995.

Warshow, Robert. *The Immediate Experience: Movies, Comics, Theatre and Other Aspects of Popular Culture*. New York: Atheneum, 1979.

Wexman, Virginia Wright. "Kinesics and Film Acting: Humphrey Bogart in *The Maltese Falcon* and *The Big Sleep*." *Journal of Popular Film and Television* 7, no. 1 (1978): 42–55. In Jeremy G. Butler, ed., *Star Texts: Image and Performance in Film*, 203–13. Detroit, Mich.: Wayne State University Press, 1991.

"What Is a Playboy?" *Playboy* (April 1956): Subscription Page.

Whitfield, Stephen J. *The Culture of the Cold War*. 1991. Baltimore, Md.: John Hopkins University Press, 1996.

Whyte, William F. *Street Corner Society: The Social Structure of an Italian Slum*. 1943. Chicago: University of Chicago Press, 1955.

Whyte, William H. *The Organization Man*. 1956. London: Jonathan Cape, 1957.

Wiener, Jon. "When Old Blue Eyes Was 'Red.'" *The New Republic* (March 31, 1986). In Ethlie Ann Vare, ed., *Frank Sinatra and the American Dream*,. 64–9. New York: Boulevard Books, 1995.

Wilder, Alec. *American Popular Song: The Great Innovators, 1900–1950*. New York: Oxford University Press, 1972.

Wilkinson, Rupert. *American Tough: The Tough-Guy Tradition and American Character*. Westport, Conn.: Greenwood Press, 1984.

Wilson, Earl. *Sinatra*. London: W. H. Allen, 1978.

Wilson, Sloan. *The Man in the Grey Flannel Suit*. 1955. London: Pan Books, 1958.

Wiseman, Thomas. *The Seven Deadly Sins of Hollywood*. London: Oldbourne Press, 1957.

Wood, Nancy. "Dining alla Sinatra." *Screen Romance* (February 1945). Available online at http://www.songsbysinatra.com/reprints

Yarwood, Guy. *Sinatra on Sinatra*. London: Omnibus Press, 1982.

Zehme, Bill. *The Way You Wear Your Hat: Frank Sinatra and the Lost Art of Livin'*. New York: HarperCollins, 1997.

Zollo, Burt. "Open Season on Bachelors." *Playboy* (June 1954): 37–38.

Frank Sinatra Filmography

Anchors Aweigh. MGM, 1945.

Around the World in 80 Days. Michael Todd Company/United Artists, 1956.

Assault on a Queen. Sinatra Enterprises/Seven Arts/Paramount, 1966.

Can Can. Suffolk-Cummings/Twentieth Century Fox, 1960.

Cannonball Run II. Warner Bros./Golden Harvest/Arcafin B.V., 1984.

Cast a Giant Shadow. Mirisch/Llenroc/Bryna/Batjac, 1966.

Come Blow Your Horn. Essex-Tandem/Paramount, 1963.

Detective, The. Arcola-Millfield/Twentieth Century Fox, 1968.

Devil at 4 O'Clock, The. LeRoy/Kohlmar/Columbia, 1961.

Dirty Dingus Magee. MGM, 1970.

Double Dynamite. RKO, 1951.

First Deadly Sin, The. Artanis/Cinema Seven/First Deadly Sin Company/ Filmways, 1980.

Four for Texas. SAM Company/Warner Bros., 1963.

From Here to Eternity. Columbia, 1953.

Guys and Dolls. Samuel Goldwyn Company, 1955.

Higher and Higher. RKO, 1943.

High Society. MGM, 1956.

Hole in the Head, A. SinCap/United Artists, 1959.

House I Live In, The. RKO, 1945.

It Happened in Brooklyn. MGM, 1947.

Johnny Concho. Kent Productions/United Artists, 1956.

Joker is Wild, The. AMBL Productions/Paramount, 1957.

Kings Go Forth. Ross-Eton/United Artists, 1958.

Kissing Bandit, The. MGM, 1948.

Lady in Cement. Arcola-Millfield/Twentieth Century Fox, 1968.

Las Vegas Nights. Paramount, 1941.

List of Adrian Messenger, The. Joel Productions, 1963.

Manchurian Candidate, The. MC/United Artists, 1962.

Man with the Golden Arm, The. Carlyle/United Artists, 1955.

Marriage on the Rocks. A-C/Sinatra Enterprises/Warner Bros., 1965.

Meet Danny Wilson. Universal, 1951.

Meet Me in Las Vegas. MGM, 1956.

Miracle of the Bells, The. Jesse Lasky Productions/RKO, 1948.

Naked Runner, The. Sinatra Enterprises/Artanis/Warner Bros., 1967.

Never So Few. Canterbury/MGM, 1959.

None but the Brave. Tokyo Eiga Co. Limited/Toho Film/Artanis/Warner Bros., 1965.

Not as a Stranger. Stanley Kramer Picture Corp./United Artists, 1955.

Ocean's Eleven. Dorchester/Warner Bros., 1960.

On the Town. MGM, 1949.

Oscar, The. Green-Rouse, 1966.

Pal Joey. Essex-Sidney/Columbia, 1957.

Pepe. Columbia/Posa, 1960.

Pride and the Passion, The. Stanley Kramer Productions/United Artists, 1957.

Reveille with Beverly. Columbia, 1943.

Road to Hong Kong, The. Melnor, 1962.

Robin and the Seven Hoods. PC/Warner Bros., 1964.

Sergeants Three. Essex-Claude/United Artists, 1961.

Ship Ahoy. MGM, 1942.

Some Came Running. MGM, 1958.

Step Lively. RKO, 1944.

Suddenly. Libra/United Artists, 1954.

Take Me Out to the Ball Game. MGM, 1949.

Tender Trap, The. MGM, 1955.

Till the Clouds Roll By. MGM, 1946.

Tony Rome. Arcola-Millfield/Twentieth Century Fox, 1967.

Von Ryan's Express. Twentieth Century Fox, 1965.

Young at Heart. Arwin/Warner Bros., 1954.

Index

Page numbers in *italics* indicate illustrations.

Karen McNally is the Course Leader for Film Studies at London Metropolitan University.

The University of Illinois Press
is a founding member of the
Association of American University Presses.

Composed in 9.7/13 Cheltenham Book
with Futura Light display
by Barbara Evans
at the University of Illinois Press
Designed by Dennis Roberts
Manufactured by Cushing-Malloy, Inc.

University of Illinois Press
1325 South Oak Street
Champaign, IL 61820-6903
www.press.uillinois.edu